Christ Victorious

Studies in the Book of Revelation

Andrew D. Erwin

ISBN: 978-1-960858-34-4

Published by:

Cobb Publishing
704 E. Main St.
Charleston, AR 72933

(479) 747-8372
www.CobbPublishing.com
CobbPublishing@gmail.com

Dedicated to

Ronald & Susan Bryant

In Recognition of Your Christian Friendship and Support

Abbreviations

ABC – Anchor Bible Commentary

ABD – Anchor Bible Dictionary

BDAG – A Greek-English Lexicon of the New Testament and Other Early Christian Literature (Bauer, Danker, Arndt, and Gingrich)

BST – Bible Speaks Today Commentaries

DBI – Dictionary of Biblical Imagery

ESV – English Standard Version

ICS – Interpretation Commentary Series

ISBE – International Standard Bible Encyclopedia

IVP – Inter Varsity Press

KJV – King James Version

LWC – Living Word Commentaries

LXX – The Septuagint

MT – Majority Text

NA – Nestle-Aland Text

NICNT – New International Commentary of the New Testament

NIV – New International Version

NKJV – New King James Version

NT – New Testament

OT – Old Testament

TFTC – Truth for Today Commentaries

TNTC – Tyndale New Testament Commentaries

UBS – United Bible Societies Text

Introduction

The book of Revelation is intimidating for many to study. Understandably, it "is acknowledged to be a closed book by the majority of modern readers,"[1] meaning many modern readers simply do not understand the nature of the literature that was used. Hopefully, our study together will not further complicate matters for the reader.

A blessing is to be received by the one who "hears and does the sayings of this book." With the hope of receiving such a blessing from God, we shall walk through this marvelous book, viewing the visions and discussing the meanings and applications as best we can. Our approach will seek to keep focused on "the forest rather than the trees." We shall seek to understand the broad, overall meaning of the message, while doing our best to grasp the meanings behind the book's symbolism.

Revelation is both challenging and rewarding to study. It requires knowledge of the entirety of God's word to understand it satisfactorily. When studying Revelation, you have arrived at the mountaintop of the Bible, the crescendo, the zenith, the summit. One usually begins studying the scriptures with Genesis and the books of the Law of Israel. He is at the fertile basin of God's word. He begins to climb through the study of Israel's history from Joshua through Ezra. He pauses to appreciate the serenity of the Psalms and Wisdom literature of the OT. He scales the prophets to arrive at the Christ. It is from this perspective that he begins to see the Christian view of life in the shadow of the cross. His view of life, as it is truly meant to be lived, is only enhanced by treading

---

[1] G.R. Beasley-Murray, "Revelation," *The IVP Dictionary of the New Testament* (Downers Grove, IL: IVP, 2004), 924.

ever upward through the study of Acts and the epistles. Now, he has arrived at the top of the mountain, the Book of Revelation. Everything he has learned on this journey will be brought to bear to reach its summit. Only by trekking the climb that is the study of scripture will he understand its meaning, appreciate its message, marvel from its peak, and receive its blessings.

Any attempt to engage in a study of this book without prior knowledge of the complete word of God will inevitably lead to misguided conclusions. One must be able to recognize the manifold allusions to the inspired books which went before its writing if he is to gain true insight from its message. Moreover, a general understanding of the world in its first century context will prove to be of immense value. Revelation was never intended to be an "easy" read or study. Yet, its challenging prose and message keeps the student ever returning for more. Thus, we present for your consideration our contribution to the vast catalog of commentaries on the wonderful message of Revelation.

Apocalyptic Literature

The book of Revelation claims to be a book of prophecy (1:3; 22:7,10,18,19). Within many prophetic books of the Bible, we find a genre of writing that modern scholars have styled "apocalyptic." The name comes from Revelation 1:1 and the Greek word *apokalupsis*, which is translated into English as "Revelation" or "Apocalypse." Thus, we have the word *apocalyptic*. The genre of literature now known as apocalyptic literature refers not only to a few books and sections of scripture which have some shared characteristics, but also to a particular group of writings from the last two centuries BC and the first century AD.[2] The genre is most likely of Jewish origin but was also used by early Christians.

---

[2] Leon Morris, *Apocalyptic* (Grand Rapids, MI: Eerdmans, 1972), 19.

Including apocalyptic writings contained in the Dead Sea Scrolls found at Qumran, we have a little over thirty examples of apocalyptic literature from extrabiblical sources covering three centuries. While we cannot accept these extrabiblical documents as divinely inspired, they do help us to understand certain features and characteristics common to the genre. For example, we find themes such as a righteous remnant, deliverance, the problem of evil, the purpose and sovereignty of God, the overthrow of wicked nations, the ultimate overthrow of evil, and the end of time, to name a few.[3] Angels play significant roles in apocalyptic literature as guides for the witnesses as they describe what they see. In extrabiblical writings, pseudonyms are commonly used. Such is not the case with biblical apocalyptic writings, however. Most obviously, we find in apocalyptic literature signs and symbols used to unveil, disclose, and reveal.

The figure of speech in scripture known as *symbolism* occurs when a material object is substituted for a moral or spiritual truth.[4] The "Revelation" to John is an "unveiling," "disclosing," or "revealing" of God's word and will by using signs, symbols, visions, and allusions to OT literature of a similar nature and style. Caution must be exercised with the interpretation of signs and symbols. Signs *signify* and symbols *symbolize*. "Doubtless there are many symbols in the Scriptures, but great care and caution must be exercised in their interpretation. The different interpretations which have been given to the same so-called symbol, are sufficient to serve as a warning."[5]

Why did the Lord choose to use the genre of apocalyptic literature to convey the message of Revelation? We are not told for

---

[3] Ibid., 23 ff.
[4] E.W. Bullinger, *Figures of Speech Used in the Bible* (Grand Rapids, MI: Baker, 2003), 769.
[5] Ibid., 770.

certain in the book itself. It has been suggested that "Its code language has an obvious purpose – the same purpose the military has in communicating messages in code to its personnel in order to withhold the information from the public. [Therefore] If John had written Revelation in plain literal language, it would have precipitated a premature onslaught against the church which would have obliterated it from the Roman Empire and wiped it off the face of the earth."[6] Such an assumption seems extreme. It is hard to accept that the church would have been obliterated by the Romans had God chosen a more literal method of communication for this book.

Our view is that apocalyptic literature is the language of Divine judgement. Apocalyptic writings are used to address the conflict of good and evil and seek to console the readers and comfort them by reassuring them of the ultimate victory of good over evil – of God over Satan. The powers that be in the world are viewed oftentimes as allies and even instruments of Satan. The kingdom of men led by Satan is arrayed for war against the kingdom of God. Throughout the conflict, God remains alive and aware of the circumstances and enemies surrounding His people, and He will deliver them in the end. Yet, before deliverance comes, God's plan and purposes must be performed in the world. His will be done. Truly, this is the message of Revelation.

Moreover, apocalyptic writings cannot be understood apart from the times in which they were written. Knowing the historical context is of utmost importance to understanding the meaning of the message. The student of Revelation, for example, must consider the religious, political, and social circumstances of the day. Apocalyptic writings were given to people in times of trouble. Oftentimes, the recipients of the message were people of God who

---

[6] Foy E. Wallace, Jr., *The Book of Revelation* (Nashville, TN: Foy E. Wallace, Jr., Publications, 1966), 7.

were discouraged due to ongoing plight and persecution. Apocalyptic messages were therefore given to encourage the readers by reminding them of the power of God and that His purpose will ultimately prevail. God was not unaware, helpless, or inactive in their circumstances.

When reading the symbols and visions of apocalyptic literature, "be prepared to use your imagination to picture a world that transcends earthly reality."[7] Readers will find unfamiliar scenes and figures which will "break through our normal way of thinking and shock us into seeing things are not as they appear."[8] The odd symbols reveal to us that not only are things not as they appear, but also that they will not always continue as they presently occur. One can understand how this would appeal to readers during times of doubt and fear.

Apocalyptic literature is "scarcely literature for the masses. It cannot ever have been easy to interpret in detail."[9] The writers did not always explain their symbolism. Possibly, "Part of their reason for using bizarre symbolism will also be that they were trying to describe something that was too big for words."[10]

The use of visions and symbols makes apocalyptic literature a unique style of writing. Apocalyptic literature is both predictive and dramatic. Apocalyptic literature makes the truth come to life in a vivid and exciting way. The dramatic imagery in Revelation illustrates the power of our enemy. Satan is the real cause of suffering for God's people, the severity of the first century persecution of the church, and the wrath of God upon those who would make His people suffer. In Revelation, the glory of the Father and

---

[7] Leland Ryken, *How to Read the Bible as Literature* (Grand Rapids, MI, Zondervan, 1984), 167.

[8] Ibid., 169.

[9] Morris, *Apocalyptic,* 33.

[10] Ibid., 36.

the Son and the victory granted to the church over their foes is depicted in the grandeur of this language. As dramatic as the descriptions of the suffering saints who cry out for divine intervention may be, even more impressive is the imagery of the victory gained through the righteous reckoning of Almighty God. Truly this is a message Christians of every century need to hear and especially those for whom it was initially intended.

Prophecy

The eternal purpose of God runs as a continuous thread throughout the scriptures, and is many times hidden in prophecy only to be made known later through the fulfillment of said prophecy. Biblically speaking, prophecy is a type of language that is employed by God to reveal His will and to foretell a future event. Prophecy can be both foretelling (predictive prophecy) and "forth telling" (a method of instruction or teaching). In either case, a true prophecy is a message sent from God.

The Holy Spirit enabled prophets to bear witness to the will of God through prophecy (2 Peter 1:19-21). It is no different in the case of John and Revelation (see 1:2, 10, 19). However, we must not conclude that Revelation is *either* apocalyptic *or* prophetic. It is both prophetic *and* apocalyptic. God is *revealing/unfolding* His plan to deliver His church from ongoing and future persecution through the voice of *prophecy*. In the case of Revelation, the testimony of Jesus is revealed through the spirit of prophecy (1:3; 19:10). Revelation is therefore a message to the seven churches of Asia Minor and to "whoever has an ear to hear *what the Spirit says to the churches*" (2:11, 29).

Many of the signs, symbols, and visions in Revelation are allusions to similar things as they appeared first in the OT. When we see these allusions, we are not to conclude that they must have identical meanings or even applications. Knowing the purpose for the visions, signs, and symbols of the OT may, however, help to explain the reason for seeing something similar in Revelation.

For example, the four living creatures (Revelation 4) appeared first in the OT (Isaiah 6; Ezekiel 1-2). In the OT they are called seraphim and cherubim. By learning about them in the OT, we can understand their place in Revelation as agents of the providence of God. Two witnesses appear alongside the temple in Zechariah 4 and in Revelation 11. They serve as agents of God's protection over the construction of Jerusalem's temple in Zechariah. They prophesy against the wickedness of the Holy City, are killed, and resurrected in Revelation.

A Circular Letter

As we study Revelation, we must not forget that it was also written as a letter to seven specific churches in Asia Minor. No doubt, it was circulated and read initially by these seven churches. The additional value of the message being circulated as a letter is that it "enables the writer to specify those to whom he or she is writing and to address their situation as specifically as he or she may wish."[11] Modern readers will find that these seven churches are representative of all churches, but adjustments must be made to account for changing historical contexts.[12] Modern readers should seek to understand the book in its original context while making any and all necessary applications to their present situation.

For instance, the original readers would have known the identity of the false apostles and prophets being mentioned, of Jezebel, and the doctrine of the Nicolaitans better than we can today. How-

---

[11] Richard Baukham, *The Theology of the Book of Revelation* (Cambridge, Cambridge University Press, 1993), 13.

[12] Ibid., 17.

ever, even though we may not ever encounter the group specifically known in sacred history as the Nicolaitans, we can adapt the message given to the churches to our present context and make an application pertaining to heretical groups we may face today.

Recipients

As discussed, Revelation was first received by John the apostle and was delivered to "the seven churches which are in Asia." Some have speculated over the years as to why Revelation was given only to seven churches when nearby congregations existed in Colossae and Hierapolis as well during the first century. As a matter of historical record, a great earthquake had destroyed much of that region. Colossae, Hierapolis, and Laodicea were each destroyed by this earthquake and Laodicea was the only city of the three to be rebuilt. Perhaps these churches merged. Regardless of whether only seven churches existed in that region at the time of writing, these seven churches relate to every congregation of the Lord's church in principle.

Every church needs to know what the Lord thinks of compromising with the secular world and that is discussed. Every congregation needs to know how the Lord reacts to false doctrine in the church and that is discussed. Every church must know to persevere and remain true regardless of their immediate circumstances and that is also discussed. The principles set forth in the addresses made to these churches are timeless and valid for any congregation of the Lord's church at any place in any time. It is difficult to reason this as being merely coincidental. Rather, the selection of these churches appears to be according to the divine wisdom of God. By His selection of these seven churches, God encompasses every Christian, in every congregation, upon every continent, for all time. By choosing these seven, God was able to address timeless issues pertaining to congregational relations and controversies for as long as the world shall stand.

Furthermore, these seven churches would have been in the thick of the fight. The seven churches of Asia needed to hear from God. At the time of writing, they were enduring and could endure even more distress. Seeing the severity of the persecution at hand, and not willing to allow His people to go without encouragement to remain steadfast, while also warning and chastening those who were not staying the course, the Lord decided to make His presence known and His voice heard in this most marvelous way.

Through the seven churches of Asia, Christians everywhere are reminded that the Lord knows their hearts, He knows their present condition, He hears their prayers, and He sees their struggles, temptations, and even their compromises. He reproves, rebukes, and encourages His people to keep their faith in recognition of His will and the certainty of eternity. God's people could rest assured that just as the sun rises and sets on rulers and kingdoms of the earth, God will overthrow the wicked and rescue His people.

Author

Many times, it is said of John that he was the "disciple whom Jesus loved." Among the followers of Jesus during His earthly ministry, John appears to be His foremost friend.[13] Among the patriarchs, it was Abraham who was called "the friend of God." Among the kings, David was "a man after God's own heart." Among the prophets, Daniel was "a man greatly beloved."

A comparison of Matthew 27:56 and Mark 15:40 implies that John's mother was Salome. Salome may have been Mary's sister (John 19:25). If so, Jesus and John would have been maternal first cousins. "But this cannot be insisted upon, for it is not certain that

---

[13] James Stalker, *The Two St. Johns of the New Testament* (New York: American Tract Society, 1895), 9.

the fourth Evangelist is making the same selection from the women before the cross (of whom there were many, Matthew 27:55) as the other Evangelists."[14] Salome also provided for the Lord out of her substance (Mark 15:40-41; Luke 8:3). John's father was Zebedee. Zebedee appears to have been a successful and prosperous fisherman, seeing that he owned a boat and hired servants to help (Mark 1:19-20). The family apparently lived in Capernaum (Mark 1:21).

John and his brother James worked with their father in the family business (Matthew 4:18-22; Mark 1:16-20). The two brothers were identified as the "sons of thunder" by our Lord (Mark 3:17). Perhaps this was because of their temperament at that early age. On one occasion, after Christ was rejected by a Samaritan village, the brothers wanted to call down fire upon the city (Luke 9:51-56), as Elijah had once done (2 Kings 1:10-12). On another occasion, to the chagrin of the others, along with their mother, they solicited the Lord to allow each one to sit at His right and left hand in the kingdom (Mark 10:35-45). Again, we must observe that these events occurred while John was a relatively young man with a young faith. As his faith would grow, John would mature into a great leader in the early church.

John was first a disciple of John the Baptist. He had traveled southward from the Sea of Galilee to find John and hear his message. His heart was stirred by John's preaching of repentance and the coming kingdom. Having been baptized by John in the wilderness, he decided to remain and continue with him. He did so until the baptism of Jesus. Upon learning that Jesus was the Lamb of God who would take away the sin of the world (John 1:29, 35), John and Andrew began to follow Christ.

---

[14] Leon Morris, "John the Apostle," *ISBE*, vol.2 (revised) (Grand Rapids, MI: Eerdmans, 1982), 1107.

While Jesus was being tempted in the wilderness, John and the others had returned to their usual routine of life. Sometime after those forty days Jesus again found John, along with Peter, Andrew, and James, and called the four of them to follow Him (Mark 1:16-20). Peter, James, and John would become the closest disciples of Christ. Only these three were selected to witness the raising of Jairus' daughter (Mark 5:37; Luke 8:51), the scenes upon the Mount of Transfiguration (Matthew 17:1-2; Mark 9:2; Luke 9:28-29), and the internal conflict and agony Jesus suffered at Gethsemane (Matthew 26:37; Mark 14:33).

After the establishment of the church (Acts 2), and upon the healing of a lame man in Jerusalem, it was Peter and John who stood boldly against the hostility of the Sanhedrin (Acts 3-4). John also possessed the ability to impart miraculous gifts to others, as is evident by his laying on of hands to new converts in Samaria (Acts 8:14-25). He was one of the pillars of the church in Jerusalem, along with Peter and James (Galatians 2:9).

However, his greatest contribution to Christianity came in the form of his writings. Through the inspiration of the Holy Spirit, John has given us the Gospel of John, 1 John, 2 John, 3 John, and the book we now study – Revelation.

Traditions vary concerning the end of John's life. He is said to have lived from 90-120 years of age. Some traditions have him dying a martyr's death. Others have him dying of old age. "The dominant tradition, however, was that the apostle John moved to Ephesus in Asia Minor, and that from there he was banished to the Isle of Patmos (sometime during Domitian's reign, A.D. 81-96). Tradition also tells that he returned later to Ephesus, where he died after Trajan became emperor in A.D. 98."[15] The theory that he was exiled to Patmos seems to fit with Revelation 1:9.

Date of Writing

Two views have been predominant in the dating of Revelation. One view is that Revelation was written around 95-96 during the reign of Domitian and due to his persecution of the church.[16] The other view is for an earlier date of 65-68, during the reign of Nero and his persecution of the church. Nero's persecution was limited to Rome and no farther than Italy. However, "Domitian's persecution broke out at many points throughout the empire. Its severity was dependent to a great extent upon the policy of the local Roman rulers."[17] It seems more plausible to believe that the churches of Asia were being persecuted during Domitian's reign rather than during the reign of Nero.

While many commentators choose either the early or later persecution of the church as being that which is discussed in Revelation, reasons for believing *both* the early and later persecutions of the first century church will be discussed throughout this study. We believe the early Jewish persecution of the church is discussed in Revelation, as well as the Roman persecution of the first century. It seems that interpretations limited to only one period of persecution in the first century present a variety of pitfalls to students of the book, because two periods of persecution are historically correct and appear to be addressed.

In Revelation, we will see Jewish persecution come and go. The church is delivered by God. We will observe the destruction

---

[15] Ronald F. Youngblood (ed.), "John the Apostle," *Nelson's New Illustrated Bible Dictionary* (Nashville, TN: Thomas Nelson, 1995), 689.

[16] The earliest commentators of Revelation, Irenaeus, and Eusebius, also held to this date for the writing of Revelation.

[17] Charles Foster Kent, *The Work and Teachings of the Apostles* (New York: Scribner, 1916), 246.

of Jerusalem during the 70 AD span. The church is delivered by God. Next, we will arrive at the Rome persecution of the church, and it will also end by the deliverance of God. The assurance of God's deliverance will provide a message of comfort to the seven churches of Asia and blessing for Christians until Christ returns.

It appears that studies which maintain the early date of writing in view of the persecution prior to 70 AD are very convincing in their explanations of the images through chapter 12. However, from chapters 13-22, their explanations seem to be lacking the same ability to convince. Contrariwise, studies which wish to limit the meanings of the symbols in Revelation solely to the period of Domitian seem to be rather limited in their explanations of chapters 6-12, while being more convincing in their explanations of chapters 13-22.

By combining both Jewish and Roman persecution of the church and realizing that Revelation speaks retrospectively about events prior to 70 AD to Christians who were living in 95-96 AD, we will hope to clarify some difficulties in the various interpretations of the book. Through the various symbolism of Revelation, we believe God was teaching the seven churches of Asia who were facing Domitian's persecution that He will deliver them just as he had delivered the church from Jewish persecution.

A second reason has prompted this approach to Revelation; namely, a study of the severity of the Jewish persecution of the early church. We find it strange that something so significant to early Christians could go without reasonable recognition by many modern commentators of the book. While we are convinced that Domitian was the current and primary antagonist of the church at the time Revelation was written, the book contains a larger historical context. It is clear that two different cities – Jerusalem (representing Jewish persecution) and Rome – are discussed in Revelation.

We will find both the overthrow of "Sodom" where our Lord was crucified (Jerusalem) *and* "Babylon" the mother of harlots (Rome). By the time of Revelation, one has been defeated in their quest to stamp out Christianity, and the other is soon to be defeated. Domitian revived emperor worship, persecuted Christians for not worshipping him, and even put to death members of his own family for what he deemed "atheism" (Christianity).[18]

Christians are assured "He who was, *is*, and is to come." The same God that *was* in the OT, *is* today, and He is not finished. He is *to come*. God always was, remains, and forever will be in control of the destinies of men, the natural world, and time itself. Even during persecution, God is in control. Thus, "He that overcomes shall inherit all things; and I will be his God and he shall be my son" (21:7). Enemies of Christ believed they defeated Him at His crucifixion, yet He is alive and is to come. Those who pierced Him will see Him coming in glory and all nations of the earth will mourn at His reckoning (1:7).

The enemies of Christ could not defeat Him then and will not defeat Him now. With victory in view, Revelation was a message of hope to the Christians of the first century and it remains a message of hope for Christians today. However, it was also a message of warning to the church then just as it is now. Not only must sinful men repent (9:21), but also unfaithful Christians and unfaithful congregations of the Lord's church must repent (2:4-5; 2:16; 2:22; 3:3; 3:19).

---

[18] According to the Roman historian Cassius Dio, in 95, the last year of Domitian's reign, he put to death his cousin Flavius Clemens and banished his wife, Flavia Domitilla, who was also related to the emperor. 'The charge of atheism was made against both of them, in consequence of which many others also who had adopted the customs of the Jews were condemned. Some were put to death, others lost their property.' One of the Christian catacombs today bears the name of Domitilla, and many members of her household lie buried there.

The most important facts to glean from the book are two: (1) those who keep the faith will gain the victory. God will see to their vindication and eternal reward. (2) Those who persecute the church, do not accept the Lamb who died for them, and do not obey the commandments of God will be defeated and suffer eternally in the lake of fire which is the second death. They will not prevail. God will be victorious. He will protect His people. He will have the final say upon the earth and in the world to come.

Historical Background

Persecution against the church was rampant in the first century. The book of Acts describes the persecution of the church which began first at the hands of the Jews in Jerusalem, where the church began (Acts 2). The Sanhedrin commanded the apostles to be silent (Acts 4:18; 5:40). When they refused to be silent, they were beaten (Acts 5:40; 18:17; 21:30-32), imprisoned (Acts 5:18; 9:2; 12:2-4; 22:4-5), and some were even put to death (Acts 7:58-60; 12:1-2). Jewish persecution of the church would spread beyond the borders of Judea into Asia Minor. Our Lord twice noted the "synagogue of Satan" which was responsible for adding to the misery of the brethren in Smyrna (Revelation 2:9) and in Philadelphia (Revelation 3:9). Persecution from Jews beyond the borders of Judea is frequently discussed throughout the NT (see 2 Corinthians 11:24; Galatians 5:11; 6:12; 1 Thessalonians 2:14-16). Even some of the Jews which were converted to Christianity were responsible for disrupting the unity and harmony of their brethren by attempting to bind the Law of Moses on them.

The "zeal"[19] exhibited by the Jews in their persecution of the church extended well into the second century. Many of the church's early leaders were put to death due to the heavy hand of

---

[19] *Martyrdom of Polycarp*, 13.1.

21

Jewish persecution. While persecution first came at the hand of the Jews, it would come later from the Romans.

Our study will attempt to show how the Jewish persecution of the church is discussed retrospectively beginning with the breaking of the seals (ch.6-11) and Roman persecution is discussed beginning with the beast of the sea (ch.13-19). Chapter twelve serves and a link connecting the two persecutions. Revelation reminds Christians of how God delivered them from Jewish persecution in Judea, while also assuring them that Roman persecution will not prevail.

To understand Roman persecution of the church, we must first learn about the imperial cult, emperor deification, and emperor worship. The practice of leader worship did not originate with Rome. Many civilizations practiced some form of leader worship or another in various places around the world for centuries prior to Rome. Before any such practice occurred in Rome, there was the practice of honoring the spirits of dead ancestors, rather than a living ruler. Incidentally, this pagan practice has been transferred into the Roman Catholic Church's practice of venerated sainthood.

To trace the development of the Roman imperial cult, we must return to the reign of Augustus Octavian (27 BC-14 AD). Augustus was the adopted son of Julius Caesar. Julius Caesar was assassinated and publicly cremated in 44 BC. Upon his ashes one of his Greek freedmen erected a pillar and offered coal to the dead ruler whom he considered to be among the gods. The senate in Rome would later declare Caesar to be *Devus Julius* or "god Julius." Augustus Octavian then began calling himself *Devi Filius* or "son of a god."

Augustus would go on to create the early guidelines for the imperial cult, while being sure to include Roma, the female goddess who personified the Roman state. The Roman citizens were instructed to worship Roma and Julius, but not Augustus himself. However, the religious prestige of Julius being a god would have been shared with Augustus, his son. The cult of Roma would later be blended with the cult of the emperor in their temples, sacrifices, prayers, and rituals.

The imperial cult spread quickly throughout the empire and soon became a tool to unite its people. Imperial cult centers became rallying points for the citizenry to express devotion to the emperor and to Rome. In time, emperors increased the influence of the imperial cult so that the cult effectively became a state religion and a test of loyalty.

When Christians refused to offer worship to the emperor and regarded emperor worship as idolatry, they were considered by Romans to be atheists and enemies of the state. During their trials, a statue of the emperor was present so that Christians could offer the appropriate sacrifices and absolve them of any wrongdoing. In the eyes of the pagan Romans, Christians were the enemies of the gods, disturbing the *peace of the gods* and of the Roman state. Refusing to take part in imperial cult worship was considered treasonous. Emperor worship continued throughout first century Rome during the reigns of Tiberius, Caligula, Claudius, Nero, Vespasian, Titus, Domitian, Nerva, and Trajan with varying obligations, strictness, and intensity of enforcement.

In addition to the animosity surrounding cult worship, Nero accused Christians of starting the great fire which consumed over one-half of the city of Rome (July 18, 64 AD). Nero's persecution of Christians would last until his death in 68 AD and would be confined to the city of Rome and its surrounding area. The Roman historian Tacitus provides us with the grizzly details and madness of Nero's persecution.

He writes, "Nero fastened the guilt and inflicted the most exquisite tortures on a class hated for their abominations, called Christians by the populace. Christus, from whom the name had its origin, suffered the extreme penalty during the reign of Tiberius at the hands of one of our procurators, Pontius Pilatus, and a most mischievous superstition, thus checked for the moment, again broke out not only in Judaea, the first source of the evil, but even in Rome, where all things hideous and shameful from every part of the world find their center and become popular. Accordingly, an arrest was first made of all who pleaded guilty; then, upon their information, an immense multitude was convicted, not so much of the crime of firing the city, as of hatred against mankind. Mockery of every sort was added to their deaths. Covered with the skins of beasts, they were torn by dogs and perished, or were nailed to crosses, or were doomed to the flames and burnt, to serve as a nightly illumination, when daylight had expired."[20]

In 55 AD, the senate erected a statue to Nero in the temple of Mars Ulto.[21] Beginning in 65 AD, Nero was depicted on coins as "god" and "Apollo the Lyre Player" while wearing the crown of a deified emperor. Even though he rejected the proposal to build a temple to the "divine Nero" as was proposed by the senate, he did construct in his palace a 100 ft. bronze statue of himself as the sun with a star-shaped crown. He was greeted with such blasphemous praises as "O Divine Voice," "lord of the whole world," and "master and god." Shortly before his suicide, he was declared an "enemy of the state" and was never consecrated by the senate.

---

[20] Tacitus, *Annals*, 15.
[21] Ibid., 13.

Nero's persecution is often alluded to in the NT (see 1 Peter 1:6; 4:12-19). In Hebrews 10:32-35 and 12:3-7, we find two passages which could either refer to Jewish or Roman persecution of the church, depending on who we believe to have been the first recipients. It seems most likely that those who first received the homily of Hebrews were Jewish Christians living in and around the city of Rome during the early stages of Nero's persecution, as they had not yet suffered bloodshed (Hebrews 12:4).

Vespasian was consecrated by his son, Titus. Titus was hailed as "savior of the world" though his salvation was not believed to be salvation from sin. Domitian consecrated Titus upon his ascension to the throne. Domitian will play a prominent role in our study of Revelation. He was the last emperor of Rome to persecute the church during the first century. Domitian demanded to be addressed as "our lord and god" while still alive and all who refused were punished. Emperor deification and rituals such as incense, prayers, and vows became obligatory. Imperial cult rituals like these were used as a means of identifying Christians and persecuting them. Refusal to worship his image was deemed "atheism" and the penalty could be as severe as death.

His persecution extended beyond the limits of the city itself and broadly into the empire. Domitian was so vicious that many wondered if Nero had come back to life.[22] "In this persecution many eminent Christians suffered; but the death of Domitian soon delivered them from this calamity. In the year 95, 40,000 were

---

[22] Ray Summers, *Worthy Is the Lamb* (Nashville, TN: Broadman & Holman, 1951), 81-85.

supposed to have suffered martyrdom."[23] Domitian's reign of terror ended when conspirators stabbed him to death on September 18, 96 AD. His wife was among the conspirators.[24]

However, the existence and practices of the imperial cult did not end with Domitian. Trajan (98-117) allowed a temple to be erected in his name at Pergamum. A letter from Pliny, the governor of Bithynia during the time of Trajan, showed the cult in its political operation. Sadly, in this letter we find many Christians recanting their faith and confession of Christ.

Pliny writes: "Those who denied they were, or had ever been, Christians, who repeated after me an invocation to the gods, and offered adoration, with wine and frankincense, to your image, which I had ordered to be brought for that purpose, together with those of the gods, and who finally cursed Christ—none of which acts, it is said, those who are really Christians can be forced into performing—these I thought it proper to discharge. Others who were named by that informer at first confessed themselves Christians, and then denied it; true, they had been of that persuasion, but they had quitted it, some three years, others many years, and a few as much as twenty-five years ago. They all worshipped your statute and the images of the gods, and cursed Christ."[25]

Hadrian (117-138) was identified with Zeus. He also once again destroyed Jerusalem and renamed it Aelia Capitolina and declared it to be a pagan city. A temple to the Roman god Jupiter was erected on the temple mount and Jews were forbidden from entering the city.

---

[23] John McClintock and James Strong, *Cyclopedia of Biblical, Theological, and Ecclesiastical Literature*, vol. 7 (Grand Rapids, MI: Baker, 1981), 965.

[24] Brian W. Jones, "Domitian," *ABD*, vol. 2 (New York: Doubleday, 1992), 222. See also, Donald L. Jones, "Roman Imperial Cult," *ABD*, vol. 5 (New York: Doubleday, 1992), 806-09.

[25] Pliny, *Letters*, 10. 96, 97.

Antoninus Pious (138-161) sentenced Polycarp to death by burning for refusing to say, "Caesar is lord" and offer incense to him. During the reign of Marcus Aurelius (161-180) the senate allowed cult priests to use Christians in the arena rather than gladiators.

Commodus (180-192) demanded divine honors just as did Nero and Domitian. Septimius Severus (193-211) received the title of "lord." Christian persecution continued during his reign.

In 249, Decius restored the worship of consecrated emperors and demanded oaths and offerings in his honor. He ordered Christians to do the same. His successor, Valerian, continued the practice. In 284, Diocletian attempted to revive the imperial cult and demanded to be called "lord and god."

During the reign of Constantine I (306-337), a quite astonishing and historic transition occurred as Christianity became recognized as the only state religion. Christians enjoyed protection due to imperial favor for a brief time. From the death of Constantine to the end of the empire (476), some Roman emperors were sympathetic to Christians while others were antagonistic. It was during the reign of Theodosius 1 (379-395), who also adopted Christianity as Rome's state religion, that all traditional gods and the imperial cult were officially abandoned.

Schools of Interpretation

The *preterist* school of thought claims that, except for specific happenings surrounding the Lord's return, every apocalyptic message in the book was fulfilled during the time of John and the years immediately following. This school of thought has two divisions: the *right wing* and the *left wing*. The right wing preterists believe in the inspiration and accuracy of Revelation and that it foretold and pertained to the church during a time of immediate persecution. Many right wing preterists are of the belief that Revelation was given during the time of Nero and much of it referred to the destruction of Jerusalem. The left wing preterists believe that John was predicting a series of events in his immediate future which would include the rise of an antichrist and the destruction of the city of Rome.

The *futurist* school believes that nothing beyond the fourth chapter has taken place or will occur until just before our Lord's return. This school is primarily made up of those who are pre-millennial dispensationalists.

The *continuous historical* school views Revelation as an ongoing struggle between the church and the world from its beginning until the second coming of Christ. The scholars of this school point to the Roman Catholic Church, the Holy Roman Empire, current issues, governments, and wars as being fulfillments of the messages from Revelation.

The *parallelist* school considers the principles behind the visions while taking the message to be quite literal. This view of the book sees parallel accounts throughout Revelation, thus foretelling and then re-telling God's judgments against the wicked which would persecute His church. Some see the same message of the book being told twice and some see the same message being told three times. With each parallel account the judgment scene intensifies and magnifies until ultimately ending with the judgment scene of Revelation 20:11-15. Also, the splendor of heaven and the punishment of the wicked become more vivid with each parallel account throughout the book.

It seems the conflicting ideas between the various schools of thought have contributed more to the misunderstanding of Revelation than they have helped students to find its message and meaning. Elements of truth can be found in the various interpretations of the book's signs and symbols in each of the four schools of thought.

Rules of Interpretation

Rather than being guided strictly by one of the prominent schools of interpretation which we have discussed, our study will elect to follow four significant and helpful rules of basic Bible interpretation to gain a clearer understanding of the meaning and prayerfully to follow faithfully the message of Revelation. The *first rule* we shall observe is to consider the text of the book itself. What is the historical context? What are the textual variants? What are the best translations available? What are the findings of significant word studies, etc.? The premise for this rule is simply to do our due diligence to ensure that we have an accurate rendering of the text and context before proceeding to an interpretation of it.

Secondly, we will be cross-referencing scripture to ensure that fundamental biblical teachings serve as the basis for our interpretation of the message. We will look to literal passages to grasp the meaning of figurative passages. We know if we have reached an understanding of a figurative passage which contradicts the clear meaning of a literal passage, we must study harder, for we have failed to arrive at the true meaning of the text. Cross-referencing scripture will both safeguard our interpretation of Revelation and enhance our understanding of its message.

The *third rule* worth following is to consider any allusions to other apocalyptic images. Do we find similar images elsewhere in biblical apocalyptic writings? Can an understanding of those images help us to understand better the images we find in Revelation? If we can find a scriptural answer to an apocalyptic image, our work as exegetes of the text will be greatly hastened.

The *fourth rule* to be applied throughout this study is more of a practical suggestion than a textbook rule. We will seek to provide literal wording to apocalyptic passages when possible. We will imagine the language as though it was being written in an epistle to the churches using literal language. It is a simple little tactic, but it pays great dividends in arriving at reasonable interpretations of the text.

Let us use the first apocalyptic image found in Revelation (1:4) as an example of how these four rules can help us to arrive at clear and meaningful conclusions in apocalyptic literature. The verse reads, "John, to the seven churches which are in Asia: Grace to you and peace from Him who is and who was and who is to come, and from the seven Spirits who are before His throne…" (NKJV).

We have herein identified for us the messenger – John; the recipients – the seven churches which are in Asia; a benediction of grace and truth from God – Him who is and who was and who is to come. The apocalyptic portion of the verse is found in the phrase "from the seven Spirits who are before His throne." What are these "seven Spirits" and should "Spirits" be capitalized?

The first rule of interpretation which we have stated requires an accurate rendition of the text. Some translations have capitalized "Spirits," and some have not. The capitalization of the word has caused some to interpret the statement to refer to the Holy Spirit. Studying manuscripts and translations alone does not answer our question satisfactorily.

Moving to our second rule, however, by cross-referencing scripture we find in Revelation 5:6 that seven eyes "are the seven Spirits of God sent out into all the earth." Thus, Revelation itself has provided the meaning for the vision of seven Spirits. These seven Spirits are the seven eyes of God. Does God literally have seven eyes? Such an interpretation would fail to consider the usage of the number seven in apocalyptic literature, as seven is used to denote completeness. Thus, answering one question has led to other questions.

When we apply our third rule of interpretation and seek to find any other biblical allusions to this saying, we find one in Zechariah 3:9-4:10. In that passage, we find seven eyes of the Lord "which scan to and from throughout the whole earth." We mention this OT reference because it helps to explain what these seven eyes/spirits are doing in Revelation. They are scanning throughout the whole earth. Thus, the all-seeing eye of God is completely aware of what is transpiring on the earth.

Now let us implement the fourth rule we have suggested and try to render a literal wording for the apocalyptic statement under consideration. If John were writing what he saw and heard in a literal epistle to the churches, it might read something like this:

> "John, to the seven churches which are in Asia: Grace to you and peace from Him who is and who was and who is to come, *who sees all things* from His throne..."

By following these four simple rules of interpretation we have made the capitalization of seven "Spirits" unnecessary by realizing the Holy Spirit is not really the point of the statement. We have also arrived at an accurate, applicable, and literal understanding of a figurative passage. The imagery portrays our God upon His throne with dominion and power. He is fully aware of all that is transpiring for good or evil pertaining to His church. He knows who is faithful. He knows who is unfaithful. He knows who is being persecuted and He will deliver them. Holding the future in His hands, the Father offers grace and peace to settle the spirit troubled by the continual conflict being waged in the world.

Canonicity

Beginning with Justin Martyr, Irenaeus, Tertullian, Hippolytus, Clement of Alexandria, Origen, Eusebius, Victorinus (who wrote the earliest known commentary on Revelation), and the Muratorian Canon (which includes the book), the book of Revelation has been appreciated and accepted as the divine word of God from many of the earliest Christian writings. From the time of the second and third centuries, we find allusions to various versions of the NT, quotes from these inspired writings, and even some lists beginning to appear group the books believed to be inspired.[26] Consider the following list of the historical evidence from the second and third centuries and the recognition given to Revelation.[27]

1.) Tatian (c. 120) was a disciple of John. He is said to have known and used nearly all the NT books.

2.) The *Didache* (c. 120) cites most NT books.

3.) Justin Martyr (c. 100-165) had access to the Gospels, Acts, Romans, 1 Corinthians, Galatians, Ephesians, Colossians, 2 Thessalonians, Hebrews, and Revelation.

4.) Melito of Sardis (c. Second Century) quoted from all the NT books except James, Jude, 2 John, and 3 John.

5.) Theophilus (c.115-188) seemed to have had all (or at least a bulk) of the NT books and held them with equal reverence as the OT books.

---

[26] As far as the earliest Christian writings are concerned, an author may or may not have mentioned a NT book simply because of the subject matter he was addressing. In such cases, no argument can be successfully maintained for the exclusion of certain NT books solely because a certain writer did not mention them.

[27] Compiled chronologically from H.C. Thiessen's, *Introduction to the New Testament* (Grand Rapids, MI: Eerdmans, 1966), 6-27.

6.) The Gnostic writers Basilides of Alexandria (c. 130) and Valentinus (c. 140) appear to have known and accepted in general the books of the NT.

7.) The Old Latin version (before 170) was in general use in Africa. It appears to have had all or most of the books of the NT.

8.) Muratorian Fragment (c. 170) lists all but 1 and 2 Peter, James, and Hebrews.

9.) Fragments of some Egyptian versions (as early as 200 AD) contain practically the whole NT.

10.) Clement of Alexandria (c.155-215) accepted all the books in the NT.

11.) Tertulian of Carthage (c. 150-222) believed Barnabas wrote Hebrews and therefore rejected it. Other than that, it appears that he accepted the rest of the NT.

12.) Origen of Alexandria (c. 185-253) wrote that the four Gospels, Acts, thirteen epistles of Paul, 1 Peter, 1 John, and Revelation were universally accepted as scripture, while Hebrews, 2 Peter, 2 and 3 John, James and Jude (among others) were doubted by some.

13.) Cyprian (c. 200-258) quoted from all but Philemon, James, 2 Peter, 2 and 3 John, Jude, and Hebrews.

14.) Dionysius of Alexandria (c. 200-265) used some of the "disputed books" such as 2 and 3 John as well as James.

15.) Eusebius of Caesarea (c. 265-340) seems to have accepted all the books of the NT, although recognizing some were disputed.

16.) The Chester Beatty Papyri (c. third century or earlier) contain portions of three codices of the NT, which when complete, would have included all the books in the NT.

From the evidence of the second and third centuries, the early existence and circulation of the book of Revelation is undeniable. Moreover, early Christian scholars were writing commentaries on Revelation. Such an undertaking would be strange indeed if it was not considered a part of the inspired canon of scripture.

Textual Issues

When a document is said to contain at least sixty different wordings for its title,[28] one might expect to be overwhelmed by textual variants. However, only approximately 115 variants can be found throughout the text, and none are so significant as to warrant any concern over doctrine or theological conclusions. The doctrinal and theological discussions which stem from Revelation overall, would exist with or without the variants found in the manuscripts. Any variants deemed necessary will be discussed in the text of the commentary itself, but these are few in number.

Theological Themes

Couched within its apocalyptic style, many significant theological themes can be found in Revelation. No theme to be discussed, however, will be valued more significantly than the doctrine of God and His relationship with man as pictured throughout Revelation. "The theology of Revelation is highly theocentric."[29] God is viewed as eternal, all-knowing, and all-powerful. He remains sovereign over His creation. God is righteous and just in His ways and judgments. He is compassionate toward His creation, specifically His people, yet His wrath can be provoked by man's unwillingness to repent. Only God can deliver man. Only God can bring order and a new creation out of chaos.

---

[28] Bruce M. Metzger, *A Textual Commentary on the Greek New Testament* (New York: United Bible Societies, 1971), 731.

[29] "God-centered." See Bauckham, *Theology*, 23.

The deity of Christ is coupled with the working of the Father. He is likewise eternal, bearing all the attributes of the Father. He is triumphant over death and will triumph over evil. Our ultimate victory will come through Him who "loved us and washed us in His own blood."

Certain aspects pertaining to angelology are prominent in the book of Revelation. Angels are ministers of the will of God. They are not to be worshipped. Some have fallen. Yet, all are powerful. However, their power is derived from God and is not self-perpetuating.

Anthropology can also be studied throughout Revelation. Man is loved by God. Man is cruel to man. Man can overcome evil with good or good men can be overcome by evil. Man possesses free-will. He is in danger of the possibility of apostasy. The persecution of God's people would and could cause many to yield their faith and denounce their confession of Christ. He must decide and the hour of decision is at hand.

One's understanding of biblical eschatology is increased by studying Revelation. Readers will learn something of the intermediate state of the dead, God's judgments and punishments, including final judgment, hell, and the new heavens and new earth.

As we study the text itself, we will pay close attention to the theology taught in the message. We will seek to understand more of God's relationship with man and how this relationship has come to exist. Moreover, it will be for us to learn how man's relationship with God can positively or negatively affect his relationship with fellowmen.

Outline of Revelation

A. Introduction and Benediction, 1:1-8.

B. John's First Vision of Christ, 1:9-20.

C. Christ's Message to the Seven Churches of Asia, 2:1-3:22.

    1.) Message to the Church in Ephesus, 2:1-7.

    2.) Message to the Church in Smyrna, 2:8-11.

    3.) Message to the Church in Pergamum, 2:12-17.

    4.) Message to the Church in Thyatira, 2:18-29.

    5.) Message to the Church in Sardis, 3:1-6.

    6.) Message to the Church in Philadelphia, 3:7-13.

    7.) Message to the Church in Laodicea, 3:14-22.

D. John's Vision of God and the Throne Room in Heaven, 4:1-11.

E. John's Second Vision of Christ, 5:1-14.

F. The Opening of Seven Seals, 6:1-8:1.

    1.) The Four Horsemen, 6:1-8.

    2.) The Martyrs in Heaven, 6:9-11.

    3.) The Great Day of God's Wrath Commences, 6:12-17.

    4.) Divine Protection for 144,000 of Israel, 7:1-8.

    5.) Divine Protection for a Great Multitude of the Nations, 7:9-17.

    6.) The Opening of the Seventh Seal, 8:1.

G. The Sounding of Seven Trumpets, 8:2-11:19.

    1.) Wrath upon Vegetation, 8:7.

    2.) Wrath upon the Seas, 8:8-9.

    3.) Wrath upon Fresh Waters, 8:10-11.

    4.) Wrath Displayed in the Heavens, 8:12-13.

Chapter One

Introduction and Benediction (vv. 1-3)

"The Revelation of Jesus Christ, which God gave Him to show His servants—things which must shortly take place. And He sent and signified it by His angel to His servant John, who bore witness to the word of God, and to the testimony of Jesus Christ, to all things that he saw. Blessed is he who reads and those who hear the words of this prophecy, and keep those things which are written in it; for the time is near" (vv.1-3).

In the first three verses we find the authority, author, apostle, and audience of the book of Revelation. The authority is God, the Father – "God in heaven who reveals secrets" (Daniel 2:28 ff.). The author is Christ, the Son. The apostle (the one sent with the message) is John, with the assistance of a divinely commissioned angel. The audience is His church, "the servants of Christ" – initially the seven churches of Asia Minor (1:4); but ultimately it is a message which offers something to Christians everywhere in every generation.

John's mission was to bear witness to the word of God, which is also called the testimony of Jesus Christ, and to all things that he saw. Concerning the things which he saw, these "must shortly take place," "for the time is near." In apocalyptic literature there is a common theme of judgment being imminent.[1] Such is the case here. The Lord reminds us throughout Revelation how "The Most High rules in the kingdom of men, and gives it to whomever He chooses" (Daniel 4:25). Regardless of what may be occurring in

---

[1] Morris, *Apocalyptic*, 44-45.

the lives of His people, or any amount of persecution they may be enduring, the future remains in God's hands, and His alone.

Revelation also bestows a blessing to those who read, hear (listen to), and keep the words of this prophecy and the things written therein (1:3). Seven beatitudes are found in the book.

1.) "Blessed is he who reads and those who hear the words of this prophecy, and keep those things which are written in it; for the time is near" (1:3).

2.) "Blessed are the dead who die in the Lord from now on. 'Yes,' says the Spirit, 'that they may rest from their labors, and their works follow them'" (14:13).

3.) "Behold, I am coming as a thief. Blessed is he who watches, and keeps his garments, lest he walk naked and they see his shame" (16:15).

4.) "Blessed are those who are called to the marriage supper of the Lamb!'" (19:9).

5.) "Blessed and holy is he who has part in the first resurrection. Over such the second death has no power, but they shall be priests of God and of Christ, and shall reign with Him a thousand years" (20:6).

6.) "Behold, I am coming quickly! Blessed is he who keeps the words of the prophecy of this book" (22:7).

7.) "Blessed are those who do His commandments, that they may have the right to the tree of life, and may enter through the gates into the city" (22:14).

When we combine the beatitudes in Revelation, we find that one is called to the marriage supper by hearing and keeping His word. This person will be blessed by the first resurrection. Once risen to walk a new life, a Christian must watch and keep himself pure and in Christ, thus keeping His commandments. If one lives in Christ, he will die in Christ and be blessed for all eternity. He will have right to the tree of life in the celestial city of God.

Greeting the Seven Churches (vv. 4-8)

"John, to the seven churches which are in Asia: Grace to you and peace from Him who is and who was and who is to come, and from the seven Spirits who are before His throne, and from Jesus Christ, the faithful witness, the firstborn from the dead, and the ruler over the kings of the earth. To Him who loved us and washed us from our sins in His own blood, and has made us kings and priests to His God and Father, to Him be glory and dominion forever and ever. Amen. Behold, He is coming with clouds, and every eye will see Him, even they who pierced Him. And all the tribes of the earth will mourn because of Him. Even so, Amen. 'I am the Alpha and the Omega, the Beginning and the End,' says the Lord, 'who is and who was and who is to come, the Almighty'" (vv.4-8).

John's greeting to the churches is one of grace and peace. While some hard things are soon to be spoken to these congregations, the message of the Lord was motivated by love for His church. God wanted grace and peace to prevail in His church. John brings a message to them "from Him who is and who was and who is to come" – lit. "The One being, and the One who was, and the coming One."[2] God is not merely a figure from the past, but He is present, and He is to come. God is in the past, in the present, and in the future – eternal and without beginning or end. God is not bound by time. One thousand years is as a day with the Lord (2 Peter 3:8).

---

[2] Philip W. Comfort, *The New Testament Text and Translation Commentary* (Carol Stream, IL: Tyndale House, 2008), 809.

Seven Spirits are before His throne. Let us pause here to observe that this is the first apocalyptic statement (one using a sign or symbol) found in Revelation. The meaning for the symbolism is found in Revelation 5:6. There we learn that the seven spirits are the eyes of the Lord. The symbol is thus connected which the Lord's omniscience. God is all-knowing. In Zechariah we also find that the Lord has seven eyes which scan throughout the earth (Zechariah 4:10). In both passages the symbolism conveys God's omniscience and omnipresence.

Commentators usually suggest that the seven spirits are either angelic spirits, or the Holy Spirit. However, the book itself only points to the omniscience and even omnipresence of God. The number seven is significant in apocalyptic literature. "Of the numbers that carry symbolic meaning in biblical usage, seven is the most important. It is used to signify completeness or totality."[3]

God has decreed that each week has seven days (Genesis 1:1-2:3). The blood of sacrifice had to be sprinkled seven times for complete purification (Leviticus 16:14, 19). Likewise, Christ is depicted as a Lamb with seven horns and seven eyes which are the seven spirits of God sent out into all the earth (Revelation 5:6), signifying His complete power and knowledge. Each of these cases illustrates to us how the number seven is used in scripture to convey the idea of completeness or totality.

Seven heavenly credentials of Christ are listed in this greeting as well. Jesus Christ is (1) the faithful witness; (2) the firstborn from the dead, and (3) the ruler over the kings of the earth. (4) He loved us and washed us (or "freed us" as in ESV and "released us" as in NASB) from our sins in His own blood. (5) He has made us

---

[3] Leland Ryken, James C. Wilhoit, Tremper Longman, *DBI* (Downer's Grove, IL: 1998), 774.

kings and priests (a kingdom of priests, cf. 1 Peter 2:9) to His God and Father. A doxology is included: "to Him be glory and dominion forever and ever. Amen." (6) He is coming with clouds, and every eye will see Him, even those who pierced Him. And all the tribes of the earth will mourn because of Him. (7) Christ certifies Himself, saying, "I am the Alpha and the Omega, the Beginning and the End,[4] who is and who was and who is to come, the Almighty."

Just as John is now called to bear witness to the word of God, Jesus did so faithfully while He was upon this earth (John 12:49, 50; John 17:8). Christ is also "the faithful witness" to the suffering of His people and the things happening in His church.

He is the firstborn of the dead. The idea of being "firstborn" is often connected with honor, and it would certainly be a fitting connection to make concerning Christ. Paul did so in Colossians 1:15, referring to Christ as the firstborn over all creation. Yet, Paul also spoke of Christ as the firstborn from the dead (Colossians 1:18). The dead will be raised as He was raised (John 5:28-29; Philippians 3:21; 1 John 3:2). In this sense He is the firstborn from among the dead (see also 1 Corinthians 15:42 ff.).

Christ is also ruler over the kings of the earth. The Father has given all authority in heaven and in earth to Christ (Matthew 28:18). Even though the church has suffered time and again at the hands of tyrannical rulers, Christ is still in control. All rulers of the earth will have to answer to Him. Every ruler's time is limited,

---

[4] The inclusion of the statement, "the beginning and the end" does not appear in early manuscripts and appears to be an inclusion by later scribes taken from 21:6. Revelation appears to contain an accumulation of titles for Christ as the book progress. See 1:8; 1:17; 2:8; 21:6; 22:13 (Comfort, 811).

and their days are numbered. Christ, however, is eternal and possesses true power. He will still be Lord and Christ after every persecutor of the church is sleeping beneath the sod.

Jesus died a physical death, but He is alive, and He is coming again. He will return with clouds and every eye will see Him, even those who pierced (drove the nails into) Him. All tribes of the earth will mourn because of Him. We have here a statement concerning some of the facts about the second coming of Christ. He will summon a universal resurrection of the dead in which all – both good and evil – will come forth (John 5:28-29; 1 Corinthians 15:23). Our Lord will come in power and glory (Mark 13:26; Luke 21:27; 2 Thessalonians 1:7; 1 Peter 4:12-13). The second coming will be visible to every eye (Acts 1:11). The return of Christ is revealed *only* as a single event, not two separate, distinct comings.

From scripture we learn of five distinct events to take place at His coming: (1) the last trump will sound; (2) Jesus will come in the clouds with His angels and holy ones being seen by every eye; (3) a resurrection of the righteous (dead) and wicked (dead) will take place, with the righteous meeting the Lord in the air and the wicked appearing before Him for judgment; (4) the righteous (living) will be caught up to meet Him in the air; (5) this universe, the earth, and all that is remaining will be destroyed with fire.

Jesus, however, is Alpha and remains Omega, the "beginning and the end." Just as the Father is, was, and is to come (1:4), so too is Christ. Just as the Father is Almighty, so too is Christ (1:8). Such statements proclaim the deity of Christ. The prophet Micah wrote of Christ "whose goings forth are from of old, From everlasting" (Micah 5:2). Throughout John's gospel and his epistles, attention is given to the deity of Christ. God used John to preach this essential message to the world. Jesus was in the beginning (John 1:1-3). He is "from the beginning" (1 John 1:1-2). The Word was not before or after God, but *with* God. Jesus was not only with

God, He was God. "The Word was God." Literally, "and God was the Word." He is of a divine nature possessing all the attributes of deity.[5]

An Apocalyptic Vision of Christ (vv. 9-20)

"I, John, both your brother and companion in the tribulation and kingdom and patience of Jesus Christ, was on the island that is called Patmos for the word of God and for the testimony of Jesus Christ. I was in the Spirit on the Lord's Day, and I heard behind me a loud voice, as of a trumpet, saying, 'I am the Alpha and the Omega, the First and the Last,' and, 'What you see, write in a book and send it to the seven churches which are in Asia: to Ephesus, to Smyrna, to Pergamos, to Thyatira, to Sardis, to Philadelphia, and to Laodicea'" (vv.9-11).

The beloved John had also felt the wrath of persecution, being a companion in tribulation and presumably by being banished to the isle of Patmos. Patmos was a volcanic, rocky, mostly treeless island in the Aegean Sea roughly ten miles long and six miles wide, off the coast of Asia Minor. During the Roman period, Patmos served as a place of banishment. It would become John's home because he had preached the word of God and born witness to Christ.

John received the Revelation while in the Spirit of the Lord's Day. Christians have a day in which they are to assemble into one place (Hebrews 10:25; 1 Corinthians 11:18, 20). This day is the first day of the week (Acts 20:7), the day of our Lord's resurrection. It is the Lord's Day. John was unable to assemble with his brethren due to his banishment from society. However, he was still able to worship God and enjoy spiritual peace of mind on the

---

[5] Cf. Isaiah 41:4; 44:6; 48:12 for similar statements made about God.

Lord's Day. Much like Daniel with Darius, Domitian could not take the desire to worship away from John. Though fettered by persecution and in isolation, John was willing to glorify God within the bounds of his limitations.

It was here on Patmos, while in the Spirit, that John heard from behind him a loud voice. The voice was powerful, likened to a trumpet, even like the voice of many waters (1:16). The voice said plainly, "What you see, write in a book and send it to the seven churches which are in Asia: to Ephesus, to Smyrna, to Pergamos, to Thyatira, to Sardis, to Philadelphia, and to Laodicea."

"Then I turned to see the voice that spoke with me. And having turned I saw seven golden lampstands, and in the midst of the seven lampstands One like the Son of Man, clothed with a garment down to the feet and girded about the chest with a golden band. His head and hair were white like wool, as white as snow, and His eyes like a flame of fire; His feet were like fine brass, as if refined in a furnace, and His voice as the sound of many waters; He had in His right hand seven stars, out of His mouth went a sharp two-edged sword, and His countenance was like the sun shining in its strength. And when I saw Him, I fell at His feet as dead. But He laid His right hand on me, saying to me, 'Do not be afraid; I am the First and the Last. I am He who lives, and was dead, and behold, I am alive forevermore. Amen. And I have the keys of Hades and of Death. Write the things which you have seen, and the things which are, and the things which will take place after this. The mystery of the seven stars which you saw in My right hand, and the seven golden lampstands: The seven stars are the angels of the seven churches, and the seven lampstands which you saw are the seven churches'" (vv.12-20).

When John turned to see who was speaking to him, he saw seven golden lampstands, which symbolized the seven churches mentioned (1:20). The light that emanated from the lampstand in the tabernacle/temple of the OT represented the presence of God (Exodus 25:30-31; Numbers 8:1-4). By comparison, "The new Israel, 'the church,' as a 'lampstand' is a part of the temple and is to draw its power from the Spirit, the divine presence, before God's throne in its drive to stand against the resistance of the world."[6]

Amid these lampstands was "One like the Son of Man." He was not separated from the churches, or outside of them, but *in the midst* of them (cf. Matthew 18:20; Hebrews 13:5). Christ was "clothed with a garment down to the feet and girded about the chest with a golden band" – the clothing of royalty and of OT priests. "His head and hair were white like wool, as white as snow, and His eyes like a flame of fire" – an awesome sight indeed! "His feet were like fine brass, as if refined in a furnace, and His voice as the sound of many waters." The description of Christ from head to foot is complete and attention turns to describing His voice a second time. The scene here is a combination of various OT visions of God (cf. Isaiah 6:1 ff., Daniel 7:9 and 10:6).

For those familiar with the OT, as was John, there could remain no doubt who was standing before Him. "He had in His right hand seven stars, out of His mouth went a sharp two-edged sword, and His countenance was like the sun shining in its strength." The seven stars in His hand are the seven angels of the seven churches. The angels are in the hand of Christ. Christ is in control of them. He has sent them, and He will receive them. Being found in the right hand of Christ is a matter of no small significance, as, "No man can be a Messenger of the Master and the Church save as he is held in the right hand of Jesus, and interprets, not his own idea

---

[6] G.K. Beale and D.A. Carson, *Commentary on the New Testament Use of the Old Testament* (Grand Rapids, MI: Baker Academic, 2007), 1091.

concerning the Church's well-being, nor the Church's wish concerning its function, but the will of the Master."[7]

"And when I saw Him, I fell at His feet as dead." John responded in much the same way as did Isaiah (Isaiah 6:5), Ezekiel (Ezekiel 1:28), and Daniel (Daniel 7:15; 8:17). The scene has garnered its intended response. The Son of God then comforts John. Christ comforts those who fear Him. The apostle writes, "He laid His right hand on me, saying to me, 'Do not be afraid; I am the First and the Last. I am He who lives, and was dead, and behold, I am alive forevermore. Amen. And I have the keys of Hades and of Death.'"

Hades is the realm of the dead (cf. Matthew 11:23; 16:18; Luke 10:15; 16:23; Acts 2:27, 31; Revelation 6:8; 20:13, 14). In the OT, we find the word *sheol* (Heb.) which corresponds to *hades* (Gr.) in the NT (cf. Genesis 37:35; Numbers 16:30, 33; Psalm 16:10).[8] The keys are within Christ's hand. Christ has authority over life, death, and beyond. While the Caesars were the most powerful men on earth, and often were recognized as gods in death, they could not claim even one of the credentials of Christ.

John is commanded to write these things which he has seen and will see, for they are "the things which are, and the things which will take place after this." Unlike Daniel, who was told that his vision pertained to events in the future rather than present (Daniel 10:14), John is told his vision is for things present and future. The time is at hand for God's judgments to begin.

---

[7] G. Campbell Morgan, *The Letters of Our Lord* (London: Pickering & Inglis, n.d.), 12.

[8] W.E. Vine, *Vines' Expository Dictionary of New Testament Words* (McLean, VA: MacDonald, n.d.), 527-8.

Application for Today

The blessing stated in verse three should be motivation enough for any student of Revelation to take its message seriously and seek to understand it. "Blessed is he who reads and those who hear the words of this prophecy, and keep those things which are written in it; for the time is near" (1:3). In chapter one, we have much to understand and value. In Christ, we have been loved and washed/freed/released from our sins in His precious blood (1:5). Christ has made us a kingdom of priests to God.

Regardless of what may transpire in this life, Christ remains ruler over the kings of the earth. Three parties are at the center of chapter one: the Father, the Son, and the church. From beginning to end, the Bible instructs man concerning his relationship with God. The church exists and has a reconciled relationship to the Father because of the Son. John serves as an instrument of communication as a brother in Christ to relate the things he will see and hear to his brethren in Christ.

Even though the message of Revelation was conveyed during a time of persecution (1:9), Christ was among His church. He had been there all along. He was there in the beginning of creation, He was there at the time of writing, He is there now, and He is coming back someday. At His return, a reckoning will occur (1:7). While His people may suffer persecution in this life, He has the keys of death and life to come (1:18). He will not forget His people and He will not forget those who punished them for His name's sake. While Rome was filled with imposters calling themselves a "god" or the "son of a god," Jesus is both God and the Son of God, the "faithful witness" of how things truly are, have been, and will be.

Chapter Two

The second chapter will provide specific addresses to four of the seven churches of ancient Asia Minor. In these addresses, we find the Lord's intimate knowledge of the spiritual conditions within His church. These churches are laid bare before the eyes of the Lord for good or bad. He knows and He cares. While providing both ample reason and time to repent, the Lord makes clear that the time He is granting for repentance is not infinite. Moreover, He encourages His brethren to know the period of persecution which that were currently enduring would not last forever.

The Church at Ephesus (vv. 1-7)

"To the angel of the church of Ephesus write, 'These things says He who holds the seven stars in His right hand, who walks in the midst of the seven golden lampstands: 'I know your works, your labor, your patience, and that you cannot bear those who are evil. And you have tested those who say they are apostles and are not, and have found them liars; and you have persevered and have patience, and have labored for My name's sake and have not become weary. Nevertheless I have this against you, that you have left your first love. Remember therefore from where you have fallen; repent and do the first works, or else I will come to you quickly and remove your lampstand from its place—unless you repent. But this you have, that you hate the deeds of the Nicolaitans, which I also hate. He who has an ear, let him hear what the Spirit says to the churches. To him who overcomes I will give to eat from the tree of life, which is in the midst of the Paradise of God'" (vv.1-7).

The city of Ephesus is known to have been the "supreme metropolis of Asia." At the time of writing, Ephesus was the fourth largest city in the Roman Empire, consisting of approximately 250,000 residents. It had the most important seaport in Asia Minor and three great trade routes passed through the city. Ephesus was also a "free city," meaning it had limited autonomy in the Empire.

Jesus addresses the church at Ephesus first. We are more familiar with Ephesus than with any of the other churches to be addressed since we can find its origin in the book of Acts (Acts 18:8 ff.), details of Paul's ministry in the city (Acts 19:1 ff; Acts 20:17-38), and an epistle written to them by Paul. In Paul's epistle to the Ephesians, it is interesting to note that he gave no word of rebuke, neither did he rebuke the church's leaders when he met with them (Acts 20:17 ff.). He did, however, warn of "savage wolves" who would come in and not sparing the flock, and that "from among yourselves" men would arise "speaking perverse things to draw away disciples after themselves" (Acts 20:29-30).

Christ begins by giving His approval of the many good qualities about this church. He commended their work, labor, and patience (endurance). Ephesus had been a working congregation. They had been a congregation which endured persecution and hardship. Ephesus did not forebear or compromise with those who were evil. They tested and found false apostles to be liars. "One phenomenon of the early church was the pretense of a group of false apostles, evidently claiming the credentials of the wider group of the apostles of Christ (cf. 2 Corinthians 3:1 ff.; 12:11 ff.)."[1] The church also persevered and labored for His name's sake without becoming weary. Moreover, they hated the deeds of the Nicolaitans, which Christ also hated (2:6).

---

[1] J.W. Roberts, *Revelation*, LWC (Austin, TX: Sweet, 1974), 38.

Who were these people and what were their deeds which the Lord hated? Many speculations abound concerning this group, but there is no real concrete evidence as to who they were. In the second century a Gnostic group was known by this name. However, it is uncertain whether these groups had any connection. It has been speculated that Nicolas (Acts 6:5) erred from the faith and that the Nicolaitans were his followers. Yet, it is extremely unfair and malicious to ruin a man's name without any tangible proof.

We can gather from the text that this was a divisive subgroup in the congregation at Ephesus and at Pergamos (2:15). It is also possible that the Jezebel in Thyatira was of this group (2:20). We do know that the Nicolaitans were known by another name than the divine name of Christ, they were teaching their own doctrine, and their works were hated by Christ.

While the church at Ephesus had many good qualities, the Lord had something against them. A church's good qualities do not excuse their sins. The Lord was not willing to allow their sins to continue. Even though they had many wonderful qualities, they had to make serious corrections to remain pleasing to the Lord.

The church had left their first love. The church was now in their second and third generation of members. "This is always a dangerous period in the life of a church. At such a point the youthful fire of discovery and the enthusiasm of a glorious anticipation of future hopes too often begin to diminish."[2] The Lord offered His remedy for the church to regain its first love: "Remember therefore from where you have fallen; repent and do the first works." *Remember*, *repent*, and *return*. You will recall that these are the very steps taken by the Prodigal Son in the Lord's parable to return to his father (Luke 15:11 ff.).

---

[2] Homer Hailey, *Revelation: An Introduction and Commentary* (Grand Rapids, MI: Baker, 1979),122.

The church's previous love could still be remembered. Just as they had willingly left that love, they could willingly return. The way they had fallen could be identified, and repentance could occur. The Lord stated His charge against them, commanded them to repent, and issued a warning – "or else I will come to you quickly and remove your lampstand from its place—unless you repent."

Just as Christ issued a warning for failure to repent, He remained willing to bestow a blessing to all those who will repent. Note, "He who has an ear, let him hear what the Spirit says to the churches. To him who overcomes I will give to eat from the tree of life, which is in the midst of the Paradise of God." Each of the blessings promised to the churches are eternal in nature and point to the new heavens and new earth of Revelation 21-22.

Application for Today

Many lessons can be gleaned from Christ's address to the church at Ephesus. We see that there is more to being a faithful church than maintaining a status quo, or even standing against error. While opposing false teachers is praiseworthy, churches must remain zealous in evangelism and saving lost souls. When zeal for evangelism is waning among the people of God, a church will find their future as a congregation of God's people to be in jeopardy.

Remember, repent, return. The Lord not only identifies the problem and the symptoms, but He prescribes the remedy. The church is called to *remember*. The application of this principle can be profound for struggling churches. Look back on where you were to see how you have fallen. *Repent.* Turn around. Cease practicing the things or permeating the attitude which has caused you to fall. *Return.* Do the first works. Do those things which once brought glory to God and impacted the world around you. The mission has not changed. The need has not changed. The gospel has not changed. Why, then, would a congregation change its works if they were once faithful to the mission, the need, and the gospel? They must remain steadfast.

The Church at Smyrna (vv. 8-11)

"And to the angel of the church in Smyrna write, 'These things says the First and the Last, who was dead, and came to life: I know your works, tribulation, and poverty (but you are rich); and I know the blasphemy of those who say they are Jews and are not, but are a synagogue of Satan. Do not fear any of those things which you are about to suffer. Indeed, the devil is about to throw some of you into prison, that you may be tested, and you will have tribulation ten days. Be faithful until death, and I will give you the crown of life. He who has an ear, let him hear what the Spirit says to the churches. He who overcomes shall not be hurt by the second death'" (vv.8-11).

The city of Smyrna was a port city consisting of approximately 500,000 citizens. Smyrna was known for its culture. A temple to Roma (Rome's female deity) was also in the city. Smyrna also housed an influential synagogue of Jews.

The church at Smyrna received no word of rebuke or instruction for correction. The omission of any rebuke from Christ only intensifies His rebuke of other churches. Jesus was not merely condemning for the sake of condemning. When no condemnation or rebuke was needed, none was given. Rather, this church was encouraged to hold fast amid tribulation and poverty. The word "tribulation" denotes "living in oppression or narrow straits"[3] The oppression which Christians were facing resulted in poverty (lit. stark poverty; extreme poverty; the abject poverty of a beggar).

---

[3] Simon J. Kistemaker, *Revelation* (Grand Rapids, MI: Baker, 2001), 123.

The poverty they were suffering could have occurred through several factors.

(1) They could have come from a poorer class.[4] W.B. West reminds us of James 2:5 – "Has God not chosen the poor of this world *to be* rich in faith and heirs of the kingdom which He promised to those who love Him?"[5]

(2) Ray Summers observes, "This is no doubt a reflection of the confiscation of property used by Domitian as a means of persecution."[6]

(3) William Hendrickson states, "These people were often thrown out of employment as a result of the very fact of their conversion."[7] He adds, "Becoming a Christian was, from an earthly point of view, a real sacrifice. It meant poverty, hunger, imprisonment, often death by means of the wild beasts or the stake."

(4) Mounce directs us to Hebrews 10:34 and notes that these brethren may have been the victims of mob violence and looting.[8]

The Lord says repeatedly, "*I know.*" The Lord knew their works, tribulation, and poverty. He also knew that they would suffer imprisonment, be tested, and continue in tribulation for "ten days," signifying a short period of time. The persecution they were facing would eventually end.

---

[4] Hailey, Revelation, 126.

[5] W.B. West, Jr., *Revelation through First Century Glasses* (Nashville, TN: Gospel Advocate, 1997), 43.

[6] Ray Summers, *Worthy Is the Lamb* (Nashville, TN: B&H Academic, 1999), 113.

[7] William Hendrickson, *More Than Conquerors* (Grand Rapids, MI: Baker, 1979), 80.

[8] Robert H. Mounce, *The Book of Revelation*, NICNT (Grand Rapids, MI: Eerdmans, 1977), 92.

The Lord also knew about the exploits of the synagogue of Satan. They claimed to be Jews outwardly but failed to be Jews inwardly (cf. Romans 2:28-29). In addition to the persecution being heaped upon them by Rome, these brethren also had to endure the continued antagonism of Jews who rejected the Messiah.

Christ also knew who was responsible for this persecution, "the devil" (v.10). Man can be used as an instrument for good in the hand of God, or as an instrument for evil in the hand of Satan. These Jews had ceased being the people of God and had become the synagogue of Satan. Along with their Roman counterparts, they made life extremely hard for the Lord's church in Smyrna. However, the upcoming tribulation would only last for a short time, "ten days." This appears to be "an allusion to Daniel 1:12-15, where the 'testing' of Daniel and his three friends for 'ten days' is mentioned three times."[9]

Our Savior also knew how His people could overcome the devil and his cohorts. "Be faithful until death, and I will give you the crown of life. He who has an ear, let him hear what the Spirit says to the churches. He who overcomes shall not be hurt by the second death." The second death is eternal hell or the lake of fire (20:14).

Application for Today

The riches of this great church were not counted in gold or silver, but in the "riches of His goodness" (Romans 2:4) and "the riches of His grace" (Ephesians 1:7). Materially, they were poor among the rich, but spiritually they were rich among the poor. A key feature of apocalyptic literature is revealing to the reader that things are not as they appear. These poor, downtrodden Christians

---

[9] Beal and Carson, *Commentary on the New Testament Use of the Old Testament*, 1093.

were rich in the eyes of Christ. In Christ alone can the poor among the rich become the rich among the poor (cf. Luke 16:19-31).

The earthly struggle of light and darkness, right and wrong, good and evil was being enacted upon the church in Smyrna. Good people were living godly lives and suffering unfairly for it, and they would be called to suffer more. Living godly lives often brings upon the Christian an unfair persecution from the world (cf. 1 Timothy 3:12). Yet, the message from Christ for such times is clear, "Do not fear what you are about to suffer." Moreover, "Be faithful unto death, and I will give you the crown of life."

The crown of life (v.10) is juxtaposed to the second death (v.11). This juxtaposition occurs many times in the NT (e.g., Romans 6:23). Truly, an eternal life or death decision awaited the church in their future. Keep the faith and receive the crown. Conquer or be conquered. The message is clear, do not allow a brief persecution on earth to cost you the eternal victory with Christ.

The Church at Pergamos (vv. 12-17)

"And to the angel of the church in Pergamos write, 'These things says He who has the sharp two-edged sword: I know your works, and where you dwell, where Satan's throne is. And you hold fast to My name, and did not deny My faith even in the days in which Antipas was My faithful martyr, who was killed among you, where Satan dwells. But I have a few things against you, because you have there those who hold the doctrine of Balaam, who taught Balak to put a stumbling block before the children of Israel, to eat things sacrificed to idols, and to commit sexual immorality. Thus you also have those who hold the doctrine of the Nicolaitans, which thing I hate. Repent, or else I will come to you quickly and will fight against them with the sword of My mouth. He who has an ear, let him hear what the Spirit says to the churches. To him who over-comes I will give some of the hidden manna to eat. And I will give him a white stone, and on the stone a new name written which no one knows except him who receives it'" (vv.12-17).

The city of Pergamos was a center of four of the most important pagan cults of the day – Zeus, Athene (the patron goddess), Dio-nysos, and Asklepios (who was designated *Soter*, Savior). The shrine of Asklepios, the god of healing (also known as "the Per-gamene god"), attracted people from all over the world."[10]

The Lord recognized the city of Pergamos as being the seat of Satan's throne and where Satan dwelt. Pergamos was also the of-ficial Asian center for the imperial cult.[11] Pergamos was the first city in Asia to receive permission to build a temple dedicated to the worship of a living ruler. In 29 BC Augustus granted permis-sion that a temple be erected in Pergamos to the "divine Augustus and the goddess Roma."[12]

It was here that a faithful Christian by the name of Antipas was martyred for his faith. While we are uncertain about his personal history, Christ knew him by name. The church was known by Christ for their works, holding fast to His name, and not denying Him even amid severe persecution.

However, they had begun to compromise with "the doctrine of Balaam" as they were being seduced to partake of meats offered to idols and sexually immoral practices (cf. Numbers 25:1-3; 31:16) – two practices strictly forbidden by the apostles (see Acts 15:29). The name "Balaam" became "proverbial for the false

---

[10] Mounce, *Revelation*, 95
[11] Robert North, "Pergumum," *ISBE*, vol. 3 (revised), (Grand Rapids, MI: Eerdmans, 1986), 768.
[12] Mounce, 96

teacher who for financial gain influenced believers to enter into relationships of compromising unfaithfulness."[13]

The teachings of the Nicolaitans also had a voice in the church. While Ephesus rejected these teachings and stoutly resisted them, some of the brethren in Pergamos accepted them. The connection between the names "Nicolaitan" and "Balaam" is significant. Nicolaitan (*nika loan*) is a compound word meaning "overcomer of the people." Whereas, Balaam (*bl'm*) is similar in meaning, as it denotes "ruling over the people" or even "consuming the people."[14] The application to this OT character is clear: just as Israel worshiped idols and committed fornication because of Balaam's deceitful counsel, so too was the church in Pergamos being led astray by the teachings of the Nicolaitans.[15] Balaam was threatened with being killed by the sword of the angel of the Lord (Numbers 22:23, 31). When he did not heed the word of God, he was indeed killed by the sword (Numbers 31:8; Joshua 13:22).

The Christians in Pergamos were being threatened in a similar way. Here was a congregation which had suffered by the sword of Rome. Yet, if they did not repent, they would suffer from the sharp, two-edged sword of Christ. His word would be their ultimate condemnation (Hebrews 4:12; Ephesians 6:10). That which should have been a divine blessing to the church, the word of Christ, would serve to spell their demise as a congregation. The church, if unrepentant, would become an example of apostasy.

However, just as He did in His address to Ephesus, Christ followed His rebuke with an offered blessing. "He who has an ear, let him hear what the Spirit says to the churches. To him who overcomes I will give some of the hidden manna to eat. And I will

---

[13] Beale and Carson, 1094.
[14] Ibid.
[15] Ibid.

give him a white stone, and on the stone a new name written which no one knows except him who receives it."

Hidden manna refers to God's providential care – both now and forever, spiritually, and physically. Just as God provided for the Israelites in the wilderness sojourn, He will provide for his people while sojourning in a hostile world (1 Peter 1:17). The manna was hidden to the world and known only to the people of God. Moreover, the reference to manna provides us with an intriguing comparison, as it became despised by the people (Number 11:1-10). It is also noteworthy that "some" of the manna is to be given. In the happy care of God's providence, we may expect those things which are sufficient to sustain us. The providential care we receive is neither too little nor too much. It is always just as God deems necessary according to His wisdom and will.

The complaining which characterized those who fell in the wilderness must not occur among the Israel of God today (Galatians 6:16; 1 Corinthians 10:9-10). Especially during times of persecution and suffering, Christians must remain thankful and rely upon the providential care of God as their source of strength and hope to sustain them as they patiently follow Christ, suffering as He suffered, and obeying as He obeyed (1 Peter 2:21).

The white stone could have reference to the appearance of the manna as a white bdellium stone (cf. Exodus 16:31; Numbers 11:7).[16] However, there could have been a specific meaning known especially by those of that era. Hailey writes, "In ancient courts of justice the accused were condemned by black pebbles and acquitted by white."[17]

The word only occurs twice in the NT, here and in Acts 26:10, where Paul gave his vote (lit. "pebble of voting"). If this analogy

---

[16] Ibid.
[17] Hailey, 134.

holds true, then the meaning of this symbol would demonstrate Christ's acquittal of their sins. The new name would signify a new heavenly relationship with Christ. That the name is engraved in stone would signify the permanency of the relationship. The white color would portray the righteousness of the saints in not compromising and thus "soiling their garments" (3:4) with compromise.[18]

Christ is the source and giver of such blessings, note: "I will give." Only through Christ can all true and spiritual blessings be bestowed. As is the case with the blessings promised to the other churches of Asia, many of these promises will find their fulfillment in the new heavens and new earth of chapters 21 and 22.

Application for Today

"Repent, or else." No faithful student of scripture can mistake this clarion charge from the Savior. Man's repentance has always been at the heart of Christ's preaching and ministry. "Repent for the kingdom of heaven is at hand" (Matthew 4:17). "Repent or perish" (Luke 13:3, 5). Even now all men are being called to repent through the preaching of the gospel (Acts 17:30-31; 2 Peter 3:9).

Our Lord came to address one issue – man in sin. For the world to change, man's relationship with God must change. The world is as it is because man is in rebellion to God. Christ has come to call men to repentance and to provide reconciliation for man with God through His atonement.

To repent is to overcome the world. Repentance is overcoming. To him who overcomes are the promises made and kept. Man cannot overcome the world while yet remaining obedient to it. He

---

[18] Beale and Carson, 1094.

must repent. His will must be changed by the gospel and his manner of life must be reversed from walking away from God to walking toward God, yea even *with* God.

Repentance does not occur only once in a person's life. While it must occur to obey the gospel and be converted (see Acts 2:38; 3:19), it must also occur daily. Repentance is a daily decision. "I day daily," said Paul (1 Corinthians 15:31). We too must die daily to self and to sin that we might live daily for Christ.

The Church at Thyatira (vv. 18-29)

"And to the angel of the church in Thyatira write, 'These things says the Son of God, who has eyes like a flame of fire, and His feet like fine brass: I know your works, love, service, faith, and your patience; and *as* for your works, the last *are* more than the first. Nevertheless I have a few things against you, because you allow that woman Jezebel, who calls herself a prophetess, to teach and seduce My servants to commit sexual immorality and eat things sacrificed to idols. And I gave her time to repent of her sexual immorality, and she did not repent. Indeed I will cast her into a sickbed, and those who commit adultery with her into great tribulation, unless they repent of their deeds. I will kill her children with death, and all the churches shall know that I am He who searches the minds and hearts. And I will give to each one of you according to your works. Now to you I say, and to the rest in Thyatira, as many as do not have this doctrine, who have not known the depths of Satan, as they say, I will put on you no other burden. But hold fast what you have till I come. And he who overcomes, and keeps My works until the end, to him I will give power over the nations—'He shall rule them with a rod of iron; They shall be dashed to pieces like the potter's vessels'— as I also have received from My Father; and I will give him the

morning star. He who has an ear, let him hear what the Spirit says to the churches'" (vv.18-29).

Located between Pergamos to the north and Sardis to the south, Thyatira was an important center of wool trade in the first century.[19] A trade guild of wool workers was also prominent in this community. Apparently, these trade guilds would host banquets in which meat offered to idols was readily partaken.[20] Christians who were members of these guilds were forced to choose between their faith and their livelihood. "The Pergamos church had been weakened by the heathen surroundings of Mysia, known for its famous temples dedicated to Zeus, Minerva, Apollo, Venus, Bacchus, and Aesculapius. The figure, *Satan's seat*, denotes the wickedness of these idolatrous temples and the nuptials to these gods. The name Pergamos meant 'the place of nuptials.' It was a fitting figure of Satan's seat."[21]

The "Jezebel" at Thyatira could have been teaching brethren to eat meat offered to idols in the banquets of the trade guilds. In so doing, she would have led them into spiritual adultery as Jezebel did with Israel and Baal in the OT. Thyatira also housed shrines to gods and goddesses such as Apollo and Helius. Thyatira's coins also bore the images of these false deities.

The "Son of God" addresses the church at Thyatira. Caesars would claim to be sons of gods, but only Jesus is truly the Son of God. Again, His eyes are likened to flaming fire and His feet bear the likeness of fine brass. One can imagine the intent glare to be received from one who is watching with earnest the things occurring in the church. His feet have been refined by fire having

---

[19] John E. Stambaugh, "Thyatira," *ABD*, vol. 6 (New York: Doubleday, 1992), 546.
[20] Robert North, "Thyatira," *ISBE*, vol. 4 (revised), (Grand Rapids, MI: Eerdmans, 1986), 846.
[21] Wallace, *Revelation*, 92.

walked through the world and partaken of human suffering and death.

Christ begins with a commendation for the church's "works, love, service, faith, and your patience; and as for your works, the last are more than the first" (v.19). However, the church was permitting a "Jezebel," a so-called prophetess, to teach and seduce the brethren – "My servants" – to commit fornication and to eat things offered to idols.

Jezebel lives in infamy due to her scandalous reign over Israel with her husband Ahab (1 Kings 16:31, 32; 21:1 ff.; 2 Kings 8:18; 9:22). Jezebel reintroduced Baal and Asherah worship in Israel. The Jezebel of Thyatira might have been a sister in the congregation, but it is not stated explicitly. Christ said He had given her "time to repent of her sexual immorality, and she did not repent" (2:21). Through her doctrine, she had gained followers, disciples, or "children" (v.23). Her ways were considered "the depths of Satan" (v.24).

Seeing that the brethren had permitted this woman to gain such a following without opposing her, Christ was going to take the matter of this woman into His own hands. He said, "Indeed I will cast her into a sickbed, and those who commit adultery with her into great tribulation, unless they repent of their deeds. I will kill her children with death, and all the churches shall know that I am He who searches the minds and hearts. And I will give to each one of you according to your works" (vv.22-23).

The Lord who searches and knows the minds, hearts, and works of His creation will judge righteously. A connection to Jeremiah 17:10 is found in the passage as well. Therein, God says, "I the LORD search the heart and test the mind, to give every man according to his ways, according to the fruit of his deeds." Wealth and pleasure were the motives for Israel's sin against God in Jeremiah 17:3. Believers in Thyatira may have been tempted to worship idols to maintain their status in local trade guilds, which often had pagan gods as patrons.[22]

Just as God used Assyria to destroy the wickedness from within Israel, Christ could use Rome to destroy the wickedness from within the church at Thyatira. He would allow them to suffer persecution as a means of eliminating the evil "Jezebel" that they had suffered to afflict His church with false doctrine and sexual immorality. The sentence of death was also the punishment rendered to Ahab and Jezebel and their seventy sons 1 Kings 21:17-29; 2 Kings 9:30-37; 10:1-11). Such would also be the judgment against the Jezebel in Thyatira.

The practice of fornication and adultery can be both physical and spiritual. When Christians attempt to join themselves to the world and to God, they are guilty of *spiritual* adultery (James 4:4). Truly, we cannot serve two masters (Matthew 6:24). However, the fornication could have been *physical* and literal. The false prophetess could have been teaching the brethren that such behavior was acceptable according to certain aspects of Thyatiran culture and pagan worship. In either case, she would have been guilty of teaching the brethren to do something God had forbidden.

The church at Thyatira remained silent when they should have spoken. Jesus said, "you allow that woman...to teach and seduce." To "allow" is to "*let alone*" or "*let it be*." The church had not put an end to this woman's sinful agenda. Jesus would. After all, these were *His* servants and never *her* servants.

If she was a Christian, the instructions for the church to deal with her would have been known but ignored (see Matthew 18:15-

---

[22] Beale and Carson, 1095.

17; Romans 16:17; 1 Corinthians 5:1-13; 2 Thessalonians 3:6; Titus 3:10). If she was a citizen in the community, the church should have known not to partake of her evil deeds (2 John 9-11). Either way, they were guilty of giving space to the devil by permitting her treachery against the church.

Unto the rest of the church, Christ said, "I will put on you no other burden. But hold fast what you have till I come. And he who overcomes, and keeps My works until the end, to him I will give power over the nations— 'He shall rule them with a rod of iron; They shall be dashed to pieces like the potter's vessels'—as I also have received from My Father; and I will give him the morning star. He who has an ear, let him hear what the Spirit says to the churches" (vv.24-29).

Consider the promises made to the faithful in Thyatira:

1.) No other burden will be placed upon them. Evidently, the church had one major issue to be addressed. The Lord was not going to "major in minors."

2.) He will come. Our Lord is coming again. There is a future and He is in it.

3.) Overcoming and keeping His works alive is always possible. "With God all things are possible."

4.) Power over the nations was promised. As Christ rules over the nations with the authority vested in Him by the Father (cf. 11:15), His faithful church will prosper, and rule with authority vested in them by Christ (cf. 20:4).

5.) Jesus promises the "morning star" to those who overcome and keep the faith. The morning star appears clearly in the hour before dawn and signifies the promise of a new day, a new beginning for the faithful. Jesus is the "Morning Star" (22:16) for those who keep His commandments. He is the promise of a new beginning and a new eternal day in heaven.[23]

Application for Today

Christ is among His people. He knows their works. He knows their sins. Being faithful in some aspects of the faith does not permit unfaithfulness in other areas. Christ is calling His people to complete faithfulness. Doing good works does not grant freedom to teach or permit false doctrine.

Some reflection and application should be made from modern churches when considering the actions of Jezebel, her children, and the church which remained silent. In the first place, if she was a sister in Christ, it is not permitted for women to exert such an influence in the local congregation (1 Corinthians 14:34 ff.; 1 Timothy 2:11 ff.). Questions abound. Why was this woman allowed to wield this kind of destructive influence at Thyatira? Where were the elders? Why did the brethren permit it? Who could have been so foolish as to follow her? Why did they not prove her to be a false prophetess?

The church was guilty of tolerating evil just as Corinth was at one time (1 Corinthians 5), and just as many churches do today. If we choose to do nothing, it is not because God has not told us what to do. Churches can either strive to remain pure in the eyes of God, or they can turn blind eyes to sin. While some of the brethren at Thyatira had turned their eyes toward Jezebel, it was clear that the Lord remained focused on them and her with "eyes like flaming fire" (cf. 19:12). Brethren may choose to ignore a person's sinful attempts to overthrow Christ's authority over His church and satanic agendas which corrupt the church but let us not think for a moment that the Lord will ignore them.

---

[23] Bradley S. Cobb, *War in Heaven War on Earth* (Charleston, AR: Cobb, 2022), 128.

Chapter Three

As with chapter two, chapter three will serve to remind us of the Lord's intimate knowledge of the spiritual conditions within His church. How does Christ view apathy, false teaching, and divisive sects in the church? The words of warning and comfort given in this chapter are relevant to all churches of Christ today.

The Church at Sardis (vv. 1-6)

"And to the angel of the church in Sardis write, 'These things says He who has the seven Spirits of God and the seven stars: I know your works, that you have a name that you are alive, but you are dead. Be watchful, and strengthen the things which remain, that are ready to die, for I have not found your works perfect before God. Remember therefore how you have received and heard; hold fast and repent. Therefore if you will not watch, I will come upon you as a thief, and you will not know what hour I will come upon you. You have a few names even in Sardis who have not defiled their garments; and they shall walk with Me in white, for they are worthy. He who overcomes shall be clothed in white garments, and I will not blot out his name from the Book of Life; but I will confess his name before My Father and before His angels. He who has an ear, let him hear what the Spirit says to the churches'" (vv.1-6).**

The next congregation to be addressed is the one at Sardis. The city of Sardis was founded in 1200 BC and became the capital of the ancient Lydian empire (680-547 BC). By the time of Revelation, Sardis was known to have had an influential community of Jewish exiles. The synagogue in this city was not found on the edge as the city as was usually the case in ancient cities, but in the heart of the community. It is believed to have had the capacity to seat 1,000 people and is by far the largest ancient synagogue yet to be discovered. The ancient city of Sardis came to an end with the attack of the Persian army led by Chosroes II in 616 AD.

Christ is identified as the One who has the seven Spirits (eyes, 5:6) and stars (angels, 1:20). The symbolism presents Christ as having authority over earth and heaven, being completely aware of everything that transpires. He begins His address to the church by making clear, "I know your works." The Lord rebuked Sardis because "you have a name that you are alive, but you are dead." The church was alive in name only. Although they continued to assemble as a congregation, their works were not perfect before God. Now, Christ provides the remedy for a dying church.

1.) *Be watchful* – be mindful and recognize what has happened; be careless no longer.

2.) *Strengthen the things which remain, that are ready to die* – stop the digression; do not allow any more works to die but strengthen one another and the works you are doing.

3.) *Remember therefore how you have received and heard* – go back into your history and remember how you once were faithful in welcoming and heeding the word of God. When a church no longer heeds the truth, its demise is eminent.

4.) *Hold fast* – be faithful and hold tightly to the Lord, His word, His hope, and His work.

5.) *Repent* – turn from digression and return to Christ. Every wayward Christian and dying congregation must do so to make things right with God. God will not acquit the wicked (Exodus 23:7; Nahum 1:3).

Suppose the church slept through this admonition and in their spiritual slumber gave no attention to the Lord's warning and instructions. The Lord's judgment would have come upon them as a thief and catch them unexpectedly, not knowing "what hour I will come upon you."

The analogy of Christ coming as a thief is used throughout the NT. It is used to convey the idea of finding people unaware. Many are and will remain unaware by choice. They simply choose not to "watch and be ready" and therefore, the day of His coming will overtake them as a thief in the night (Matthew 24:42 ff.; 1 Thessalonians 5:1 ff.; 2 Peter 3:10 ff.).

Oftentimes, a faithful remnant will exist in an unfaithful congregation, if only for a while. Such was the case with the church at Sardis. A faithful remnant was within the congregation and the Lord did not leave them without a word of encouragement. Note, "You have a few names even in Sardis who have not defiled their garments; and they shall walk with Me in white, for they are worthy." The color "white" in this case denotes purity (cf. 19:8). They had not defiled their garments. They remained pure in the sight of God amidst impure brethren. The white garments will appear later in the book as the attire worn by those in heaven.

Jesus is here promising heaven to those who will remain true as, "He who overcomes shall be clothed in white garments, and I will not blot out his name from the Book of Life; but I will confess his name before My Father and before His angels." Just as surely as Christ will visit the unfaithful with judgment, He will remember the faithful with mercy. The name of the faithful Christian will remain written in the Book of Life and will be confessed before the Father and His angels (Matthew 10:31-32).

The Lamb's Book of Life will also appear later in Revelation as heaven's register of the faithful (13:8; 17:8; 20:12, 15; 21:27).

The Book of Life is mentioned several times in scripture in this connection. One's name can be written there or blotted from thence (Exodus 32:31-33; Psalm 69: 27-28; Daniel 12:1; Luke 10:20; Philippians 4:3; Hebrews 12:22-23).

"He who has an ear, let him hear what the Spirit says to the churches."

Application for Today

The works of the churches were of utmost importance to Christ. In each address to the churches, the works and faithfulness of the congregation are the only matters being discussed. Christ did not mention the attendance or size of the congregation. He did not mention the size of the contribution or building. Many of the things which concern churches today were of no concern to Christ. He made no mention of youth events, light bills, building expansion or remodeling, salaries, etc. He only spoke of their works and their faithfulness.

A congregation can have a team of ministers, elders and deacons in abundance, an ornate building with a million-dollar budget, but if they are lacking in their works and their faithfulness, they must repent. Jesus gives no attention to the worldly standards of excellence which shallow minds perceive to be earmarks of greatness. He is only concerned with the works and faithfulness of His church. If a congregation is to be faithful and remain faithful to the Lord, they must also find their works and faithfulness to be of utmost and unrivaled importance. Nothing else can compare.

The Church at Philadelphia (vv. 7-13)

"And to the angel of the church in Philadelphia write, These things says He who is holy, He who is true, He who has the key of David, He who opens and no one shuts, and shuts and no one opens: I know your works. See, I have set before you an open door, and no one can shut it; for you have a little

73

strength, have kept My word, and have not denied My name. Indeed I will make those of the synagogue of Satan, who say they are Jews and are not, but lie—indeed I will make them come and worship before your feet, and to know that I have loved you. Because you have kept My command to persevere, I also will keep you from the hour of trial which shall come upon the whole world, to test those who dwell on the earth. Behold, I am coming quickly! Hold fast what you have, that no one may take your crown. He who overcomes, I will make him a pillar in the temple of My God, and he shall go out no more. I will write on him the name of My God and the name of the city of My God, the New Jerusalem, which comes down out of heaven from My God. And I will write on him My new name. He who has an ear, let him hear what the Spirit says to the churches'"(vv.7-13).

The city of Philadelphia was founded by Eumenes II, King of Pergamum (197-159 BC) or possibly by his brother, Attalus II (159-138 BC), whose loyalty had earned for him the epithet 'Philadelphus,' hence the city's name.[1] Macedonian veterans were brought here to settle sometime before 100 BC.[2] The region was settled due to its being a rich and fertile agricultural area. Vineyards were a staple in this area. However, an edict from Domitian in 92 AD ordered at least half of the vineyards in these provinces to be removed without new ones being planted. Domitian's edict brought considerable economic hardship to the area.

Philadelphia was also situated upon a fault line and was subject to frequent earthquakes. One earthquake destroyed the city in 17 AD. Tiberius relieved the city of paying any tributes for five years,

---

[1] W. Ward Gasque, "Philadelphia," *ABD*, vol. 5 (New York: Doubleday, 1992), 304-5.

[2] Robert North, "Philadelphia," *ISBE*, vol. 3 (revised) (Grand Rapids, MI: Eerdmans, 1986), 830.

giving them time and opportunity to rebuild. Due to his generosity, the city adopted a new name "Neocaesarea" and later "Flavia." In 155 AD some of the members of the church at Philadelphia were martyred along with Polycarp.

The address to the church at Philadelphia begins with some clear and definite statements regarding Christ. Christ is *holy* and He is *true*. Moreover, He "has the key of David," and He "opens and no one shuts, and shuts and no one opens." We find the "key of David" in Isaiah 22:22, and an application of that passage is here made by Christ. Note, "The key of the house of David I will lay on his shoulder; So he shall open, and no one shall shut; And he shall shut, and no one shall open." Also consider Isaiah 9:6, as the "government shall be on His shoulder." Both statements refer to the absolute authority of Christ over His kingdom – the church.

Christ has no word of rebuke for the church at Philadelphia, only praise. As in His addresses to the other churches, Christ proclaims, "I know your works." Again, we must recognize that Jesus is primarily concerned with the works and faithfulness of these churches.

Jesus opened a great door of opportunity for these brethren – "See, I have set before you an open door, and no one can shut it." A great door was opened to a church of relatively "little strength." The Lord was willing to give a great opportunity to a church with great faith. Even though they may not have been great in numbers, they (1) kept His word; (2) did not deny (disown, repudiate) His name; and (3) kept His command to persevere. Such are the churches which receive greater opportunities to serve.

As with the other cities of Asia Minor, the Jews in the community of Philadelphia were very much against the church. Once again, Jesus referred to them as "the synagogue of Satan" (cf. 2:9). They were not doing the will of God, but the will of Satan, the enemy (John 8:44). By claiming to be doing the will of God, they were committing a "lie" – and Jesus said, "...indeed I will make them come and worship before your feet, and to know that I have loved you." Here is a collective allusion to several passages in Isaiah (cf. 45:14; 49:23; 60:14), as well as Psalm 86:9. "These OT texts predict that the unbelieving Gentiles would come to bow down at Israel's feet and to Israel's God in the last days."[3] As this would occur, the Gentiles would enlarge the family of God, becoming brethren to the Jews, and comprising the new Israel of God (Isaiah 2:1-4; 62:1-2).

On many occasions in the OT, God reminded Israel of how He loved them (Jeremiah 31:3; Hosea 11:1). God destroyed the Edomites to protect Israel and in so doing proved His love for them (Malachi 1:2 ff.). In like manner, the synagogue of Satan would be destroyed, the church would be protected, and Christ's love for the church would be known.

The Lord who is true also promised them, "I also will keep you from the hour of trial which shall come upon the whole world, to test those who dwell on the earth." We are approaching this study from the perspective that the "hour of trial" was at that time the persecution of Domitian upon the church. The Lord is promising that this persecution would not have the same effect on this faithful church as it would have on unfaithful churches.

Christ's coming judgment on the churches was at hand. Therefore, He says, "Hold fast what you have, that no one may take your crown." The "crown" herein mentioned in the victor's crown. As with the white robe, to the faithful it is his prize and his reward. To live faithfully and to overcome (be a victor, conquer, prevail) is to receive the crown (2 Timothy 4:8; Revelation 2:10).

---

[3] Beale and Carson, 1097.

However, to be overcome by the world is to lose the crown. Thus, he who overcomes is victorious. Jesus says, "I will make him a pillar in the temple of My God, and he shall go out no more." The one who conquers life and death through faith in Christ Jesus will be a pillar in the temple of God, signifying that he will not be moved, his place is secure in heaven. He will be exalted in honor with a permanent place in God's heavenly temple.

Our Lord "will write on him the name of My God and the name of the city of My God, the New Jerusalem which comes down out of heaven from My God. And I will write on him My new name." God will give the Christian victor a new name and a new citizenship in the new Jerusalem (cf. 21:1 ff.). The new name signifies that God is identifying this person with Himself, His home, and His Son. Such an identification has already been done on earth with the name "Christian" (cf. Isaiah 56:5; 62:1-2; Acts 11:26) and will be done again in heaven.

Application for Today

A church does not have to be the biggest or best in the eyes of man to be right with God. Just be faithful. With faith, God can take a "little strength" and do great things. God can open doors of opportunity for such a church which no man can shut. God will also protect a church like this.

Though the kingdoms and societies around it may fall and rise only to fall and rise again, the church that is protected by God will endure. "He who has an ear, let him hear what the Spirit says unto the churches."

The Church at Laodicea (vv. 14-22)

"And to the angel of the church of the Laodiceans write, These things says the Amen, the Faithful and True Witness, the Beginning of the creation of God: I know your works, that you are neither cold nor hot. I could wish you were cold

or hot. So then, because you are lukewarm, and neither cold nor hot, I will vomit you out of My mouth. Because you say, 'I am rich, have become wealthy, and have need of nothing'— and do not know that you are wretched, miserable, poor, blind, and naked— I counsel you to buy from Me gold refined in the fire, that you may be rich; and white garments, that you may be clothed, that the shame of your nakedness may not be revealed; and anoint your eyes with eye salve, that you may see. As many as I love, I rebuke and chasten. Therefore be zealous and repent. Behold, I stand at the door and knock. If anyone hears My voice and opens the door, I will come in to him and dine with him, and he with Me. To him who overcomes I will grant to sit with Me on My throne, as I also overcame and sat down with My Father on His throne. He who has an ear, let him hear what the Spirit says to the churches'" (vv.14-22).

The city of Laodicea had existed for almost 400 years by the time of Revelation. Zeus had been recognized as the chief deity of the city from the time of its founding as he was also for the former city Laodicea was built upon, Diospolis.[4] The city was also given to emperor worship and the title of "temple warden" was given to the city by Commodus (180-192 AD) for their devotion to the imperial cult.[5] Laodicea was home to thousands of Jews, many of whom were quite wealthy. They were settled in Laodicea sometime around 213 BC.

Laodicea came under Roman control in 129 BC. By 50 BC, it was a center of financial and banking operations and by the beginning of the first century AD, it was well-known for its financial sustainability, prosperity, and prowess. Laodicea was home to

---

[4] F.F. Bruce, "Laodicea," *ABD*, vol. 4 (New York: Doubleday, 1992), 229-31.
[5] Ibid.

several textile products, such as its ravenous black wool. The chief medical center of Phrygia was housed here and may have been sponsored by the temple of Men Karou, an Anatolian deity, which was also located in the city. It is believed that eye salve was produced in this medical center from "Phrygian powder."[6]

Water was also piped into the city through an aqueduct. The water provided for a water tower, water basin, feeding chambers, bath houses, and a public fountain house. The city also boasted two theaters, a council chamber, a gymnasium, and a stadium. Christianity was brought to Laodicea by the time of Paul's epistle to the Colossians (cf. Colossians 2:1), although we are not certain of the details of the early evangelistic efforts conducted in the city.

The Lord's address to the Laodiceans begins with a proclamation of a few of His credentials. He is "the Amen, the Faithful and True Witness, the Beginning of the creation of God." That Christ is the *"Amen"* denotes that His words will be fulfilled. His words are true, everlasting, and established forever. Christ is the *"Faithful and True Witness"* as He sees and knows what is happening in and to His churches. His witness, in a judicial sense is faithful and true. The word translated "witness" is *martus* which is also the basis for the English word *martyr*. Christ's faithful witness to the words of His Father led to His crucifixion by the hands of the Jews in Jerusalem. Yet, His witness was faithful and true, just as it remains today.

Recognizing Christ as the *"Beginning of the creation of God,"* denotes His is role in creation as its Beginner, Author, Source, and Lord (John 1:1-3; Colossians 1:15-17). He is the First and the Last, the Beginning and the Ending, the Alpha and the Omega. He was

---

[6] G.L. Borchert, "Laodicea," *ISBE*, vol. 3 (revised) (Grand Rapids, MI: Eerdmans, 1986), 72-4.

there in the creation of the universe, and He will be there at the end of the universe (2 Peter 3:10-13).

Christ begins His address by rebuking the Laodiceans. Unlike other occasions, when Christ would begin His address with words of commendation, here He begins with words of condemnation. "I know your works, that you are neither cold nor hot. I could wish you were cold or hot." Cold water serves a purpose and hot water serves a purpose. The church at Laodicea was serving no purpose. The members of the church would have been all too familiar with lukewarm water as their water would have become lukewarm after having been piped through the aqueduct system they used.

"So then, because you are lukewarm, and neither cold nor hot, I will vomit you out of My mouth." Being "lukewarm" is generally associated with a lack of zeal, indifference, and apathy for the Lord's work. The church and citizenry of the city saw themselves as being rich and having need of nothing. Yet, their self-perception was far different that Christ's true perception of them.

The Lord said, "...you are wretched, miserable, poor, blind, and naked" and He counseled them "...to buy from Me gold refined in the fire, that you may be rich; and white garments, that you may be clothed, that the shame of your nakedness may not be revealed; and anoint your eyes with eye salve, that you may see."

Once again, Jesus uses a metaphor which would have been familiar to the members of the church. The eye salve produced by the city's medical center gave prominence to the center and the city. The Lord was herein explaining their need to correct their spiritual vision more than any need they had to correct physical vision. If they could see the importance of physical vision, as Christians, they should realize the greater importance of spiritual vision. The church needed: (1) true riches which could only come from Christ – i.e., "gold refined in the fire"; (2) moral purity – i.e., "white garments" to clothe themselves; and (3) a corrected perspective of life as a Christian – i.e., "eye salve" to anoint their eyes and cure their spiritual blindness.

"As many as I love, I rebuke and chasten." We must not confuse Christ's rebuke of these people with animosity or hatred. Jesus loved this church too. However, His love did not and would not excuse their sins. "Therefore be zealous and repent."

The address to Laodicea closes with an invitation: "Behold, I stand at the door and knock. If anyone hears My voice and opens the door, I will come in to him and dine with him, and he with Me. To him who overcomes I will grant to sit with Me on My throne, as I also overcame and sat down with My Father on His throne."

Christ remained ready to save. He was standing and knocking at the door. He wanted their fellowship. He remains prepared to dine with whosever welcomes Him. Christ is ready to bless and those who overcome will be exalted by Christ and with Christ (Matthew 19:28 ff.). "He who has an ear, let him hear what the Spirit says to the churches."

Application for Today

What does Christ think about the apathetic and lukewarm church? Obviously, He is not happy with the condition. His stomach is turned by such. Yet, in mercy and tender patience, His love remains. He pleads for repentance. However, if sinful churches refuse to repent, the day will come when Christ will no longer consider them to be lampstands in the world.

Only by true faith in Christ can churches be a light in a world of darkness. Any light which may beam from a congregation is merely reflective. The light emanates from the Son and reflects off of those who walk as children of light to bring life and immortality to light through the gospel. Without His light, any church, regardless of history, location, or era, would be useless.

How essential is zeal to shine this light! The addresses to the seven churches are bookended with warnings about apathy. One church had left their first love. Another had become lukewarm. Both churches were situated in cosmopolitan communities. Both churches knew riches. Both churches knew industry. But, in the midst of their work-a-day world, they were in danger of making their faith an afterthought. The Lord would not let this happen without first issuing a word of warning and remedy.

For the Christian to endure faithfully in the world, faith and a personal relationship with God must be foremost, centermost, and utmost. Christians cannot become satisfied with giving God the leftovers, else they themselves become leftover at the final judgment.

Chapter Four

In chapter four, Revelation transfers from scenes on earth to visions in heaven, from the current affairs of the churches in Asia to the activities occurring in the throne room of Almighty God with all its radiance and splendor.

"Until now the symbols in Revelation have been relatively straightforward and their meaning relatively easy to understand. From here onward they become more difficult and complex."[1] Our guidelines stated for interpreting Revelation in our introduction will become more useful as we proceed in our study.[2]

God has seen the persecution on earth. He has judged to condemn and destroy the powers of evil that are contesting His sovereignty and afflicting His people. Each act of judgment to come upon the world will be issued from the throne of God. Evil must perish under His judgment. God's rule from heaven will be contrasted against the satanically inspired power on earth with all its destructive effects and idolatrous claims.[3]

Judgment will not come, however, without God first giving mankind ample reason and opportunity to repent. As man continues to harden his heart against God, the judgments become more severe and greater in scope, until ultimately climaxing with the final judgment of Satan, his angels, and all mankind (20:11-15). The wheel of God's judgment turns slowly, but make no mistake, it grinds to powder (Matthew 21:44).

---

[1] Bruce M. Metzger, *Breaking the Code: Understanding the Book of Revelation* (Nashville, TN: Abingdon, 1993), 47.

[2] See pg. 35-39 in the Introduction.

[3] Bauckham, 40-43.

Down through the vast and distant history of humanity many rulers and dominions have come and gone, yet One remains. Many a Pharaoh, King, and Emperor have led armies into battle, yet only One will remain victorious. Untold nobles have sat on thrones of ivory and gold, crowned with jewels rare and precious, yet none has ever exceeded or will ever rival the splendor of the glory-circled throne upon which He sits who is, was, and is to come, the Almighty, the great "I AM."

When John was invited in the Spirit to witness and portray the celestial court of God, it was for the express purpose of bringing calm assurance and quieting the worries of the people of God. God remains where He ever has been and will remain, sovereign over His creation and the creatures who possess it.

Such has always been the case when a theophany[4] occurs in scripture. Isaiah received a similar vision during a time of spiritual wickedness and laxed leadership in Judah with a looming threat of Babylonian conquest (ch. 6). Isaiah saw, "the Lord sitting on a throne, high and lifted up, and the train of His robe filled the temple. Above it stood seraphim; each one had six wings: with two he covered his face, with two he covered his feet, and with two he flew." Their proclamation was one of honor and glory to God: "Holy, holy, holy is the Lord of hosts; The whole earth is full of His glory!"

The voice of God shook the posts of the temple, and the area was filled with smoke. Isaiah exclaimed, "Woe is me, for I am undone! Because I am a man of unclean lips, And I dwell in the midst of a people of unclean lips; For my eyes have seen the King, The Lord of hosts." After being cleansed, the Lord commissioned Isaiah with a message of judgement and desolation for Judah. Yet, a remnant and a "holy seed" remained in their future.

---

[4] A theophany is a manifestation or appearance of God to human beings.

In Ezekiel (1-3) we find another case of theophany intended to reveal a message of divine judgment. Ezekiel beheld "a whirlwind coming out of the north, a great cloud with raging fire engulfing itself; and brightness was all around it and radiating out of its midst like the color of amber, out of the midst of the fire." Like John, he also saw four living creatures, although their appearance was a little different from John's vision. Ezekiel heard a voice that came from above the firmament" and witnessed "a throne, in appearance like a sapphire stone; on the likeness of the throne was a likeness with the appearance of a man high above it."

The Lord's appearance is described from His waist upward as "the color of amber with the appearance of fire all around within it; and from the appearance of His waist and downward I saw, as it were, the appearance of fire with brightness all around. Like the appearance of a rainbow in a cloud on a rainy day, so was the appearance of the brightness all around it. This was the appearance of the likeness of the glory of the Lord."

God commissioned Ezekiel to go "to the children of Israel, to a rebellious nation that has rebelled against Me; they and their fathers have transgressed against Me to this very day. For they are impudent and stubborn children...For you are not sent to a people of unfamiliar speech and of hard language, but to the house of Israel, not to many people of unfamiliar speech and of hard language, whose words you cannot understand." God gave Ezekiel a scroll to eat, "Then He spread it before me; and there was writing on the inside and on the outside, and written on it were lamentations and mourning and woe."

In Ezekiel we find God's presence was just as real in Babylon as it was for Isaiah in the temple of Jerusalem. God was equally able to bless or punish Israel in Babylon as He was in Judah. Both visions are meant to demonstrate God's greatness and majesty, with three great truths presented. First, we are reminded that God had not forgotten His people. Second, God is glorious beyond our ability to picture. Third, God is almighty and omnipresent.[5]

In both instances of theophany, God made His presence known. The gods of Babylon have appeared to be victorious over the God of Jacob. As a result, the people of God felt defeated. The defeat they would and did suffer, however, was not due to God's lack of power, but because of their lack of faith and obedience. The Jews were being punished for the sins. Their exile in Babylon was an act of divine judgment and justice.

God foretold in Isaiah what he explained in Ezekiel. As the people of God lingered in doubt, frustrated by their own rebellious and stubborn spirit, God appeared to Ezekiel as only He could. He appeared for the purpose of calling Ezekiel to the prophetic office. Ezekiel was called to carry and convey the message of God to the people of God in exile – word for word. Such an appearance proved necessary for Ezekiel and occurred more throughout his life. Truly, his prophetic life was a ceaseless reflection of this experience.[6] God was preparing Ezekiel to preach to the captives in Babylon.[7] The prophet would need courage, trust, and assurance that he was truly serving God. Assurance was granted in most significant ways. As with Moses and Isaiah, when the Lord appeared to them, Ezekiel was forever changed.[8]

We find this to be true for John as well. The vision he received no doubt served to strengthen him and remind him of the greatness of the God he served. In Revelation, some of the children of God undoubtedly felt defeated by Rome as the gods of Rome appeared

---

[5] Denny Petrillo, *Ezekiel*, TFTC (Searcy, AR: Resource Publications, 2004), 38-39.

[6] Frank Chesser, *The Man of Chebar: A Study of Ezekiel* (Huntsville, AL: Publishing Designs, 2018), 17.

[7] Ibid.

[8] Ibid., 15-17.

to be victorious over the true God. Christians who would aposta-tize would be punished along with the Romans for their iniquities. God's punishment would again be an act of His sovereign judg-ment and justice.

A Vision of God the Father (vv. 1-11)

"After these things I looked, and behold, a door standing open in heaven. And the first voice which I heard was like a trumpet speaking with me, saying, 'Come up here, and I will show you things which must take place after this'" (v.1).

The chapter begins with a vision of a door standing open in heaven and an invitation is extended for John to "come up here" and be shown "the things which must take place after this" (v.1). The significance of the open door represents access to the Father. John is being invited into the presence of the royal court and throne room in heaven. A man cannot intrude upon such a sacred scene as this. He must be invited and welcomed. John is permitted to enter the celestial court to be shown the things which will take place on earth. What would become human history will have its origin in heaven.[9]

John saw "a throne set in heaven, and One sat on the throne" (v.2). Only One could occupy the throne John saw. It was not Nero, or Domitian, or any earthly ruler. The One occupying the throne was none other than the Everlasting, the Ancient of Days.

"And He who sat there was like a jasper and a sardius stone in appearance; and there was a rainbow around the throne, in appearance like an emerald...Before the throne there was a sea of glass, like crystal...from the throne proceeded lightnings,

---

[9] Mounce, 133.

thunderings, and voices." (vv.3-5). Every color and every precious stone are truly God's handiwork. Every "good and perfect gift" known to man emanates from God Himself. They exist because He exists.

An audience surrounds the throne. John saw **"twenty-four thrones, and on the thrones I saw twenty-four elders sitting, clothed in white robes; and they had crowns of gold on their heads" (v.4).** Twenty-four is a significant number to us. The OT speaks of twelve sons of Israel and the NT speaks of twelve apostles of the Lord. These two sets of twelve appear again in Revelation (cf. 21:12, 14). The twenty-four elders could symbolize the leaders in Israel in the OT and of the early church in the NT, representing the leaders of the people of God throughout history, but we cannot say for sure.

These men "fell down before Him who sat on the throne and worshipped Him, even casting their crowns before the throne, saying: 'You are worthy, O Lord, To receive glory and honor and power; For You created all things, And by Your will they exist and were created'" (vv.10-11). No matter how great the man, he is still just a man, a creature, and all his praise, glory, and honor should be duly given to God, the Creator. The elders before the throne of God clearly recognize their debt to God and proclaim their devotion to Him.

The **seven spirits of God** are mentioned again (v.5). They are represented as seven lamps of fire burning before the throne. In 5:6 they will be revealed as the seven eyes of the Lord. By comparing the two passages, the metaphors convey divine knowledge. God's sees and knows all that transpires in heaven and on earth. He is not unaware of the suffering of His saints.

John also saw **"four living creatures full of eyes in front and in back. The first living creature was like a lion, the second**

living creature like a calf, the third living creature had a face like a man, and the fourth living creature was like a flying eagle" (v.6). Isaiah and Ezekiel had similar visions of four living creatures when they beheld God's throne scene. In Isaiah, the creatures are identified as seraphim. In Ezekiel they are identified as cherubim. Placing an exact definition of the words cherub and seraph is extremely difficult. Not even the etymology of the words is known.

The cherubim (pl. of cherub) first appear in scripture as divinely appointed guardians, and this seems to be their most constant task. In Genesis 3:24, the cherubim are placed at the east of Eden, together with the flaming sword "to keep the way of the tree of life." The symbolism of the guardianship of the cherubim was seen in the tabernacle. In the tabernacle, there were two cherubim of solid gold upon the golden slab of the "lid," or "mercy-seat," facing each other, with wings outstretched above, so as to constitute a throne on which the glory of the Lord appeared, and from which He spoke (Exodus 25:18-22; 37:7-9; Numbers 7:89; Hebrews 9:5). There were also cherubim woven into the texture of the inner curtain of the tabernacle and the veil (Exodus 26:1, 31; 36:8, 35).

Cherubim are seen as the chariot of the Lord (1 Chronicles 28:18). As attendants of God, they bear the throne upon which He descends from His high abode. In Psalms 18 we read, "He bowed the heavens also, and came down; And thick darkness was under his feet. And he rode upon a cherub and did fly; Yea, he soared upon the wings of the wind" (Psalms 18:9-10). Hence, the Lord, or, as the fuller title goes, the Lord of Hosts, is repeatedly styled "He that is seated (throned) above the cherubim" (Psalms 80:1; 99:1; 1 Samuel 4:4, and elsewhere).

In Ezekiel, they are represented as four living creatures, each with four faces, man, lion, ox (replaced in the parallel chapter by cherub), and eagle (1:10; 10:14), having the figure and hands of men (1:5,8), and the feet of calves (1:7). Each has four wings, two of which are stretched upward (1:11), meeting above and sustaining the "firmament," that is, the bottom of the Divine throne (1:22; 10:1), while two are stretched downward, conformable the one to the other, to cover their bodies (1:11, 23). In appearance, the living creatures resemble coals of fire (compare 10:2,6 f, where the "man clothed in linen" is told to fill both his hands with coals of fire from between the cherubim), burning like torches, the fire flashing up and down among the creatures, a bright fire out of which lightning goes forth (1:13). Thus, the creatures run and vanish as the appearance of a flash of lightning (1:14). The cherubim do not turn as they change direction, but always go straight forward (1:9,17; 10:11), as do the wheels of the cherubic chariot with rings full of eyes round about (1:18; 10:12). The cherubim represent the spirit, or will, in the wheels: at the direction of the spirit, the wheels are lifted from the bottom and the chariot moves upward (1:19 f; 10:16 f). The cherubim are thus the moving force of the vehicle.

Ezekiel's cherubim are clearly related to the seraphim in Isaiah's inaugural vision. Like the cherubim, the seraphim are the attendants on God as He is seated upon a throne high and exalted; they are also winged creatures: with twain they cover their faces, and with twain they cover their feet, and with twain they fly. Like the Levites in the sanctuary below, they sing a hymn of adoration: "Holy, holy, holy, is Yahweh of hosts: the whole earth is full of his glory."

The "four living creatures" of Revelation 4:6 ff. allude to those in Ezekiel and Isaiah. Full of eyes before and behind, they are amid the throne, and round about it. One resembles a lion, the other a calf, and the third a man, and the fourth a flying eagle. Each of the creatures has six wings. **"They have no rest day and**

night, saying, Holy, holy, holy, is the Lord God, the Almighty, who was and who is and who is to come" (v.8).

John then witnesses a worship scene suddenly burst in jubilation before God's throne. They cry out: **"Holy, holy, holy, Lord God Almighty, Who was and is and is to come!"** Compare this scene with the scene in Isaiah. The living creatures gave glory and honor and thanks to the Father, "who sits on the throne, who lives forever and ever." No matter how powerful these heavenly agents might be, they are subject to the will and power of God.

Application for Today

The scene of Revelation 4 is awe-inspiring. Faithful men are represented with robes and crowns, with great dignity and honor. But all the dignity and honor they know, and share is due to the One seated upon the throne. The four living creatures are powerful, awesome creatures. Yet, all the power, knowledge, and ability they possess is because of Him who sits upon the throne. God reigns over all. The world is His and the fullness thereof. The heavens are His handiwork, strown across the sky as a cascading ocean of diamonds. All things great and small owe their existence to Him who sits on the throne and lives forever and ever, Amen.

While the kingdom was suffering countless trials and diabolical cruelty on earth, God was reigning in heaven where He has ever been. Nothing had changed. He was witnessing the persecution and was to come and He was soon to act. At His command were four living creatures beyond human imagination. Even though suffering was occurring on earth, God was working according to His infinite wisdom in heaven with powers and through agents beyond our comprehension.

Such is often the case during times of suffering. Man may not know or even fathom what God is doing or how He is going to come to his rescue, but he must rest assured that God knows, and He cares (1 Peter 5:7). God will work His wonders in due time.

With God in mind, could any saint rightfully fear Rome, or any man, or any government? Things are not as they appear. Rulers often arrive with great force and ferocity, and depart with a whimper, or with shame, only to live in memory and infamy. Yet, God remains. Philosophies spring from the earth, and for a time appear as lasting full-flowing rivers of life and wisdom, only to dry and disappoint the thirsty soul searching for life's meaning. Yet, God's word remains living and active. Untold idols have been fashioned from wood, stone, and minerals, never to speak, never to listen, never to intercede in times of need. These lifeless figurines continue to collect dust in museums, shrines, and homes even today, serving no good, offering no help, hearing no prayer, speaking no wisdom. Yet, God remains seated upon His throne and is alive forevermore.

The kingdom of Christ has been established upon the ruins of the kingdoms which opposed Him and upon the ash heaps of shrines to false gods whose devotees once persecuted and oppressed His people. These have faded into obscurity, but the kingdom of God remains. We have nothing to dread from the kingdoms of the earth as long as we remain faithful to Him who is truly in control of history and eternity.

Chapter Five

A great many heroic and good men have graced the lives and societies of our world throughout history. But even "the best men are men at best." The greatest men and women have weaknesses and frailties and err in judgment from time-to-time.

Throughout scripture, we are introduced to mighty and holy angels, heavenly messengers and ministers endued with unfathomable power to intercede in the lives of men at the behest of their sovereign Creator. Yet, no angel among the multiplied thousands upon thousands could possess the scroll held in the right hand of the Majesty on High. The combined populace of heaven and earth, both great and small, living, and dead, could only watch and wait to hear and to see the message which was to be unfolded from the scroll with its seven-fold seal.

As John weeps over the hopelessness and unworthiness of all creation, man and angel alike, One appears. Only One. The "matchless supernal One." One is worthy. One is able. Only One is allowed to receive and to reveal the message of the scroll. How might this One be described? A Lion. A Lamb. Both are equally fitting metaphors to describe the person and the ministry of the Son of God, the Christ, the crucified Savior of the world.

The significance of the imagery is profound and clear. In true apocalyptic prose, the introduction of the book of Revelation is repeated (1:1-2). God the Father – the only true and living God – has a message to disclose to His oft-persecuted children. His message will be revealed through His only begotten Son, Jesus Christ. The penman of the message is none other than the beloved apostle and servant and companion in suffering, John. As the celestial scene unfolds, our attention is gripped, and our imagination is captivated along with John's by the vividness and uniqueness of the transpiring drama before us.

A Vision of the Lamb of God (vv. 1-14)

A scroll with a seven-fold seal and writings on the inside and on the back captures John's attention. The scroll was held **in the right hand of Him who sat on the throne (v.1).** A mighty angel appears and inquires of the court, **"Who is worthy to open the scroll and to loose its seals?"** The silence was deafening as **"no one in heaven or on the earth or under the earth was able to open the scroll, or to look at it" (vv.2-3).**

The unworthiness of man and angel caused John to weep much, but one of the twenty-four elders calmed his troubled soul, saying, **"Do not weep. Behold, the Lion of the tribe of Judah, the Root of David, has prevailed to open the scroll and to loose its seven seals" (v.5).**[1]

In the midst of the heavenly throne room, John witnessed a Lamb standing, **"as though it had been slain, having seven horns and seven eyes, which are the seven Spirits of God sent out into all the earth" (v.6).** The Lamb had once been slain. He is the Lamb of God who was slain to take away the sins of the world (John 1:19-24; Isaiah 53:7).

OT sacrifices involving a lamb served to foreshadow the ultimate sacrifice of Christ. In Exodus 12 we can see that the Passover lamb was to be given as a Passover sacrifice for those within the sanctified house. In 1 Corinthians 5:7, Paul teaches us that Jesus is the ultimate reality of the Passover sacrifice. His blood sanctifies all those within the house (cf. Ephesians 5:26; 1 Timothy

---

[1] The designations of Christ as "the Lion of the tribe of Judah, the Root of David" are taken from OT prophecies of the Messiah (Genesis 49:9; Isaiah 11:1, 10; Jeremiah 11:19; 23:5; 33:15; Zechariah 3:8).

3:15). Just as the Passover lamb was without spot (Exodus 12:5) so too is Jesus (1 Peter 1:19). Our Lamb was a vicarious offering given by God for the atonement of the world (Hebrews 2:9).

In Exodus 29:38-42 the Jews were instructed to make two offerings a day. One in the morning and one in the evening, with a lamb being used as the sacrifice for sin, continually. Jesus did this once for all when He offered up Himself (Hebrews 10:14). The daily offering served the Jew in the same way that Christ serves the Christian. He is our daily or perpetual sacrifice for sin. The sacrifice was to be made at the door (Exodus 29:42), and only the priest on the Day of Atonement could go within the veil (Leviticus 16:2, 12). We may enter within the veil at any time through hope since for us our Lord Jesus has already entered (Hebrews 10:19-20). Through Jesus everyday can be a day of atonement and of personal fellowship with God.

The Lamb of Revelation 5:6 has **"seven horns and seven eyes, which are the seven Spirits of God sent out into all the earth."** "Horns were symbolic of strength and honor (Psalm 89:17, 24) and particularly associated with the Davidic king (1 Samuel 2:10) and hoped-for salvation (Luke 1:69)."[2] That there were seven horns could only represent a fullness and absoluteness of strength and honor and power possessed by the Lamb. He is all-powerful and all-knowing.

The Lamb takes the scroll from God. He is the only One with authority to do so. He has been given all authority in heaven and earth (Matthew 28:18 ff.). Upon receiving the scroll, a worship scene in the throne room commences. The four living creatures

---

[2] Ian Paul, *Revelation,* TNTC (Downer's Grove IL: IVP Academic, 2018), 133.

and the twenty-four elders worship the Lamb with the same devotion with which they worshipped the Father (4:8, 11). Just as the Father is worshipped in heaven, so too is the Lamb given glory, honor, and thanks.[3] The prayers of the saints are depicted as "golden bowls full of incense." Christ knows, hears, cares, and intercedes on behalf of the prayers of the saints (cf. Hebrews 4:13-16). He is fully aware of all that is transpiring on earth.

Musical instruments such as harps and bowls of incense were common fixtures in ancient courts of royalty and are only fitting for this scene depicting the Royal court of heaven. We mustn't make the oft too common mistake of believing that since these things are found in Revelation that they belong in the worship of the Lord's church on earth. Nowhere in the NT do we find authorization for these items to be used in Christian worship to God. Man has no more authority to dress in animal costumes to resemble the four living creatures than to use mechanical instruments of music in Christian worship.

In passages speaking of worship and praise to God we read of the church or of individual Christians singing hymns in eight different passages.[4] We do not have one passage in the New Testament which authorizes the use of mechanical instruments in the church or Christian worship. God has commanded us to sing. He has commanded us concerning the types of songs we are to sing – psalms, hymns, and spiritual songs. He has commanded us concerning corporate worship – teach and admonish *one another*. God has provided every instruction necessary to accomplish worship in the music of the church, and instrumental music is not included.

"You are worthy to take the scroll, And to open its seals; For You were slain, And have redeemed us to God by Your

---

[3] Compare this scene with Daniel 7:9-14 and see the same imagery.

[4] Romans 15:9, 11; 1 Corinthians 14:15, 26; Ephesians 5:19; Colossians 3:16; Hebrews 2:12; James 5:13

blood Out of every tribe and tongue and people and nation, And have made us kings and priests to our God, And we shall reign on the earth" (vv.9-10).

It was a new song; we have a "new and living way" (Hebrews 10:20). Christ has made us a kingdom – His kingdom – of priests to God. The Lord's church is His kingdom Matthew 16:16-18; Hebrews 12:22-29). His kingdom is comprised of all nations (Matthew 28:18-20; Mark 16:15-16). His church is a royal priesthood (1 Peter 2:5, 9). Just as Israel was called to be a kingdom of priests in the OT, the designation is continued for God's people in the NT.[5]

John saw and **"heard the voice of many angels around the throne, the living creatures, and the elders; and the number of them was ten thousand times ten thousand, and thousands of thousands, saying with a loud voice: Worthy is the Lamb who was slain To receive power and riches and wisdom, And strength and honor and glory and blessing!" (vv.11-12)**

An innumerable company of angels offer a sevenfold praise to Christ. The angels of heaven worship Him. He is not merely another angel (cf. Hebrews 1:4 ff.). He is God (Isaiah 9:6-7; John 1:1-3), and worthy of all the praise due to the Father.

John observed **"every creature which is in heaven and on the earth and under the earth and such as are in the sea, and all that are in them, I heard saying: Blessing and honor and glory and power Be to Him who sits on the throne, And to the Lamb, forever and ever! Then the four living creatures said, "Amen!" And the twenty-four elders fell down and worshiped Him who lives forever and ever" (vv.13-14).**

---

[5] See also our comments for Revelation 1:5.

Creation in its entirety worships the Father and the Lamb in one accord. Every creature whether in earth or heaven, living or dead cannot resist praising God. There are occasions in scripture when the Father is spoken of as God, as well as the Son, as well as the Spirit. Each are deserving of our praise as being Divine, as being God, or the Godhead (Acts 17:29; Colossians 2:9).

Application for Today

Seeing the adoration given to the Father and the Son in heaven should evoke in our consciences the need and desire to offer such adoration to the Godhead on earth. Our worship must be spiritual, uplifting, and vibrant. Periods of worship together as the church should be considered some of life's most treasured moments. Too often Christians go about their worship with drudgery, apathy, and cold formality. God is deserving of so much more.

For worship to become more meaningful, the object of our worship and the reason for our worship must be clearly understood and appreciated. As Jesus told the Samaritan woman, "You worship what you do not know."

"Give unto the Lord the glory due to His name; Worship the Lord in the beauty of holiness" (Psalm 29:2). "Oh, worship the Lord in the beauty of holiness! Tremble before Him, all the earth" (Psalm 96:9).

Let us remember that we are coming before the Lord God when we worship. And, "Let us come before His presence with thanksgiving; Let us shout joyfully to Him with psalms. For the Lord is the great God, And the great King above all gods" (Psalm 95:2-3). "Oh come, let us worship and bow down; Let us kneel before the Lord our Maker. For He is our God, And we are the people of His pasture, And the sheep of His hand" (Psalm 95:6-7).

Worship is not something we do out of obligation to God; but something we offer in appreciation of God. "Worthy is the Lamb who was slain To receive power and riches and wisdom, And strength and honor and glory and blessing!" (Revelation 5:12)

Chapter Six

Wild speculations run rampantly through a vast number of commentaries on the book of Revelation concerning the identities of the four horsemen of chapter six. Whatever meaning is assigned to the first four seals, it must not be isolated from the historical and contextual setting of the book. Sound reasoning must also be applied by the student when seeking to ascertain the meaning of the fifth and sixth seals opened in chapter six.

We find in this chapter an unfolding drama set to apocalyptic prose. The drama begins retrospectively. Imagine that a curtain is being raised, and as each seal is opened and the imagery ensues, a new actor is appearing in the drama. Chapters six through eleven are to be understood as a single unit, or Act I in the drama, culminating in the destruction of Jerusalem (11:8, 13) as an act of divine judgment upon the Jews for rejecting Christ and persecuting His church. Chapter twelve will serve a two-fold purpose as a summary to chapters 6-11 and as a segue to chapters 13-19.

Before beginning our study of the forthcoming chapters, let us review our principles for interpreting the symbolism found in the book. The *first rule* we shall observe is to consider the text of the book itself. What is the historical context? What are the textual variants? What are the best translations available? What are the findings of significant word studies, etc.?

Secondly, cross-reference scripture to ensure that fundamental biblical teachings serve as the basis for our interpretation. Look to literal passages to grasp the meaning of figurative passages.

The *third rule* worth following is to consider any allusions to other apocalyptic images. Do we find similar images elsewhere in biblical apocalyptic writings? Can an understanding of those images help us to understand better the images we find in Revelation?

The *fourth rule* to be applied throughout this study is more of a practical suggestion than a textbook rule. We will seek to provide literal wording to apocalyptic passages when possible. We will imagine the language as though it was being written in an epistle to the churches using literal language.

The Four Horsemen (vv. 1-8)

John is invited to **"Come and see"** the images to appear with the breaking of the seals. The first of which is **"a rider upon a white horse. He has a bow, wears a crown which was given to him, and went out conquering and to conquer" (vv.1-2).** "In Scripture the horse is generally mentioned in connection with the concepts of strength, terror, warfare, and conquest (Isaiah 30:16; 31:1; Job 39:22-28). In the Apocalypse we have the same association of ideas (9:7; 14:20; 18:13; 19:11)."[1]

The "bow" carried by the rider has been a subject of debate among scholars and commentators of Revelation. Some believe it indicates the Parthian threat of invasion which loomed for Rome in the first century.[2] The Parthians were "a warlike federation of tribes across the Euphrates, the eastern boundary of the Roman Empire."[3] However, no definite historical context needs to be supposed in this case, as Parthian conquest had little to do with Jewish

---

[1] William Hendrickson, *More than Conquerors*, 113.

[2] e.g., M. Eugene Boring, *Revelation*, ICS (Louisville, KY: John Knox Press, 1989), 122.

[3] Grant R. Osborne, *Revelation: Verse by Verse* (Bellingham, WA: Lexham Press, 2016), 124.

persecution against the church and the climactic destruction of Jerusalem in chapter eleven, which closes this section of the book.

Others believe it signifies weaponry in general, conveying the idea of mankind's lust for war.[4] Hence, the rider on the white horse would convey God's use of man and his insatiable desire to conquer his fellowman as the first act of judgment rendered in the scene. Such an interpretation is certainly plausible and fits with the actions of the other three horsemen. It also fits with the use of horsemen in OT apocalyptic writings.

In Zechariah 1:8-15; 6:1-8, we find horses and chariots patrolling the earth and executing judgment upon the nations at the behest of God. The similarities in these two accounts may imply that the symbolism of the horsemen in Revelation is rooted in Zechariah.[5]

If this connection is to be made, then the horsemen would be "commissioned by God to patrol the earth and to punish those nations on earth that they find to have oppressed His people. By analogy, the horses in Revelation 6:1-8 may signify that the natural and political disasters throughout the world are caused by Christ in order to judge unbelievers who persecute Christians and to vindicate His people."[6] If this is the proper interpretation for the first rider, then he would represent God's judgment on the Jews and Jerusalem at the hands of Rome in the first century AD. It seems this interpretation is likely as it fits will the ideas presented in the following judgments and the book's context.

However, an alternative interpretation should also be considered. The rider of the white horse in Revelation 19:11 is identified

---

[4] Mounce, 154; Osborne, 124.
[5] Ferrell Jenkins, *The Old Testament in the Book of Revelation* (Marion, IN: Cogdill Foundation, 1972), 43.
[6] Beale and Carson, 1103.

as Christ. Also, the rider of chapter six is wearing white and is crowned – symbols associated with Christ throughout the Revelation. White has already been viewed as the color of purity and holiness in Revelation 2:17. If the first seal is an image of Christ, the horseman would symbolize a heavenly mission of conquest.[7] God is also portrayed carrying a bow in the OT (cf. Psalm 7:12; Habakkuk 3:8-13), as is Christ (Psalm 45:5).

The rider is also conquering, which is another idea associated with Christ in Revelation and in the writings of John (John 16:33; Revelation 1:13; 2:26, 27; 3:21; 5:5; 6:16; 7:9, 10; 11:15; 12:11; 14:1, 14; 17:14; 19:11; 20:4; 22:16). The Messianic Psalm 45:3-5 provides an interesting parallel as well. Note, "Gird Your sword upon Your thigh, O Mighty One, With Your glory and Your majesty. And in Your majesty ride prosperously because of truth, humility, and righteousness; And Your right hand shall teach You awesome things. Your arrows are sharp in the heart of the King's enemies; The peoples fall under You."

According to this view, Christ is presented as the first horseman, victorious, and "carrying out the content of the hitherto sealed book...not in military strength or war, but in the gospel to conquer the souls of men according to God's plan."[8]

The two interpretations are valid and neither does harm to the historical or contextual settings of the book. In one case, the first horseman represents God's judgment on the Jews through the military might of Rome. He is the first of four horsemen to execute God's judgment on the Jews. In the second case, Christ is presented conquering the world with His gospel.

The next horseman to appear is riding "**on a fiery red horse and is wielding a great sword. He is charged to take peace**

---

[7] Hailey, 188.
[8] Hailey, 189.

from the earth, and that people should kill one another" (vv.3-4). At first glance we might think warfare is the object of this symbol. However, the sword this rider carries is the *machaira* or the "short sword." It is the same type of sword used by Abraham in Genesis 22:6, 10. The killing that was to be done was literally a "slaughtering" of mankind (see Revelation 5:6; 5:9; 5:12; 6:9; 13:8; 18:24), or "murder" (1 John 3:12).

The imminent church historian, Philip Schaff provides insight for how such swords and similar knives might have been ruthlessly used in Palestine during the first century. "After the accession of Felix,[9] assassins, called "Sicarians" (from sica, a dagger), armed with daggers and purchasable for any crime, endangering safety in city and country, roamed over Palestine."[10]

If we are to understand these horsemen to represent woes upon the Jewish people as acts of divine retribution and vindication for persecuting the church of Christ, then the "slaughtering" being done in this passage would refer to man's humanity to man, brother against brother, through acts of violence, assault, robbery, and murder. Civil and societal peace has been taken from the land as a demonstration of God's judgment and punishment upon the people. We see a pattern of this behavior in godless societies today. Whenever and wherever God's will is not followed, man will demonstrate atrocious acts of violence against each other.

If the first rider on the white horse represents Christ, then the second rider on the fiery red horse would likely represent the persecution of the church at the hands of the Jews. Thus, Jesus came conquering with the gospel, and as a result carnage followed in the form of persecution against His people. Our Lord certainly

---

[9] Cf. Acts 23:24 ff.

[10] Philip Schaff, *History of the Christian Church: Apostolic Christianity AD 1-100* (vol.1) (New York: Scribner's, 1889), 394.

warned of such (cf. Matthew 10:34). Seeing that both interpretations remain plausible, we must continue reading to see if the context of the chapter will serve to clear up the matter of identifying the meaning of the riders.

When the third seal is broken a third rider appears mounted this time upon "**a black horse and he had a pair of scales in his hand**" (**v.5**). "In the ancient world food was distributed by rationed amounts (using scales) when it became scarce...Severe food shortages are in view."[11] We know from Acts and several of Paul's epistles that a famine did occur in Palestine (cf. Acts 11:27-30). During Paul's third missionary journey he collected monetary support to relieve suffering saints in Jerusalem and Judea (cf. Romans 15:25-26; 2 Corinthians 8-9).

John heard a voice amid the four living creatures saying, "**A quart of wheat for a denarius, and three quarts of barley for a denarius; and do not harm the oil and the wine**" (**v.6**). Wheat for bread came at a day's wages (Matthew 20:2). Such oppression would leave little for clothing, shelter, etc. However, the famine was not yet completely devasting, as the oil and wine which were basic food staples went untouched.[12] Greater and severer punishment was yet to come.

Later, John will see that those without the mark of the beast were unable to buy and to sell (Revelation 13:17). The first century Christian was all too familiar with the looting of his goods (Hebrews 10:34). However, looting and famine are different calamities. One is natural the other manmade. The mark of the beast and subsequent sufferings came from the hands of Rome and does not fit with this scenario of the third seal. Thus, the rider of the

---

[11] Beale and Carson, 1103. Cf. Leviticus 26:26; 2 Kings 7:1; Ezekiel 4:10, 16.

[12] Ibid., cf. Deuteronomy 7:13; 11:14; 28:51; 2 Chronicles 32:28; Nehemiah 5:11; Psalm 104:14-15; Jeremiah 31:12; Hosea 2:8, 22; Joel 1:10; 2:19; Micah 6:15; Haggai 2:12.

black horse is not a picture of Roman persecution, but of divine retribution upon the inhabitants of the land.

With the opening of the fourth seal, a fourth horseman appears. John beheld **"a pale horse. And the name of him who sat on it was Death, and Hades followed with him. And power was given to them over a fourth of the earth, to kill with sword, with hunger, with death, and by the beasts of the earth" (vv7-8).** Death with the afterlife (hades) following is obviously depicted. The rider was to kill (as in warfare) with sword (a sword of battle), with hunger (famine), with pestilence (plagues), and by wild beasts of the earth. Christ held the keys to hades and death (1:18). He remains in control of these events. These are acts of divine judgment.

A study of Ezekiel 14 will help us to understand the symbolism of this horse and rider.[13] Israel's attitude toward God was described as "persistent unfaithfulness" (v.13). They had become like Sodom and Gomorrah in the scarcity of righteous souls. God uses a hyperbole when He says, "Even if these three men, Noah, Daniel, and Job, were in it, they would deliver only themselves by their righteousness" (v.14, 20). The hyperbole continues as God again speaks of the destruction of the people. God speaks of the same four means of destruction in Ezekiel 14 as He does in Revelation 6 – sword, famine, wild beasts, and pestilence (vv.15-21). As God allowed these punishments to afflict unfaithful Israel (and other nations) in the OT, and cities were brought to desolation by them because of their sins, so too would these souls suffer in death and the hereafter if they did not repent. Judea and Jerusalem would be destroyed.

---

[13] Similar passages are found in Leviticus 26:18 ff; and Jeremiah 15:2 ff.

The contents of the fourth seal appear to help us identify the rider from the first seal as we can now explain the entirety of the picture. Christians were not being warned and were not the intended subject of the calamities brought on by these acts of divine judgment. Retribution was being dealt out to the fourth part of the "earth" not the church (v.8). By understanding how the larger context (through chapter eleven) addresses the fall of Jerusalem – "where also our Lord was crucified" (11:8) – and the historical context of Jewish persecution of the church, we can reasonably interpret the symbols of the four horsemen as follows:

(1) The White Horse and Rider represents Roman conquest of Judea leading to the destruction of Jerusalem in 70 AD.

(2) The Red Horse and Rider represents the cruelty manifested among assassins and the like which were running amuck in Palestine during that time.

(3) The Black Horse and Rider represents the famine which was experienced in Judea.

(4) The Pale Horse and Rider represents God's continued judgments upon the people and the land for their refusal to repent.

We should also note that these calamities did not occur consecutively, but often simultaneously.

The Cry of the Martyrs (vv. 9-11)

The opening of the fifth seal provides John with a vision of martyred souls **"who had been slain for the word of God and for the testimony which they held" (v.9).** They are situated "under the altar" which can only refer to the altar in heaven (8:3, 5; 14:18). In Revelation, heaven in presented as the temple of God

(11:19; 14:15; 15:5).[14] The allusion here is to the altar of burnt offering, not the altar of incense. As with the offering of the animal sacrifices of the OT, the blood of the martyred saints was being poured out as an offering (cf. Philippians 2:17; 2 Timothy 4:6).[15]

The martyred saints are crying out for God's righteous vindication. **"How long, O Lord, holy and true, until You judge and avenge our blood on those who dwell on the earth?" (v.10)**

They seek immediate retribution. They call upon Him who is "Lord, holy, and true" knowing that He will not acquit the wicked (Numbers 14:18). However, God's judgments are not yet complete. As Revelation unfolds, we will see an intensification of the scope and nature of His judgments against Judea.

The martyred were to **"rest a little while longer, until the number of their fellow servants and their brethren, who would be killed as they were, was completed" (v.11).** A white robe, the garment of a heavenly one (cf. Revelation 7:9, 13; Daniel 7:9; Matthew 28:3),[16] was given to each of them (cf. 19:8).

That a number exists signifies to us that God had in His mind how long He would allow the persecution to continue. Everything which was occurring was in the hands of Almighty God. God remained sovereign, supreme, and in control, even during a time of great persecution.

Cosmic Upheaval (vv. 12-17)

The opening of the sixth seal presents God's continued judgments using OT language once again. What follows is the language of divine judgment. John witnesses **"a great earthquake;**

---

[14] See also Psalm 18:6; Habakkuk 2:20; Micah 1:2.
[15] Roberts, 67.
[16] Ibid.

and the sun became black as sackcloth of hair, and the moon became like blood. And the stars of heaven fell to the earth, as a fig tree drops its late figs when it is shaken by a mighty wind. Then the sky receded as a scroll when it is rolled up, and every mountain and island was moved out of its place" (vv.12-14).

When we find the use of this language in the OT, it often refers to God's overthrow of wicked civilizations (cf. Isaiah 34:1 ff; Zephaniah 1:14 ff). For example, this imagery was used to describe the overthrow of Babylon (Isaiah 13:10-13), Edom (Isaiah 34:4), Egypt (Ezekiel 32:6-8), and other enemy nations of Israel (Habakkuk 3:6-11). It was used with reference to Judah as well (Jeremiah 4:23 ff). This dramatic language is also used to prophesy of the establishing of the church (cf. Joel 2:10, 30-31; Acts 2:14 ff).[17] Here we find this language is being used again to refer to the defeat of those of who had been persecuting the church.

In Matthew 24:29-31 this language is used in connection to the tribulation suffered during the destruction of Jerusalem (vv. 21-22, 29) and to the time of His return (vv. 30-31). Because of this connection, many commentators believe the sixth seal pertains to the final judgment and the end of the world. However, that judgment scene does not occur in Revelation until 20:11-15. Moreover, wicked kings and men remain alive after this dramatic series of events. They will be destroyed with the earth at the second coming and final judgment.

"And the kings of the earth, the great men, the rich men, the commanders, the mighty men, every slave and every free man, hid themselves in the caves and in the rocks of the mountains, and said to the mountains and rocks, 'Fall on us and hide us from the face of Him who sits on the throne and from

---

[17] Beale and Carson, 1105.

the wrath of the Lamb! For the great day of His wrath has come, and who is able to stand?'" (vv.15-17).

Here we have another OT allusion, this time to Hosea 10:8 and the overthrow of wicked Samaria. The Hosea passage reads: "Also the high places of Aven, the sin of Israel, Shall be destroyed. The thorn and thistle shall grow on their altars; They shall say to the mountains, 'Cover us!' And to the hills, 'Fall on us!'"

In the sixth seal of Revelation, God is likewise foretelling the end of those who persecuted the church and the passing of the hypocritical religious system they had developed and used to crucify His Son and slay His children.

Application for Today

Some souls lose faith when they are tried by evil, pain, and suffering. Such a person will express a loss of faith by claiming that if God truly existed, He would not allow their suffering to happen. In such cases of disbelief, God is blamed rather than considering His cause. Evil does not originate with God, and He does not tempt us with evil (James 1:13). Yet, God does allow our faith to be tried and to become stronger by such trials as a means of perfecting us and making us more useful for His service (cf. Jeremiah 12:5).

We live in a world that is marred by sin. Sufferings can go from bad to worse. God may indeed be looking down through the corridor of time and know of some greater challenge we will be called to face. He may be allowing something to test us in order to prepare us for that which is greater. Trials are used by God as a means of revealing our weaknesses to us (cf. Philippians 3:10-15). We may not yet understand why certain things happen in our lives. But we can rest in the assurance that "God shall reveal even this unto you."

Peter writes of the trying of our faith (1 Peter 1:7) and encourages us to follow in Christ's steps when facing such trials (2:21; 3:17; 4:12-19). Even though we may not know why we are called upon to suffer, we must remain vigilant (5:8) and steadfast in the faith (5:9). We must have an attitude which is expressed thusly, "I must keep the faith. I must endure" (cf. 2 Timothy 4:6-8; Revelation 2:10).

We may not know why, and we may not understand all His reasons, but we can know God will see us through, even unto a home in heaven someday. Regardless of whatever the church may face or be called to endure, God is in control. He remains as He has always been. His attributes are immutable. His word is sure. His judgments are righteous and holy. Yet, we must realize that God works according to His will, not ours. His schedule, not ours. His wisdom, not ours.

Faith is required and increased during times of despair. Faith is required to endure. Faith is increased after we endure. "Count it all joy" to know that God lives, cares, and acts according to His infinite wisdom on behalf of His dearly loved children. Such has always been true and will forever be true. Let us be thankful that we know God, have God, and let us love God evermore.

Chapter Seven

The opening of the first six seals provided us with scenes of God's judgments on sinful men and the dire circumstances the church was facing in the world. In chapter seven an interval occurs between the opening of the seals, wherein we are provided with scenes of the church on earth and in heaven. God has not forgotten His people. Quite the opposite. He has sealed them with a mark of ownership, identifying them as His own. Moreover, He has kept His promise to those who have come through earth's tribulation and this period of persecution at the hands of nonbelievers, granting them peace and glory in His presence. They, like their Savior, are victorious over all enemies natural and spiritual.

As we seek to ascertain the meaning of the symbols in chapter seven, particularly the 144,000, we should keep in mind that chapters six through eleven are presenting a retrospection of the first persecution inflicted on the church at the hands of Jews in Jerusalem and Judea. Revelation was written in the mid-90s AD. Jerusalem was destroyed in 70 AD. The temple in Jerusalem is no more to be, but the temple in heaven would remain forever. These scenes look back upon what has already transpired and provide hope for what is transpiring in the present, and what will transpire in the future.

After the scenes of Jerusalem's destruction are conveyed in chapter eleven, another interval will occur in chapter twelve. Chapters thirteen through nineteen will present a picture of Roman persecution of the church and the ultimate overthrow of their empire. Christ and His kingdom will prove to be victorious over Rome and endure long after the ancient city and the empire seated therein have faded into history.

Four Angels at the Four Corners of the Earth (vv. 1-3)

Four angels appear before John, standing **at the four corners of the earth, holding the four winds of the earth (v.1).** "The idea of the earth having four quarters or angels from which the four winds blow is a convention frequently mentioned in the Old Testament (Isaiah 11:12; Ezekiel 7:2; four winds – Zechariah 2:6; Daniel 7:2; 8:8; 11:4)...Furthermore, the idea of the winds as God's avenging spirits or of the Lord coming in vengeance, riding upon the clouds or winds, is so commonplace in the Old Testament that it is difficult to mistake (Isaiah 19:1; 66:15; Psalms 18:10; 104:3 ff; Jeremiah 4:11-13; 23:19)."[1]

As the vision is introduced, a continuation of judgment is imminent. But before God's judgment continues in chapter eight with the sounding of the seven trumpets, the servants of God on earth must be sealed, denoting His protection from the wrath He will pour out upon the earth. **Another angel ascends from the east carrying the seal of the living God (v.2).** Just as each new day brings hope with a sunrise from the east, so too does this angel appear. His purpose is to **"seal the servants of God on their foreheads" (v.3)** before any further harm occurs on earth.

Seals were commonly used in this era. They were used for branding cattle and tattooing slaves to mark ownership. Soldiers and those in service of the emperor were marked. Members of trade guilds were marked on the hand, brow, or neck to seal them as religious devotees in consecration to the deity and as members of a sacred militia.[2] In the context of Revelation 7:2-3, the seal

---

[1] Roberts, 70.

[2] Fritz Rienecker and Cleon Rogers, *Linguistic Key to the Greek New Testament* (Grand Rapids, MI: Zondervan, 1980), 828-9.

served to mark, identify, and distinguish the people of God to protect them from the judgments to come when the trumpets would sound (chaps. 8-11).

The 144,000 are Sealed (vv. 4-8)

The number of those who were sealed was **144,000 "of all the tribes of the children of Israel" (v.4).** Judah is listed first rather than Reuben who was the firstborn (v.5). Students of scripture should not consider this to be out of place, as Christ was from the tribe of Judah (Genesis 49:10; Revelation 5:5). All the other tribes would bow to Judah (Genesis 49:9) and be incorporated into the tribe of Judah through Christ at the time of the restoration of all things (cf. Ezekiel 34:23-25; 37:15-25; Acts 3:21).

The omission of Dan and the inclusion of Manasseh and Joseph are also unique to the listing of the tribes (vv.6, 8). Dan had become synonymous with idolatry by this time and even Satan was said to be the prince of this tribe.[3] The exclusion of Dan could be for this reason. However, the list is not intended to be taken literally. The ten tribes of the northern kingdom of Israel had long since vanished into obscurity. The number represents the faithful church in Judea which would be spared when the trumpets are sounded.

The number "12" conveys completeness or totality in apocalyptic symbolism. 12,000 x 12 = 144,000. Here we have the full or total number in apocalyptic language, not a literal counting of souls, for those who would be sealed and spared as the following events occur. The symbolism reminds us of the numbering of Israel prior to entering Canaan. These saints are numbered as they too are on their way to the eternal land of promise.

---

[3] Mounce, 169.

The church is referred to as such throughout the NT (cf. James 1:1; 1 Peter 1:1; Luke 22:30; Matthew 19:28; Galatians 6:16; Philippians 3:3). What can be said of the whole can also be said of the part. If the church is spiritual Israel in total, consisting of both Jews and Gentiles, then the church in part, no matter how small, could be considered part of spiritual Israel.

The text says these people are **"of all the tribes of the children of Israel."** Jewish Christians could be called children of Israel in both senses, literally and spiritually (cf. Romans 2:28-29). Seeing that the context of Revelation at this point is addressing the first wave of persecution thrust upon the church, which came in Judea at the hands of disbelieving Jews, and upon Jewish Christians, reason calls for us to see this number as standing for Jewish Christians who were to be spared during the continued judgment of the Jewish people in Judea. Jerusalem would fall, the temple would be destroyed, and the Jewish system would be fulfilled, but the church which began there would remain.

A Multitude in Heaven (vv. 9-17)

Just as God would deliver Jewish Christians from Jewish persecution, He also promised to deliver Gentile Christians from Roman and Jewish persecution where the church had spread. One who was currently suffering persecution at the hands of Rome might wonder about his fate. Will God protect him too? The answer and necessary assurance are provided in the next vision, as John writes, **"After these things I looked, and behold, a great multitude which no one could number, of all nations, tribes, peoples, and tongues, standing before the throne and before the Lamb" (v.9).**

John witnessed a great multitude comprised of souls from all nations, all tribes, all peoples, all languages, standing before the throne God and before the Lamb. They were with the Lord. God's promise to Abraham is fulfilled as the nations of the earth have come to be blessed through his Seed, Christ (cf. Genesis 12:3 ff; Galatians 3:16). They were clothed in garments of white robes, signifying purity, and victory; and they had palm branches in their hands, signifying a glad "Hosanna" to be raised (cf. John 12:13).

"Salvation belongs to our God who sits on the throne, and to the Lamb!" (v.11). Moreover, **"All the angels stood around the throne and the elders and the four living creatures, and fell on their faces before the throne and worshiped God, saying: 'Amen! Blessing and glory and wisdom, Thanksgiving and honor and power and might, Be to our God forever and ever. Amen'" (v.12).**

One of the twenty-four elders asks John, **"Who are these arrayed in white robes, and where did they come from?"** To which John could only reply, **"Sir, you know" (vv.13-14).** The elder replies, **"These are the ones who come out of the great tribulation, and washed their robes and made them white in the blood of the Lamb" (v.14).** After having endured great tribulation by holding fast to the faith, scarlet stains of sin had been erased and replaced by a pure white created by the cleansing power of Christ's atonement.

Beyond the borders of Judea, the tribulation against the church spread to every place Jesus was confessed as Lord. As we study the book of Acts, we find the historical record of such distress. Persecution followed Paul on his missionary journeys from one Gentile city to another, back to Jerusalem to face rioting from his kinsmen, and then to face imprisonment in Rome where he would eventually suffer martyrdom after being imprisoned a second time. Throughout the Roman world the church was called to endure hardships, perils, and persecution. Those who endured are now seen in the happy care of God, to know eternal bliss in the light of His love forevermore.

"Therefore they are before the throne of God, and serve Him day and night in His temple. And He who sits on the throne will dwell among them. They shall neither hunger anymore nor thirst anymore; the sun shall not strike them, nor any heat; for the Lamb who is in the midst of the throne will shepherd them and lead them to living fountains of waters. And God will wipe away every tear from their eyes" (vv.15-17).

The temple of God no longer stands on a hill in Jerusalem, representing a heavenly reality. "The Lord is in His holy temple. The Lord's throne is in heaven" (Psalm 11:4). The doors to the true temple in heaven have been opened, and all who enter may be free from hunger, thirst, heat, and sadness. Such is significant to our continued study of Revelation as these are a few of the very elements of judgment soon to face the world as it stands condemned by God for refusing to repent. While the church in heaven is delivered from these calamities, the church on earth will have to persevere a little while longer, until heaven becomes their home too.

Application for Today

Come what may, God remains in control. He knows His people and His watchful eye and protection is ever upon them. God will not allow His people to suffer more than they are able to endure (1 Corinthians 10:13).

Being a Christian, however, does not free a person from the dangers of persecution. But "if God is for us, who shall be against us?" For the faithful child of God, "to die is gain" and we must never fear the one "who is able to destroy the body" above the One who can "destroy both body and lose in hell."

The thought of the Christian's ultimate salvation is central to the chapter as is the proper response to "so great a salvation." When considering our salvation from sin, death, and punishment, and the blessings resulting from the blood of Christ and the grace of God, what can we do but praise Him! "Blessing and glory and wisdom, Thanksgiving and honor and power and might, Be to our God forever and ever."

God is the source of all blessings, glory, and wisdom. We can experience these blessings because of our relationship with Him as His children. As we recognize His greatness, we offer thanksgiving for His honor and power and might, our God and Father forever and ever, Amen. May our worship on earth be as spontaneous as was this scene in heaven! Let it flow naturally and suddenly and frequently as we reflect on the goodness and power and providence of God.

Chapter Eight

Chapter eight begins with a deafening silence. As the children of Israel were instructed to "stand still, and see the salvation of the Lord" when crossing the Red Sea (Exodus 14:13), the martyred souls who have cried for vindication are in quiet stillness, soon to behold both the wrath and the salvation of the Lord. God is righteous to repay with tribulation those who trouble the church (2 Thessalonians 1:6). The world has caused the church to pass through a period of great tribulation (Revelation 7:6; Acts 8:1). In righteousness, God will now repay the world for the evil they have sown.

As was the case with the Egyptian plagues, we can see man's heart being hardened and a refusal to repent in chapter eight. Not only are the plagues of Exodus mirrored here, but also the outcome of a hardened heart and deliverance from persecution.

With the 144,000 sealed by God on earth and the great multitude redeemed in heaven, Christians have been provided assurance with God's promises. Now, the wrath and fury of God is to be unleashed in the world, while the church will be preserved. Christians can rest assured of God's protection and deliverance in times of tribulation and persecution. Their prayers are heard and answered. Sinful men will come and go, but the kingdom of God will endure forever.

Seven Angels with Seven Trumpets (vv. 1-6)

"When He opened the seventh seal, there was silence in heaven for about half an hour" (v.1).

In the OT especially, silence like this is associated frequently with a forthcoming judgment upon a nation. In those instances, the earth is commanded to keep silent before the Lord (cf. Amos 8:2-3; Habakkuk 2:20; Zephaniah 1:7-18; Zechariah 2:13). Such must be the intended effect of this scene in Revelation. Only here, the silence is in heaven. The vast host of heaven is awaiting and preparing for their summons to act and to witness God's vindication of His people. "It was the silence of dreadful suspense, fearful expectation, a calm before the storm."[1]

The silence lasted for about half an hour. "A similarity exists between the silence and the cessation of singers and trumpets in the cleansing of the temple by Hezekiah when the king and all the congregation 'bowed themselves and worshipped' (2 Chronicles 29)."[2] In Chronicles the cessation and silence occurred between periods of worship and offerings. Here, the silence occurs between the worship of chapter 7 and the judgments of chapters 8-11.

Following the brief period of silence, John saw **"the seven angels who stand before God, and to them were given seven trumpets" (v.2).** It may be that these seven angels are the ones introduced in 1:20 and serve as angels to the seven churches (ch. 2-3). In Jewish apocalyptic literature, we read of seven archangels as well.[3] The significance of the trumpets can also be found in the OT, where they were used to call the people to worship (Leviticus 23:24; Numbers 29:1), gather a troop for battle (Numbers 10:9), alert people of danger (used metaphorically in Ezekiel 33:1-6), and signal God's forthcoming judgment (on the nations per Joel 2:1, 15 ff. and upon Judah per Zephaniah 1:14 ff.).[4] In Revelation, they are used to signal God's acts of judgment against those who

---

[1] Wallace, 167.

[2] Ibid.

[3] Beale and Carson, 1111; Metzger, 63-64; see Jewish apocalyptic books of Tobit 12:15 and Enoch chapter 20.

[4] Paul, 170.

have been persecuting His people and engaging in wickedness (8:20-21).

In 8:3, we see a continuation of the scene from 5:8, wherein we first read of the prayers of the saints being represented as golden bowls full of incense. In this passage, **"another angel, having a golden censer, came and stood at the altar. He was given much incense, that he should offer it with the prayers of all the saints upon the golden altar which was before the throne."** The heavenly altar again combines the imagery of the altar of incense and the altar of burnt offering (Exodus 27; Exodus 30). In heaven, these are not two separate altars, but one.[5] The imagery in Revelation symbolizes the prayers of troubled saints ascending before God as they seek deliverance from their oppressors, as **"the smoke of the incense, with the prayers of the saints, ascended before God from the angel's hand" (v.4).**

"Then the angel took the censer, filled it with fire from the altar, and threw it to the earth. And there were noises, thunderings, lightnings, and an earthquake" (v.5).

The symbolism of this verse depicts the prayers being heard as God begins His response. The censer is filled with fire as it is mingled with the prayers of the saints and thrust toward to the earth from the throne room of heaven. Earth is filled with noises, thunderings, lightnings, and an earthquake. God's judgment has begun.

However, we should not conclude that this is the final judgment as some commentators have done. The judgment is a continuation of God's judgment of Israel for their rejection of Christ and persecution of the church. This judgment will conclude in chapter eleven. Judgment upon the house of Israel for their obstinance and arrogance is foretold in similar language by Malachi. Note, "For

---

[5] Osborne, 150-151.

behold, the day is coming, Burning like an oven, And all the proud, yes, all who do wickedly will be stubble. And the day which is coming shall burn them up, Says the Lord of hosts, That will leave them neither root nor branch. But to you who fear My name The Sun of Righteousness shall arise With healing in His wings; And you shall go out And grow fat like stall-fed calves. You shall trample the wicked, For they shall be ashes under the soles of your feet On the day that I do this, Says the Lord of hosts" (Malachi 4:1-3). The triumph of Christ and His gospel and His people is foretold by Malachi and continued in Revelation with the sounding of the trumpets.

"So the seven angels who had the seven trumpets prepared themselves to sound" (v.6).

"The trumpet is a favorite instrument of apocalyptists since it summons people's attention to God's communication."[6] The scenes to follow correspond with the ten plagues God sent upon Egypt. Just as the Israelites were once enslaved and sorely mistreated by Pharoah, the church has been in a similar distress in Jerusalem (Acts 8:1), i.e., "Sodom and Egypt where also our Lord was crucified" (Revelation 11:8). The purpose of the forthcoming plagues parallels the purpose of the plagues upon Egypt as God makes His presence known in defense of His people. He has heard their cry and His response will serve to demonstrate His power and remind humanity of His sovereignty over all created things. Just as the plagues in Egypt should have induced Pharoah to heed Moses, these plagues upon Judea should have convinced the Jews to heed a Prophet greater than Moses (Deuteronomy 18:15-19; Acts 7:37).

---

[6] Metzger, 63-64.

First Trumpet: Vegetation Is Struck (v.7)

"The first angel sounded: And hail and fire followed, mingled with blood, and they were thrown to the earth. And a third of the trees were burned up, and all green grass was burned up" (v.7).

The scene corresponds to the seventh plague in Egypt (Exodus 9:13 ff.), which would have resulted in widespread famine. The extent of the punishment has also increased since the opening of the seals from one-fourth to one-third of the earth being affected. However, God's judgment is not all-encompassing. Life on earth is still possible. It is not intended to destroy man completely as did Noah's flood, but to humble him to the point of repentance.

Throughout the OT, and especially in the book of Isaiah, hail and fire were used by God as weapons in the destruction of His enemies (Isaiah 30:30-33), idolaters (Isaiah 28:17 ff.), and the rebellious (Isaiah 28:2 ff.).[7] Concerning the blood that was mingled with the hail and fire, "From the time immediately following the flood God has demanded blood for blood (Genesis 9:6); that blood can be expiated only by the blood of the one who shed it (Numbers 35:33)."[8] Thus, the blood of the Christians who have been martyred is now being brought upon the heads of those who shed it.

Second Trumpet: The Seas Are Struck (vv. 8-9)

"Then the second angel sounded: And something like a great mountain burning with fire was thrown into the sea, and a third of the sea became blood. And a third of the living creatures in the sea died, and a third of the ships were destroyed" (vv.8-9).

---

[7] Hailey, 219.
[8] See also Isaiah 26:21; Joel 3:19; Psalm 79:10.

Mountains were quite significant in the OT for good and for evil (cf. Psalm 48:1 ff.; Isaiah 2:2-4; 11:9; Micah 4:2; Isaiah 41:15; 64:1; Amos 4:1) and mention of their destruction conveyed the fall of a nation (as with Babylon in Jeremiah 51:25, 42).

The picture that appears with the sounding of the second trumpet seems to present a volcanic eruption. "If, as is likely, Revelation was written after AD 79, when the sudden eruption of Vesuvius completely engulfed the city of Pompeii with molten lava and destroyed ships in the Gulf of Naples, then John's readers, from reports they had heard of the catastrophe, would have had no difficulty picturing 'something like a great mountain, burning with fire, [being] thrown into the sea.'"[9]

Many commentators also note how the destruction of sea trade pictured in this vision would have had an obvious effect on the economy of any society and would have served as another form of punishment delivered from God. While this is no doubt true and plausible, the larger picture should not be obscured. We find in these visions that God has complete control over every created thing. The grass of the field can flourish or wither under His command. The waters and life of the sea can provide food and nourishment and wealth to humankind, or they can be turned to blood and yield no benefit. Evil men cannot escape the judgment of God on land or at sea.

Third Trumpet: The Fresh Waters Are Struck (vv. 10-11)

"**Then the third angel sounded: And a great star fell from heaven, burning like a torch, and it fell on a third of the rivers and on the springs of water. The name of the star is Wormwood. A third of the waters became wormwood, and many**

---

[9] Metzger, 64.

men died from the water, because it was made bitter" (vv.10-11).

A meteorite-type of burning star next crashes to the earth with pinpoint accuracy, this time affecting the rivers and springs, mankind's source of drinking water. God's punishments continue to reach one-third of humankind, denoting His judgment is increased but not final. Animal life and vegetation have been damaged, the sea has been cursed, and now water for drinking is contaminated by blood. The allusion to the Exodus plagues continues (cf. Exodus 7:15-24; Psalm 78:44).

The crashing star is named "Wormwood" which is a bitter herb and was used in OT times to poison drinking water (cf. Jeremiah 9:15; 23:15). "A figurative understanding of wormwood as a metaphor for the bitterness of punishment is confirmed from the indisputable metaphorical use elsewhere in the OT, where it also represents severe affliction as a consequence of divine wrath (see Deuteronomy 29:17-18 [again in connection with idolatry]; Proverbs 5:4; Lamentations 3:15, 19; Amos 5:7; 6:12 [cf. Hosea 10:4])."[10]

That "many men died from the water" indicates the consequences of the plagues upon mankind. By cursing the earth, God is cursing those whose survival is dependent upon it. This too is a common theme in the OT, especially in the books of poetry and prophecy. God is willing and able to bless the land for those who fear Him and yet He remains righteous in cursing the land for those who refuse Him and mistreat their fellowman (Nahum 1:2-15; Psalm 107).

---

[10] Beale and Carson, 1113.

Fourth Trumpet: The Heavens Are Struck (v. 12)

"Then the fourth angel sounded: And a third of the sun was struck, a third of the moon, and a third of the stars, so that a third of them were darkened. A third of the day did not shine, and likewise the night" (v.12).

Not only does God reign over all earth but also heaven. The sun, the moon, the stars, are in His hand. We find God's control over the heavens in Egypt (Exodus 10:22), in the conquest of Canaan (Joshua 10:13), and during the crucifixion of Christ (Amos 8:9; Luke 23:44).

The heavens remain at His command to bless or to curse. God's power over the entirety of His created order is on display. "Early Jewish tradition understood the plague of darkness to have symbolic significance – for example, as representing estrangement from God and eternal judgment."[11] Spiritual darkness and light are often contrasted in the NT. The lost abide in darkness of ignorance and sin while the saved walk in light of wisdom and truth. Here darkness blankets one-third of the heavens, but it is not complete and darkness for all.

Three More Woes to Come (v. 13)

"And I looked, and I heard an angel flying through the midst of heaven, saying with a loud voice, 'Woe, woe, woe to the inhabitants of the earth, because of the remaining blasts of the trumpet of the three angels who are about to sound!'" (v.13)

The NKJV is the primary text we have been using in this study. As with the KJV, the underlying Greek text[12] states that an *angel*

---

[11] Ibid.
[12] The Majority Text (MT)

is heard flying in heaven. However, more recent translations present an *eagle* flying in heaven (ESV; NASB; NIV). The more recent translations are based on a different Greek text.[13] Most of the older manuscripts have an eagle (*aetos*) as the object.

If "eagle" is the correct object in the text, it would fit with OT metaphorical language which used eagles in announcements for coming judgments (cf. Jeremiah 48:40; 49:22; Ezekiel 17:3). Of special interest is the use of the "eagle" metaphor in Hosea 8:1, wherein Israel is being judged for their rejection of God's covenant and rebellion to His law.

If "angel" is the correct object of the text, the wording would clearly fit the overall context and prominence placed upon angels in the book of Revelation. Obviously, this is a minor matter in understanding the message of Revelation, but interesting, nonetheless.

Whether God used an eagle or an angel to present His message, the message was loud and clear: **"Woe, woe, woe to the inhabitants of the earth, because of the remaining blasts of the trumpet of the three angels who are about to sound!"** Four woes have passed, but God's judgment is not complete. Three woes remain. As with the opening of the seven seals, the sounding of the seven trumpets falls into two groups of four and three.[14] Thus far, man has been affected indirectly by the first four plagues. With the remaining three, man will be affected directly.

Application for Today

An article from March of 2022 states that "The group Open Doors USA figures that 360 million Christians last year [2021] lived in countries where persecution was 'significant.' Roughly

---

[13] Nestle-Aland and United Bible Societies (NA; USB)
[14] The chapter divisions placed in English Bibles for chapters two and three also list the addresses to the seven churches in groups of four and three.

5,600 Christians were murdered, more than 6,000 were detained or imprisoned, and another 4,000-plus were kidnapped. In addition, more than 5,000 churches and other religious facilities were destroyed."[15]

Christianity remains the most persecuted religion in the world. Countries where Christian persecution is most severe include Afghanistan, North Korea, Somalia, Libya, Yemen, Eritrea, Nigeria, Pakistan, Iraq, Iran, India, Saudi Arabia, Russia, and China. Christians in these countries are praying for God's intervention just as those did in Revelation. Now consider the devastation in these countries. Is this a coincidence? Far from it! "Let it never be said that God has not done all in his power, even to the devastation of His own perfect earth, in order to bring men to their senses."[16] The very thing these countries need most is the very thing they suppress with vigor – true Christianity.

As with the natural disasters in Revelation chapter eight, the natural calamities happening around the globe, and in these countries especially, should not be misconstrued as the direct result of environmental pollutants, but as demonstrations of the wrath of God upon the wickedness of man.

The calamities of this chapter served a three-fold purpose: (1) they served as God's vindication of His people and as an answer to their prayers; (2) they served to punish mankind [which we believe at this point in Revelation were Jews prior to 70 AD] for their rebellion toward His Son and wicked treatment of His people; (3) they were intended to bring man to repentance through suffering the severity and punishment of His wrath.

---

[15] https://www.cato.org/commentary/christianity-worlds-most-persecuted-religion-confirms-new-report
[16] Michael Wilcock, *The Message of Revelation: I Saw Heaven Opened*, BST (Downers Grove, IL: IVP, 1975), 95.

Is this not also the case in the world today? How often do natural disasters occur? How often do countries go to war? No political party or policy can correct the world's downward trajectory. Only God can do that. Only when mankind humbles himself before God and serves his Creator with all his heart, soul, mind, and strength will he begin to experience all the blessings found in Christ. But as man continues to rebel against God and persecute His people, God will continue to punish man by every means at His disposal.

God is allowing man's iniquity to run its course with crime, drugs, homelessness, and public upheaval, thus reaping the sown seed of unrighteousness. Society is devouring itself without God. We are witnessing the self-destruction of human society because God is not in it. Sin will destroy an individual, a family, a city, a nation, and ultimately the world. Sin knows no limits. Man created these problems, but he cannot cure them. Only by turning to God, His Son, His word, and His kingdom can the suffering of this present evil age be treated and healed.

Chapter Nine

In our introduction to this study, we offered four rules to guide us through our interpretation of the apocalyptic signs and symbols of the book of Revelation. The *first rule* to be followed is to consider the text of the book itself. *Secondly*, cross-reference scripture to ensure that fundamental biblical teachings serve as the basis for our interpretation. The *third rule* worth following is to consider any allusions to other apocalyptic images. The *fourth rule* to be applied is to provide literal wordings for apocalyptic passages when possible. The four rules we have suggested will serve to assist us as we move forward in our study. By keeping these rules in mind, perhaps we can arrive at a clear understanding of the book's message.

The apocalyptic imagery will increase in both frequency and difficulty from chapter nine onward. For instance, only six verses were used to describe the first four trumpets (8:8-12); whereas the entirety of chapter nine will be devoted to the fifth and sixth trumpets. One-third of mankind will be affected by the demonic forces unleashed in the sounding of trumpets five and six. Only those who were sealed by God (7:3 ff.) will be protected from the devastation to come.

Fifth Trumpet: The Locusts from the Bottomless Pit (vv. 1-12)

"Then the fifth angel sounded: And I saw a star fallen from heaven to the earth. To him was given the key to the bottomless pit. And he opened the bottomless pit, and smoke arose out of the pit like the smoke of a great furnace. So the sun and the air were darkened because of the smoke of the pit" (vv.1-2).

The sounding of the fifth trumpet reveals a fascinating vision to John. He saw a "star fallen" (lit. which had fallen, NASB)[1] from heaven to earth. In Revelation, there are more than a dozen verses which contain images of stars.[2] The seven angels are depicted as seven stars (1:16, 20; 2:1). Christ is the Morning Star (22:16). A volcanic star turns the freshwater bitter (8:11). Stars may also represent the tribes of Israel (12:1). Stars are found often in apocalyptic warnings for times of great calamity or historic change (Isaiah 13:10; Joel 2:10; 3:15; Matthew 24:29; Mark 13:25), and as we have noted, for denoting certain persons or beings.[3]

To ascertain the usage and meaning of the star metaphor used in this passage, we will first consider the clues found within the immediate context. The star of this passage is referred to with a personal pronoun, "he," and he receives a key to the bottomless pit. Personality is thus determined by these clues. Whoever the star is, he is a person or being. Secondly, he has fallen from heaven to earth. Thirdly, he is associated with the bottomless pit. In Revelation 20:1, we find an angel who has the key to the bottomless pit as well. However, the angel of 20:1 did not fall from heaven but descended or "came down" from heaven as in 10:1; 18:1, just as did the sheet which Peter saw "descending" from heaven when he was in Joppa (Acts 10:11).[4]

---

[1] *Pipto* can denote various means of falling. In Revelation, we find various ones falling in humility and devotion before God (7:11;11:16). We also find a church that had fallen in sin (2:5). Babylon would also fall in the sense of being defeated (14:8; 18:2). However, in this sense, it is to move rapidly in a downward trajectory from s higher point (see also 8:10). The star is not simply lighting upon the earth as a bird on a pole. The star is crashing toward the earth. See *BDAG*, 815-6.

[2] Leland Ryken, James C. Wilhoit, Tremper Longman, "Stars" *DBI* (Downers Grove, IL: IVP, 1998)813.

[3] Ibid.

[4] *BDAG*, 514.

The bottomless pit also provides clues for interpreting the meaning of the fallen star and the complete picture of the passage. In NT times the bottomless pit or abyss is spoken of as a place of torment, punishment, and confinement for the wicked. Legion begged the Lord not to send them into the abyss (Luke 8:31, NASB). The angels that sinned were committed to pits of darkness (2 Peter 2:4, NASB; cf. Jude 6), or more literally "to the deepest abyss."[5]

Thus far, all signs are pointing to the fallen star being a fallen angel. We have observed how the scriptures speak of angels which sinned. Therefore, it would not be a violation of any literal passage to conclude that this figurative passage denotes the same meaning. An angel fell from heaven. He was given the key to the abyss where other fallen angels are kept in punishment and confinement. Additional information is provided in v. 11, as the name of the angel of the bottomless pit is given. His name "Abaddon" in Hebrew and "Apollyon" in Greek. In both languages the name means "destroyer." Jesus described Satan's threefold agenda as coming to "kill, steal, and destroy" (John 10:10). Upon the joyous return of the seventy, Jesus also beheld Satan fall as lighting to the earth (Luke 10:18).

Concerning Satan, twice in the OT a double meaning is used when referring to him. Isaiah depicts both the king of Babylon and the devil in the same context as one's actions and haughtiness mirrored the other. Note, "How you are fallen from heaven, O Lucifer, son of the morning! How you are cut down to the ground, You who weakened the nations! For you have said in your heart: 'I will ascend into heaven, I will exalt my throne above the stars of God; I will also sit on the mount of the congregation On the farthest sides of the north; I will ascend above the heights of the clouds, I

---

[5] George Ricker Berry, *Interlinear Greek-English New Testament* (Grand Rapids, MI: Baker, 1984), 604.

will be like the Most High.' Yet you shall be brought down to Sheol, To the lowest depths of the Pit" (Isaiah 14:12-14).

"Isaiah saw the king of Babylon as possessing an enormous amount of disgusting pride and arrogance. In cultivating aspirations that exceeded his stature and ability, he paralleled the ultimate ruler with an exaggerated sense of his own accomplishments: Satan."[6] Isaiah and Revelation present the devil as being cast down from heaven to be ultimately banished into "the lowest depths of the Pit."

In Ezekiel, the king of Tyre mirrors the working and thinking of Satan as well. This "prophetic device is well attested in the Old Testament and should not cause special concern,"[7] as the "fluidity of language can be seen elsewhere as the near fulfillments of many prophecies do not embrace the totality of the language as the final judgment does."[8]

Note, "You were in Eden, the garden of God...You were the anointed cherub who covers; I established you; You were on the holy mountain of God; You walked back and forth in the midst of fiery stones. You were perfect in your ways from the day you were created, until iniquity was found in you" (Ezekiel 28:13-15).

"The historic fall of Satan, otherwise not directly described in the Bible but alluded to in a number of passages, supplied the background terminology and metaphor for this text, just as it did for Isaiah 14...the fall of the king of Tyre will be but a small indication of what the fall of Satan will be like in the final day."[9]

---

[6] Walter C. Kaiser, Jr., Peter H. Davids, F.F. Bruce, Manfred T. Brauch, *Hard Sayings of the Bible* (Downers Grove, IL: IVP, 1996), 303. See also, Gleason L. Archer, *Encyclopedia of Bible Difficulties* (Grand Rapids, MI: Zondervan, 1982), 269.

[7] Ibid.

[8] Ibid., 316.

[9] Ibid.

Paul also warns Timothy when selecting elders how pride was the motivation and condemnation of the devil (1 Timothy 3:6). Not only did Satan convince himself he could overthrow God, he convinced other angels to join him (cf. Matthew 25:41; 2 Peter 2:4; Jude 6; Revelation 12:4). When Satan attempted to stop the resurrection of Christ, Michael was there to stop him (Revelation 12:7). Jesus was victorious over Satan and the grave (Hebrews 2:14), swallowing death in victory (1 Corinthians 15:54-55).

For these reasons, we conclude this passage in Revelation is depicting Satan's fall and the limited authority given to him over the demonic spirits of the abyss for the purpose of tormenting humankind. The text now moves to a description of these spirits and their commission to injure mankind.

"Then out of the smoke locusts came upon the earth. And to them was given power, as the scorpions of the earth have power. They were commanded not to harm the grass of the earth, or any green thing, or any tree, but only those men who do not have the seal of God on their foreheads" (vv. 3-4).

A thick smoke from the bottomless pit clouds the air as from it rushes forth a dreadful army of locusts to blanket the sky. Throughout the OT the locust is a symbol of destruction (cf. Deuteronomy 28:42; 1 Kings 8:37; Psalm 78:46).[10] Such is the meaning here. The lives of wicked men will be tormented by these agents of Satan, leaving only devastation in their wake.

The imagery of the scene serves to remind the readers of the plague of locusts (Exodus 10:12-15). Deuteronomy 28 is also significant to understand the imagery of the text.[11] Therein, God foretells the time when Israel would suffer the plagues of Egypt for

---

[10] Mounce, 193-4.
[11] Beale, 1114.

their unfaithfulness and disobedience to Him. Locusts were included in this warning (vv.38-42). As a result, the people would have a "trembling heart, failing eyes, and anguish of soul" (v.65) among the nations to which they were driven.

"And they were not given authority to kill them, but to torment them for five months. Their torment was like the torment of a scorpion when it strikes a man. In those days men will seek death and will not find it; they will desire to die, and death will flee from them" (vv. 5-6).

Even though these locusts represent the agents of Satan, they were still subject to the ultimate power and authority of God. Yes, they were powerful, but they were not all-powerful. Compare this scene with the scenes of Job 1:12 and 2:6 wherein Satan's power is limited by God.

The locusts were similarly given power to torment wicked men, but they were not allowed to kill them. Moreover, the torment would last for a limited time of five months. The duration of time denotes that this is not an end but a means to an end. God is not willing to see them perish, but repent (2 Peter 3:9).

Also like the language of Deuteronomy 28, "In those days men will seek death and will not find it; they will desire to die, and death will flee from them." Death was more desirous than living. Such would certainly describe the severity and dire circumstances of a city under siege (cf. Jeremiah 8:3) as was Jerusalem in the summer of 70 AD.

Joel uses similar language to depict either the Assyrian or Babylonian[12] conquest of Judah and Jerusalem (see Joel 1:4-2:11). "It is this symbolic locust, swarming from the smoke of the abyss as a 'scourge upon the earth,' that is employed in the vision here, to

---

[12] Whether Joel is interpreted as early or late among the prophets will determine whether the invading armies were Assyrian or Babylonian.

signify the woe being pronounced by the angel of the fifth trumpet upon Jerusalem and the land of the Jews. By the same symbol Joel described the invading armies of Israel's Old Testament history (Joel 1:4-6) – a striking parallel."[13]

"The shape of the locusts was like horses prepared for battle. On their heads were crowns of something like gold, and their faces were like the faces of men. They had hair like women's hair, and their teeth were like lions' teeth. And they had breastplates like breastplates of iron, and the sound of their wings was like the sound of chariots with many horses running into battle. They had tails like scorpions, and there were stings in their tails. Their power was to hurt men five months" (vv. 7-10).

Placing this scene alongside the one in Joel 1-2 will provide even more striking similarities. The vision of Revelation should have evoked strong emotions in the first readers who were familiar with Joel's prophecy and its meaning. The vivid picture of an invading army coming to destroy everything in its path is clear. The true king over this army is Satan. **"And they had as king over them the angel of the bottomless pit, whose name in Hebrew is Abaddon, but in Greek he has the name Apollyon" (v. 11).**

The name of the angel of the bottomless pit is *Abaddon* in Hebrew and *Apollyon* in Greek. In both languages the name means "destroyer." We believe this to be none other than the devil whose threefold agenda was to "kill, steal, and destroy" (John 10:10). See the previous comments from 9:1-2.

Putting this apocalyptic scene in literal terms, as best we can, yields the following interpretation: The Jewish people who had been persecuting the church were acting out a devilish agenda. They had "sowed the wind" in their rejection of Christ and His

---

[13] Wallace, 179.

kingdom. Now, they were going to "reap the whirlwind" and receive punishment according to their deeds. They would desire death over life under the dreadful invasion of this army governed by Satan. Their punishment, however, would not be final. Time was granted for them to repent. **"One woe is past. Behold, still two more woes are coming after these things" (v. 12).**

Sixth Trumpet: The Angels from the Euphrates (vv. 13-21)

"Then the sixth angel sounded: And I heard a voice from the four horns of the golden altar which is before God, saying to the sixth angel who had the trumpet, 'Release the four angels who are bound at the great river Euphrates'" (vv. 13-14).

Mounce provides us with some insightful comments on this passage and the identity of these four angels. "Attempts to identify the four angels with any definiteness have not been successful. Apparently they are not mentioned elsewhere in apocalyptic writings...In our immediate context the four angels appear to be in charge of the limitless horde of demonic horsemen who ride across the pagan world spreading terror and death. They correspond to the king of the locusts in 9:11 and like him seem to disappear into the demonic forces they release."[14]

"So the four angels, who had been prepared for the hour and day and month and year, were released to kill a third of mankind" (v.15).

The four angels had been placed at the Euphrates, bound there until the hour, day, and month purposed by God, and released at His command. The Euphrates River was the northern border for the Promised Land. It was also a boundary between Israel and countries to its north. The angels would unleash an army from this direction to kill one-third of "the earth," those not sealed by God

---

[14] Mounce, 200.

as His own. The wrath of God intensifies in this vision. Death is the punishment. No longer is sinful man being punished indirectly. The refusal to repent has brought upon them the judgment of death.

"Now the number of the army of the horsemen was two hundred million; I heard the number of them. And thus I saw the horses in the vision: those who sat on them had breastplates of fiery red, hyacinth blue, and sulfur yellow; and the heads of the horses were like the heads of lions; and out of their mouths came fire, smoke, and brimstone" (vv.16-17).

The number is not to be taken literally and is closer to the Greek "tens of thousands times ten thousand...and is approximately the total world population in the first century."[15] A similar number is used in reference to the army of God (cf. Psalm 68:17; Daniel 7:10).[16] It is as though the entire world is arrayed for battle against these people who have been persecuting the church of Christ – a fearsome and foreboding sight indeed!

Described in a most vivid and fascinating manner, the army is arrayed with "breastplates of fiery red, hyacinth blue, and sulfur yellow." The horses had powerful heads like lions and from their mouth proceeded "fire, smoke, and brimstone."

"By these three plagues a third of mankind was killed—by the fire and the smoke and the brimstone which came out of their mouths" (v.18).

---

[15] Paul, 181.

[16] David L. Roper, *Revelation 1-11*, TFT (Searcy, AR: Resource Publications, 2002), 371.

Fire, smoke, and brimstone are synonymous with punishment from the Lord (cf. Genesis 19:24; Psalm 11:6; Isaiah 34:9-10; Ezekiel 38:22).[17] These elements will be used again in eternal punishment (Revelation 14:10-11; 19:20; 20:10; 21:8).

"For their power is in their mouth and in their tails; for their tails are like serpents, having heads; and with them they do harm" (v.19).

An allusion to Job's portrait of the of the sea dragon as a source of cosmic evil may be in play here (cf. Job 41:18-34).[18] However, "The correct background is probably Ezekiel's picture of Gog and Magog (Ezekiel 38, 39). The former prophet's vision of invading armies had been fulfilled by the Assyrian and Babylonian invasions, but Ezekiel had seen the hordes of King Gog of the land of Magog invading a returned and resettled Israel who dwelt securely and would be protected by God's 'great shaking,' as God would enter into judgment with him with pestilence and bloodshed, and with torrential rains and hailstones, fire and brimstone (Ezekiel 38:19-23)."[19]

From nose to tail, these beasts were deadly, evoking fear and melting the hearts of those in their paths. They were innumerable and unstoppable. Defeat was certain and inevitable.

"But" with hardened and impudent hearts, **"the rest of mankind, who were not killed by these plagues, did not repent of the works of their hands, that they should not worship demons, and idols of gold, silver, brass, stone, and wood, which can neither see nor hear nor walk. And they did not repent of**

---

[17] Ibid., 373.

[18] Beale, 1115.

[19] Thompson, 83. See our comments on 20:7-10 for further discussion of Gog and Magog in Ezekiel and Revelation.

their murders or their sorceries or their sexual immorality or their thefts" (vv. 20-21).

Man can reach such a state of spiritual depravity that his heart is hardened by the deceitfulness of sin (Hebrews 3:13). Here we have the typical list of OT idols derived from their demonic source harkening back to the writings of the Law (Deuteronomy 4:28), the Psalms (Psalm 115), and the Prophets (Jeremiah 10). The spiritual state of the people was reminiscent of the time of Jeremiah just before the destruction of Jerusalem, Solomon's Temple, and Babylonian captivity (cf. Jeremiah 9:9, 11).

If we were to put the vision of the sixth trumpet into literal terms, it might read something like this: According to the plan of God, at the time appointed by God, a mighty army of almost unimaginable strength and ferocity, coming from beyond the border of the Euphrates River, would be used to punish the nonbelievers for their sins and persecution of His kingdom. Yet, even after the severity of their conquest, the people would not repent.

As we continue reading Revelation, we will learn that these people dwelt in the city where our Lord was crucified – Jerusalem. History teaches us that the army used to destroy Jerusalem was Roman, led by Titus, and was from beyond the Euphrates River.

Application for Today

"Therefore say I unto you, The kingdom of God shall be taken from you, and given to a nation bringing forth the fruits thereof. And whosoever shall fall on this stone shall be broken: but on whomsoever it shall fall, it will grind him to powder" (Matthew 21:43-44). Christ's words found fulfillment in the first century church. The gospel was first preached to the Jews. Some obeyed and became Christians. The majority resisted and rejected their Savior. Moreover, they slammed the heavy hand of persecution down upon the church. The apostles, especially Paul, turned to the

Gentiles and began congregations in their cities. Jewish persecution from the synagogues in those cities followed Paul like a shadow.

The nation which sprang from the seed of the kingdom was the Lord's church (1 Peter 2:9). As the church was bringing fruit to God amid vicious trials, their prayers ascended to God, and the stone of God's righteous vindication was prepared to drop. "The way of the unfaithful is hard" (Proverbs 13:15). And "The wages of sin is death" (Romans 6:23). Moreover, "The LORD is slow to anger and great in power, And will not at all acquit the wicked. The LORD has His way In the whirlwind and in the storm, And the clouds are the dust of His feet" (Nahum 1:3).

Those who had been terrorizing the people of God were soon to realize all of these hard realities. God's judgment will begin with Jerusalem (Sodom and Egypt, 11:8) and conclude with Rome (Babylon, 18:21). Of the three societies, only the kingdom of God will remain (Daniel 2:44; Hebrews 12:28). For Christians who are living under the heavy hand of persecution, these truths are not only essential to remember but necessary to endure. God will vanquish the enemies of His people and ultimately provide a heavenly reality for us where no enemy will exist.

Chapter Ten

Chapter ten begins an interlude between the sounding of the sixth and seventh trumpets. The section begins with the appearance of a mighty angel endowed with divine attributes, causing many commentators to speculate on his identity. However, the angel, who is simply God's special representative, is sharing in the glory of God himself.[1] The angel will commission John in a manner similar to the commissioning of Ezekiel, yet for the purpose of preparing the apostle with a "renewed commission for his mission in communicating to men the consummation of God's redemptive purpose."[2]

The interlude is reminiscent of chapter seven, between the opening of the sixth and seventh seals. Readers of Revelation are kept in suspense as the drama is heightened. "It is therefore more than an 'interlude'; it serves to intensify expectation and interest in the great proclamation of 11:15."[3] The interlude, therefore, must be considered more than a mere literary device. "It is part of life. Men cannot predict how God's judgments will operate. They take unexpected courses. There are delays which give opportunity for repentance."[4]

The mighty angel will descend to earth with a little book in his hand. John is told to take the book and consume it. He found the

---

[1] Sean P. Kealy, *The Apocalypse of John* (Collegeville, MN: Liturgical Press, 1990), 155.

[2] George Eldon Ladd, *A Commentary on the Revelation of John* (Grand Rapids, MI: Eerdmans, 1972), 140.

[3] Edward A. McDowell, *The Meaning and Message of the Book of Revelation* (Nashville, TN: Broadman, 1951), 106.

[4] Leon Morris, *The Revelation of St. John*, TNTC (Grand Rapids, MI: Eerdmans, 1980), 136.

book to be sweet as honey in taste, but bitter in his stomach. "This signifies to him the burden of prophesying things still worse than those he had told before."[5] John is once more seen as an active participant in the unfolding drama of Revelation. He is not just a witness to the Revelation, but a participant in it.

The Mighty Angel with the Little Book (vv. 1-7)

"I saw still another mighty angel coming down from heaven, clothed with a cloud. And a rainbow was on his head, his face was like the sun, and his feet like pillars of fire" (v.1).

The descriptions given to the angel in v. 1 show us that he was sent from God. "The pattern here of a divine angel of the Lord appearing in order to commission a prophet is a reflection of the same repeated pattern in the OT (e.g., Exodus 3:2-12; Judges 6:22; 2 Kings 1:3-15; 1 Chronicles 21:18)."[6]

"He had a little book open in his hand. And he set his right foot on the sea and his left foot on the land, and cried with a loud voice, as when a lion roars. When he cried out, seven thunders uttered their voices" (vv. 2-3).

The angel was sent from heaven with "a little book open in his hand." His feet were set on land and sea, signifying God's dominion over the earth in its entirety. His loud voice was reminiscent of God's voice in the prophets, as a lion's roar (Isaiah 31:4; Amos 3:8; Hosea 11:10). Seven thunders uttered their voices, evoking the imagery of Psalm 29 and the greatness of the voice of God (see also Job 37:4-5; Psalm 18:3; Psalm 77:18).

"Now when the seven thunders uttered their voices, I was about to write; but I heard a voice from heaven saying to

---

[5] W.S. Thompson, *Comments on the Revelation* (Memphis, TN: Southern Church Publications, 1957), 103.

[6] Beale, 1116.

me, 'Seal up the things which the seven thunders uttered, and do not write them'" (v.4).

Much speculation has been given in commentaries concerning the content of the voices of the seven thunders, when in fact, John is the only human being to know or have heard them. Whatever was said was not intended to be included in the message of Revelation. The secret things belong to the Lord (Deuteronomy 29:29; 2 Corinthians 12:1-4).

The Lord has authority over the contents of scripture in general and the book of Revelation specifically. Not even John, who witnessed and heard and knew the message spoken in the seven thunders, could add to or take from God's desired content for His revealed word. Man would do well to recognize this truth and follow it accordingly.

"The angel whom I saw standing on the sea and on the land raised up his hand to heaven and swore by Him who lives forever and ever, who created heaven and the things that are in it, the earth and the things that are in it, and the sea and the things that are in it, that there should be delay no longer, but in the days of the sounding of the seventh angel, when he is about to sound, the mystery of God would be finished, as He declared to His servants the prophets" (vv.5-7).

The next scene to unfold presents the mighty angel of chapter ten with his right hand[7] raised toward heaven and solemnly swearing by God that the delay would be no longer, the seventh trumpet was about to sound. The culmination of the mystery God declared to His prophets was at hand.

What was this mystery spoken to the prophets? The word "mystery" in the NT denotes a subject or prophecy of old which

---

[7] Manuscript evidence is strong for the inclusion that it was his "right hand" that was raised (cf. ESV, NASB).

needed further revelation to provide its fulfillment. Prior to such revelation, the subject's full meaning was "hidden" in the sense that complete understanding was not yet attained on the part of the hearer. The idea behind the word "mystery" is that of a battle strategy. The strategy has been hidden, not yet fully revealed, until the time of execution. Of the eternal strategy of God, Paul wrote, "But we speak the wisdom of God in a mystery, the hidden wisdom which God ordained before the ages for our glory, which none of the rulers of this age knew; for had they known, they would not have crucified the Lord of glory" (1 Corinthians 2:7-8).

In the context of Revelation 10, the mystery which was to be spoken through John was the end of the Jewish state as foretold in the prophets and in connection with God's eternal plan to redeem mankind (cf. Daniel 7-12; Zechariah 14; Romans 16:25-26).

"The Old Testament prophets never dealt with specific events beyond the coming redemption, the permanent establishment of the spiritual kingdom, the termination of the Jewish theocracy, the persecution of the saints, and the destruction of the fourth world empire (the Roman Empire – see Daniel 2:7).[8] Thus, "the angel's message looked not to the end of time but to the completion of God's mystery, the gospel, the firm establishment of His kingdom and power, and the destruction of world powers."[9]

The kingdom of Christ would continue to expand after the fall of Judaism and the end of the Jewish state. "The destruction of Jerusalem, the demolition of the temple, the downfall of Judaism, and the end of the Jewish state, which politically and practically ended the Jewish dispensation, were all a part of the divine mystery. The Mosaic law had been 'nailed to the cross,' 'abolished'

---

[8] Hailey, 246.
[9] Ibid.

and 'taken away'; but the Jewish state continued, and in that sense the Jewish dispensation functioned, until 'the days of the voice of the seventh angel' which sounded final doom."[10]

John Eats the Little Book (vv. 8-11)

"Then the voice which I heard from heaven spoke to me again and said, "Go, take the little book which is open in the hand of the angel who stands on the sea and on the earth. So I went to the angel and said to him, 'Give me the little book.' And he said to me, 'Take and eat it; and it will make your stomach bitter, but it will be as sweet as honey in your mouth'" (vv.8-9).

John's eating the little book reminds us of the events and effects described in the book of Ezekiel. God instructed Ezekiel to "...open your mouth and eat what I give you" (2:8). God would personally "feed" Ezekiel the message he was to preach. Such is the meaning here in Revelation 10. With the act of eating the scroll we can see that God wanted Ezekiel and now John to be thoroughly consumed with the message they were to preach.

Though he was an aged man, God still had a purpose for John and a work to accomplish. In both cases of Ezekiel and John, the scroll/book was like honey in sweetness.[11] Possibly, the sweetness of the scroll signifies the divine origin of it, and the sensation of joy to be experienced from preaching the word of God. The bitterness, however, would no doubt denote the hurt experienced by a true servant of God when encountering the bitter resistance and rejection of men to the word he was commissioned to speak.

"Then I took the little book out of the angel's hand and ate it, and it was as sweet as honey in my mouth. But when I had eaten it, my stomach became bitter. And he said to me, 'You

---

[10] Wallace, 207-208.

[11] The manna from heaven also tasted like honey (Exodus 16:31).

must prophesy again about many peoples, nations, tongues, and kings'" (vv.10-11).

Here we find the work God had in mind for His aged, faithful apostle. He was to "prophesy again about many peoples, nations, tongues, and kings." The message given to John did not end with the destruction of Jerusalem and the Jewish state. It was not limited to one certain event or a single nation. Beginning in chapter 12 the focus will shift to the church in the wilderness and the enemy that was the Roman Empire. The destruction of Rome as an enemy to the church will be foretold in chapters 13-19.

John's commission in Revelation would therefore extend to many peoples, nations, tongues, and kings (cf. Acts 9:15). In Revelation 14:6, we will find the message to be preached to every nation, tribe, tongue, and people was the everlasting gospel. In the style of apocalyptic literature, the Great Commission is therefore restated (cf. Matthew 28:18-20; Mark 16:15-16; Luke 24:46-47).

Application for Today

Revelation 10 is a beautiful but oft complicated chapter, due in large to the speculations of commentators. Much ado is given to the identity of the mighty angel. Is it Michael? Is it Gabriel? The fact is, we do not know. Much attention is devoted to the sayings of the seven thunders. Again, we do not know. Nor were we intended to know. When covering this chapter a sad indictment is to be made, sad indeed. It is sad to see such time and energy afforded to the questions we cannot answer while so little time and energy is dedicated to the precious truths we can glean. In our application section we shall observe four such truths.

First, we learn that God works on His schedule. His answers and vindication may or may not arrive immediately or always to our satisfaction. This is not for us to question, but to trust. God "who lives forever and ever, who created heaven and the things that are in it, the earth and the things that are in it, and the sea and the things that are in it" alone determines "that there should be delay no longer." It is not for Christians to speculate why, when, or how, but to trust in the certainty of the righteous, just, and ultimate judgment of God.

Secondly, God's word, the Bible, contains only those things which He in His infinite wisdom decreed to be revealed to man. The holy prophets and apostles spoke and wrote as they were guided by Him. Some things were not to be revealed. In scripture, we have the things which were disclosed finally, fully, and freely by a Creator who desires to reconcile His creation to Himself. The word we possess has been given to that end and to communicate to us everything we need to know about our relationship with God and how that one relationship affects all other relationships in life.

Thirdly, we must observe John's role as the aged apostle, even the *last* remaining apostle. Even in his old age, God had work for him to do, a mission to accomplish, and not a small one at that! At an age believed to be north of 90 years, John was instructed to bring a message before "many peoples, nations, tongues, and kings." His work was not finished and thus his life was not finished. God was not finished with him. There was no retirement for John. No sequestering to a life of ease to eat, drink, be filled and merry. The old war horse still had a battle to fight and who better to fight it! Might we learn from this not to quit using our talents and abilities before God is finished with us? Might we see that the sword must remain in hand, and the armor of God adorned until "the time of our departure is at hand?" Let us not give up on our work in the kingdom prematurely. If we will remain prepared, perhaps our greatest opportunity will come when we least expect it.

Lastly, like the prophets of old and as with gospel preachers who desire to be true to the word today, John was given a message that was sweet for those who heed his message, but bitter to those who refuse it. The sweetness and bitterness are experienced by the messenger too. Sweet are the joyous occasions when a messenger of God's truth can have a role in helping someone become reconciled to their heavenly Father. Yet, bitter are the memories of those who mocked, refused, debated, and delayed obedience to the gospel. The word of God is truly a double-edged sword. On one side of the blade is the goodness of God and on the other, severity. Both are calling men to repentance. And both the goodness and the severity of God must be proclaimed by His messengers.

Chapter Eleven

Chapter eleven is a continuation of the interlude that began in chapter ten. For this reason, many commentators will combine these two chapters under a shared theme or chapter in their works. In this chapter we will find the culmination of judgment against Jerusalem. Our study has been building to this point since chapter 6:1.

The Two Witnesses (vv. 1-6)

"Then I was given a reed like a measuring rod. And the angel stood, saying, 'Rise and measure the temple of God, the altar, and those who worship there. But leave out the court which is outside the temple, and do not measure it, for it has been given to the Gentiles. And they will tread the holy city underfoot for forty-two months. And I will give power to my two witnesses, and they will prophesy one thousand two hundred and sixty days, clothed in sackcloth'" (vv.1-3).

The reed which grows alongside rivers served as an instrument of discipline (Psalm 2:6-9; 110:1-2; Job 9:34; Revelation 2:27) as well as an ancient measuring stick. The reed in this passage served as a standard of measurement. John was instructed to take the reed he was given and "measure the temple of God, the altar, and those who worship there." Metaphorically speaking, all men will be judged by "reed" or the standard of measurement which is the word of God (cf. John 12:48).

We find a parallel apocalyptic passage in Ezekiel 40-48. In Ezekiel, we have a vision of Ezekiel measuring a new temple and all its buildings, walls, and sacrificial implements, along with priestly allotments of land and the priests' duties. Ezekiel's vision depicted the Lord in His glory and presence returning to dwell again among the people in Jerusalem and offered hope for the future for the Jewish captives in Babylon.

The significance we place on the measuring of the temple in Revelation 11 should be considered in view of the stated destruction of the "holy city." Many commentators view Rome as the object of destruction in this chapter. We disagree. In scripture, the holy city is none other than Jerusalem (cf. Nehemiah 11:1), the "city of God" (cf. Psalms 46:4; 48:1; 87:3).

If the vision of Revelation 11 follows a similar thought of the vision in Ezekiel 40-48, the measuring of the temple would denote future purpose rather than destruction (see also Zechariah 1:16-17; 2:1-5). Two temples existed in Jerusalem. One was the physical temple, Herod's Temple, which was destroyed in 70 AD, along with the city of Jerusalem, as was foretold by Christ (Matthew 24:1-2; Luke 21:6, 20, 24). The second temple was the spiritual temple of the Lord's church (cf. 1 Corinthians 3:16-17; 1 Timothy 3:15; 1 Peter 4:17).

Which of these temples was preserved during the destruction of Jerusalem? The days of Jerusalem's destruction were shortened for the sake of saving/delivering the elect (Matthew 24:22). The "elect" is a familiar term used for the church in the NT (cf. Romans 8:33; Colossians 3:12; 1 Peter 1:2). Thus, the church in Jerusalem would be spared during the destruction of the city. The Jewish church had already been numbered and sealed by God – the 144,000 (Revelation 6:3 ff.). Therefore, we conclude the measuring of the temple in this passage refers to God's protection of His church – the Israel of God (Galatians 6:16) – during the plundering and destruction of the city of Jerusalem and greater Judea in 70 AD. Those outside the temple, the Jews who did not repent and convert to Christ, would be trodden under foot by the Gentiles, i.e., Titus' Roman army.

The holy city would be trodden underfoot for "forty-two months." Rome was given power to destroy the holy city and permitted to persecute the saints for a short while. It is interesting to note that the Roman forces began their conquest of Judea in early 67 and destroyed Jerusalem in the late summer of 70 – approximately three and a half years or 42 months.[1] In apocalyptic terminology, however, where numerology is significant, this number presents half of seven. Seven denotes completeness in Revelation as it does in other apocalyptic writings. Here we have half of that number. The remaining three and one-half years will be mentioned in chapter thirteen.

Three and one-half years are dedicated to the destruction of Jerusalem and three and one-half years are given to the beast of the sea to persecute the church (13:5). Adding the two sums brings the total to seven, signifying the duration of persecution for the church in the first century as communicated in the apocalyptic style of the book of Revelation.

"And I will give power to my two witnesses, and they will prophesy one thousand two hundred and sixty days, clothed in sackcloth" (v.3).

The significance of two witnesses is steeped in OT scripture. The law required a minimum of two witnesses for a just judgment to be rendered (Numbers 35:30; Deuteronomy 17:6; 19:15).

To identify the two witnesses, we must first look at their work (prophesying) and the duration of their work (1,260 days). The length of days coincides with the number of months (42), totaling three and one-half years. The text does not say these days run simultaneously with the months, but it does not say they run consecutively either. The reader of Revelation is left to decide.

---

[1] See Cobb, 275; Wallace, 213-215.

The two witnesses are adorned in sackcloth, the garment of mourning. "In the OT the wearing of sackcloth primarily refers to such mourning in the face of judgment, though sometimes repentance is also in mind. Twenty-seven out of approximately forty-two occurrences of the word 'sackcloth' in the OT refer only to mourning, and an additional thirteen include mourning together with repentance (e.g., Genesis 37:34; 2 Samuel 3:31; Isaiah 37:2; Daniel 9:3)."[2] In this passage a case could be made for the sackcloth representing both mourning and repentance.

"These are the two olive trees and the two lampstands standing before the God of the earth. And if anyone wants to harm them, fire proceeds from their mouth and devours their enemies. And if anyone wants to harm them, he must be killed in this manner. These have power to shut heaven, so that no rain falls in the days of their prophecy; and they have power over waters to turn them to blood, and to strike the earth with all plagues, as often as they desire" (vv.4-6).

Numerous identities have been given to these men.[3] We must keep in mind that this is apocalyptic literature and look for what is being symbolized by these two witnesses. Returning to the four guides we have followed for interpreting Revelation will prove to be helpful once more.

The *first rule* we observe is to consider the text of the book itself. We have cited the text of the NKJV, and it is free from any major textual issues in this passage. The historical context is the destruction of the holy city, Jerusalem, which occurred in 70 AD.

Secondly, by cross-referencing scripture we find two witnesses which foretold the destruction of Jerusalem. Daniel prophesied about the calamity to befall Jerusalem (Daniel 9:26-27; 11:31;

---

[2] Beasley, 1119.
[3] Cobb lists 14 suggested identities in his work, 278.

12:11-13). Jesus also foretold the destruction of the city and temple (Matthew 24:2-35; Luke 21:20-24).

The perspective of the "witnesses" in Revelation 11 makes use of the figure of speech known as *personification*. The prophecies of Daniel and Christ are being represented as two men "standing before the God of the earth" prophesying in the garment of mourning and judgment – sackcloth, while endowed with all the power of a prophet of God, akin to the powers exhibited by Moses and Elijah.

The *third rule* worth following is to consider any allusions to other apocalyptic images. A parallel apocalyptic passage is found in Zechariah 4. The two olive trees of Zechariah's vision can be identified as certain individuals – Zerubbabel and Joshua the high priest. The olive trees represented these men as the "two anointed ones, who stand beside the Lord of the whole earth" (Zechariah 4:14). In the case of Zechariah's vision, the two anointed ones were kept by God as they rebuilt the temple. In Revelation, the two anointed ones are kept by God as they foretell the destruction of the temple, while also witnessing to the construction of the spiritual temple, the kingdom of God on earth, the Lord's church.

The *fourth rule* to be applied is to provide literal wording to apocalyptic passages when possible, imagining the language as though it was being written using literal language. A literal rendering of this passage could read as follows: The city of Jerusalem will be destroyed, but the church in that city will be protected by God. The prophecies of Daniel and Christ stand as two witnesses of the calamity that will transpire. They have been sent from God. The veracity of the witnesses has been confirmed by God through miracles (cf. Mark 16:20; Hebrews 2:1-4). The witnesses are protected by God for the purpose of prophesying against the holy city. Their message has been communicated and confirmed. It stands.

The truthfulness of the prophecies of Daniel and Christ should not be questioned but believed.

The Witnesses are Killed (vv. 7-10)

"When they finish their testimony, the beast that ascends out of the bottomless pit will make war against them, overcome them, and kill them" (v.7).

The beast represents Satan. He wages war on the prophecies of Daniel and Christ concerning the destruction of the temple and Jerusalem, causing the residents to reject the message of the witnesses with violence. Satan is ever waging war for the destruction of the scriptures. We see evidence of this today. The devil does not want man to believe in the inspiration of the Bible or its veracity. The Bible condemns him and saves man. Satan is opposed to the objective truth of scripture. He does not want man to be warned, comforted, or set free by it.

By causing the Jews to disbelieve the words of Jesus and twist the words of Daniel, the devil has temporally overcome the prophecies concerning Jerusalem's destruction. He has done so to the destruction of the lives in that city, the lives of those who disbelieved the word of God.

"And their dead bodies will lie in the street of the great city which spiritually is called Sodom and Egypt, where also our Lord was crucified" (v.8).

The bodies (the scriptures) lie dead in Jerusalem, where our Lord was crucified. Jerusalem had once again become as Sodom to the Lord (cf. Isaiah 1:9-10, 21; Jeremiah 23:14; Ezekiel 16:49-56) and would suffer the same fate of divine judgment and destruction. Just as Lot was told to flee from Sodom, Christians were told to flee from Jerusalem (see Matthew 24:15-22).

Egypt corresponds to spiritual bondage. Jerusalem was igno-rantly under the bondage of sin (cf. Romans 10:3; 1 Corinthians 2:8; 2 Corinthians 4:4). Egypt also corresponds to a nation which kept God's people in bondage and suffering. Judea had become such a nation.

"Then those from the peoples, tribes, tongues, and nations will see their dead bodies three-and-a-half days, and not allow their dead bodies to be put into graves. And those who dwell on the earth will rejoice over them, make merry, and send gifts to one another, because these two prophets tormented those who dwell on the earth" (vv.9-10).

Any message of judgment leading to destruction is tormenting to people refusing to repent. Such was the case with these proph-ecies which stood as witnesses against Jerusalem. While the peo-ple believed they had put an end to the divine message, their vic-tory was short-lived lasting only three and one-half days, signify-ing an incomplete and temporary triumph over God's message.

For a while, the Jewish rebellion against Rome was valiant and victorious. It may have seemed that the yoke of the Roman Empire might soon be broken. Each victory over Rome, regardless of how small, was of great significance and inspiration to the Jewish peo-ple fighting the war.

The Witnesses are Resurrected (vv. 11-14)

"Now after the three-and-a-half days the breath of life from God entered them, and they stood on their feet, and great fear fell on those who saw them. And they heard a loud voice from heaven saying to them, 'Come up here.' And they as-cended to heaven in a cloud, and their enemies saw them" (vv.11-12).

The Jewish sense of victory was fleeting, and their hope for independence would be dashed to pieces along with their great city. The prophecies of Daniel and Christ would live. "For ever, O Lord, thy word is settled in heaven" (Psalm 119:89, KJV).

The judgment of God against Jerusalem stood. Great fear swept through the city as they saw their end was at hand. God glorified His witnesses for all to see. Such is the case with every inspired prophecy of scripture. It is given by God, and though men may strive to defeat it, the word of God will live and abide forever. The word has been sent by God and has returned to God, signifying its fulfillment. The prophecies of Daniel and Christ will stand as witnesses on the judgment day for those who did not believe, repent, and obey (cf. John 12:48).

"In the same hour there was a great earthquake, and a tenth of the city fell. In the earthquake seven thousand people were killed, and the rest were afraid and gave glory to the God of heaven. The second woe is past. Behold, the third woe is coming quickly" (vv.13-14).

Earthquakes are synonymous with God's judgment throughout scripture (cf. Psalm 18:7; Isaiah 29:6; Ezekiel 38:19-20; Nahum 1:5; Haggai 2:6). Seven thousand were killed denoting a complete number in apocalyptic terms. God's judgment against Jerusalem was complete. "The rest" who "were afraid and gave glory to the God of heaven" probably refers to the Christians who were delivered from the destruction and others who may have repented because of it.

"The second woe is past. Behold, the third woe is coming quickly." The first of three "woes" (8:13) came in 9:1-12 with the unleashing of a demonic army led by Satan (cf. Daniel 11:31; 12:12:7). The second "woe" has now ended with the destruction of Jerusalem (9:13-11:14).

A third "woe" is yet to come. The destruction of Jerusalem was not the end of God's judgment. An eternal judgment against those who turned God's holy city into "Sodom" was yet to come (Revelation 11:18; 20:11-15).

Seventh Trumpet: The Kingdom Proclaimed (vv. 15-19)

"Then the seventh angel sounded: And there were loud voices in heaven, saying, 'The kingdoms of this world have become the kingdoms of our Lord and of His Christ, and He shall reign forever and ever!'" (v.15)

The martyred saints once again appear in heaven, in the presence of God. They have been vindicated. They worship the Lord and His Christ for the victory He has granted to His people. God will be sovereign over the earth.

They shout a proclamation of victory: "The kingdoms of this world have become the kingdoms of our Lord and of His Christ, and He shall reign forever and ever!" The kingdom of Christ would endure and live beyond Jewish persecution and the destruction of Jerusalem. Not only did Daniel's prophecy concerning Jerusalem come true, but his prophecy concerning the church would as well. "And in the days of these kings (Roman) the God of heaven will set up a kingdom which shall never be destroyed; and the kingdom shall not be left to other people; it shall break in pieces and consume all these kingdoms, and it shall stand forever" (Daniel 2:44).

"And the twenty-four elders who sat before God on their thrones fell on their faces and worshiped God, saying: 'We give You thanks, O Lord God Almighty, The One who is and who was and who is to come, Because You have taken Your great power and reigned. The nations were angry, and Your wrath has come, And the time of the dead, that they should be judged, And that You should reward Your servants the prophets and the saints, And those who fear Your name, small

and great, And should destroy those who destroy the earth'" **(vv.16-18).**

The twenty-four elders once again appear and are once again praising God for His eternality, His power, and His reign. God has overcome the ones who raged against Him. He has judged them and rewarded His servants. God has prevailed.

They praise God for His righteous vindication of His people and His judgment of the wicked. Here we have the two-fold judgment of God presented in the form of the heavenly praise. God will judge both the evil and the good (Ezekiel 18:19-24; 2 Corinthians 5:10).

"Then the temple of God was opened in heaven, and the ark of His covenant was seen in His temple. And there were lightnings, noises, thunderings, an earthquake, and great hail" (v.19).

God's temple is still standing, which His true temple in heaven (Psalm 11:4; Acts 17:24). The presence of the ark of His covenant reminds us of God faithfully keeping His covenant with those who are His. The ark of the covenant was taken away from Israel, and was not to be remembered under the new covenant God would make with them (Jeremiah 3:16; 31:31-34). Yet, it is seen here as a reminder of His covenant with Israel in much the same way as the rainbow colors in heaven remind us of His covenant with Noah and mankind after the flood.

The lightening, noise, thunder, earthquake, and hail represent His great power over the heavens and the earth. This is true throughout the apocalyptic writings of scripture. God is almighty. God will remain and His kingdom will stand after all the kings and kingdoms of this earth have fallen. "Who can be likened unto the Lord?" (Psalm 89:6)

Application for Today

The word of God stood as a witness against Jerusalem. Rather than repenting and obeying, most of the Jews chose to ignore or falsely interpret the true meaning of the prophecies which foretold their destruction. God's word came to pass just as He said it would.

For modern readers, we must ask the question of ourselves, for our own soul's sakes, is God's word testifying against us? Are we choosing to ignore or am I interpreting falsely the warnings God has given us?

Will we have boldness on the day of judgment (1 John 4:17)? Some, He will commend by saying: "Come, you blessed of My Father." Christ will sentence others to outer darkness where there will be weeping and gnashing of teeth. Every soul should be found asking "Will I stand before my Lord as a faithful, obedient Christian – a child of God?"

We must be found reading, understanding, and obeying the word of God (2 Timothy 2:15; Romans 10:17). Some were spared in Jerusalem – the elect. Others were destroyed – the proud and impenitent. It will be this way on the day of the final judgment as well. Let us live in Christ that we may die in Christ to live with Him for eternity.

Chapter Twelve

Chapter twelve serves a two-fold purpose in our study of Revelation. Using apocalyptic visions, chapter twelve summarizes chapters 6-11 while providing a segue to chapters 13-19. As we noted earlier in our study, whenever the book itself provides the meaning for a sign or symbol, interpreters of Revelation must let the meaning which is being provided stand. There is no reason to assign another meaning when God has already given it. When this mistake is made, the true meaning will inevitably be lost. By letting God's given meanings stand for themselves, we will be enabled to have a much clearer picture of what John has viewed, heard, and described.

The Woman, the Dragon, and the Child (vv. 1-6)

"Now a great sign appeared in heaven: a woman clothed with the sun, with the moon under her feet, and on her head a garland of twelve stars. Then being with child, she cried out in labor and in pain to give birth" (vv.1-2).

We must first observe that John is witnessing a "great sign" as it appears in heaven.[1] A sign is intended to signify something. What is being signified by a woman giving birth to a child?

Let us first look at what the chapter says about the woman. Her appearance is heavenly, even divine, as she is clothed with the sun and the moon is under her feet. Upon her head we find a garland

---

[1] "Ch. 12 begins a new division of our work, one which might be called the 'book of signs.' The word 'sign' does not occur in chs. 4-11, but appears seven times in chs. 12-19. Three of these signs are in heaven (12:1, 3, 15:1) and four are on earth (13:13, 14, 16:14, 19:20)." J. Massyngberde Ford, *Revelation*, ABC (Garden City, NY: Doubleday, 1975), 194-5.

of twelve stars, which likely alludes to Israel. She clearly represents something that is divine although she herself is not a deity. She experiences labor and pain in birth. She is also in need of protection. The woman gave birth to a Child **"who was to rule all nations with a rod of iron;"** who was **"caught up to God and His throne" (vv.4-5).** Moreover, the rest of her offspring "keep the commandments of God and have the testimony of Jesus Christ" (v.17).

Personification is once again being utilized in Revelation, but who or what does the woman personify? Perhaps the easiest explanation is to say that she personifies Israel as the nation which gave birth to the Christ through the offspring of Abraham. However, Israel in and of itself was just another nation. It was God's covenant with Israel that made them special (Deuteronomy 7:6). God's promise to Abraham produced the Christ (Genesis 12:3).

The "offspring" of this promise "keep the commandments of God and have the testimony of Jesus Christ" (cf. Galatians 3:26-29; 6:16). It seems more plausible to us to say that this personification corresponds to God's plan of redemption which was first foretold in Eden (Genesis 3:15). God's plan of redemption gave birth to the "Child who was to rule all nations with a rod of iron" (cf. Psalm 2:9). Those who are in covenant with God through His plan of redemption "keep the commandments of God and have the testimony of Jesus Christ."

It is also fitting that the plan of redemption should be adorned with the twelve stars which seems to represent Israel, as through Israel the prophets spoke, and the Christ came. The twelve stars adorn the woman; yet they are not the woman. The woman is greater than her apparel, just as God's plan of redemption was greater than Israel, its law, and its government. Israel was the vehicle for God's plan of redemption which brought forth the Christ, His gospel, and His church.

"And another sign appeared in heaven: behold, a great, fiery red dragon having seven heads and ten horns, and seven diadems on his heads. His tail drew a third of the stars of heaven and threw them to the earth. And the dragon stood before the woman who was ready to give birth, to devour her Child as soon as it was born" (vv.3-4).

The second sign John witnessed appearing in heaven was of "a great, fiery red dragon." The identity of the dragon is provided in verse 9: "the great dragon was cast out, that serpent of old, called the Devil and Satan." Satan appears with seven heads, ten horns, and seven diadems. Seven diadems (crowns of governing authority) rest upon seven heads (the authorities/kings or kingdoms). The seven heads (kings/kingdoms) have ten horns. Horns denote power. Hence, seven kings/kingdoms had ten horns meaning some kings/kingdoms possessed greater power than others (cf. Daniel 7-8). All had authority; but none had all authority.

Throughout Israel's OT history many nations came and went which sought their destruction and to destroy God's covenant promises along with them (Daniel 11:28, 32). Ultimately, even the Jewish government in Jerusalem came to seek the destruction of the plan of redemption (the woman) and her Child (the Christ).

With his tail, the dragon "drew a third of the stars of heaven and threw them to the earth." The Lord spoke of the devil and his angels (Matthew 25:41), just as Peter and Jude wrote of "the angels that sinned" (2 Peter 2:4) and "did not keep their proper domain" (Jude 6). It seems these "stars of heaven" drawn away by Satan represent the angels which fell with him. Similar terminology is also used in Daniel 8:10, where we find some of the host of heaven cast down and trampled.

Having his evil forces aligned for battle, the devil "stood before the woman who was ready to give birth, to devour her Child as soon as it was born." We know this symbolism is historically true from the narratives given concerning the birth of Christ and the diabolical scheming of Herod (cf. Matthew 2).

"She bore a male Child who was to rule all nations with a rod of iron. And her Child was caught up to God and His throne" (v.5).

Despite the devil's efforts through Herod, Christ was born. He was crucified. Yet, His crucifixion did not stall the plan of redemption; rather, it fulfilled the precious promises of God's salvation through His resurrection and ascension to heaven. Thus, the "Child was caught up to God and His throne" (cf. Acts 1:9-2:36; Ephesians 4:8; Hebrews 1:8, 13).

"Then the woman fled into the wilderness, where she has a place prepared by God, that they should feed her there one thousand two hundred and sixty days" (v.6).

The number of days the woman is protected coincides with the time designated for the destruction of Jerusalem. While Jerusalem is being destroyed, the plan of God is being preserved along with His people (her offspring). Jesus said as much in Matthew 24:22. Note, "And unless those days were shortened, no flesh would be saved; but for the elect's sake those days will be shortened."

The temple of God was measured and divinely protected (11:1). Many Christians escaped Jerusalem and other Judean cities during this period. Eusebius wrote of one such example which occurred before the destruction of Jerusalem, when early Christians fled to Pella in the region of the Decapolis across the Jordan River.

Satan Thrown Out of Heaven (vv. 7-12)

"And war broke out in heaven: Michael and his angels fought with the dragon; and the dragon and his angels fought, but they did not prevail, nor was a place found for them in

heaven any longer. So the great dragon was cast out, that serpent of old, called the Devil and Satan, who deceives the whole world; he was cast to the earth, and his angels were cast out with him" (vv.7-9).

John's vision expands from earth to include heaven. Once more, the vision corresponds to Daniel where Michael plays a prominent role in protecting the people of God (Daniel 10:13; 12:2 ff.). In Revelation Michael is once again seen fighting against and defeating the devil and his forces. Keeping in mind the nature of apocalyptic literature, it is difficult to determine if these are actual events or symbolic of a spiritual message.

Satan is waging war in the spiritual realm. Christians must realize that the war we are fighting against evil on earth is also being fought in heavenly places (cf. Luke 10:18; Ephesians 6:12). We too must know that just as the devil cannot prevail in heaven against Michael and his angels, he cannot triumph over our fight of faith on earth. Moreover, just as the devil is here cast from heaven, he will again be "cast into the lake of fire and brimstone…to be tormented day and night forever and ever" (Revelation 20:10, KJV).

Especially of note here is that the devil's work is to deceive the whole world. For now, the whole world is under his sway (1 John 5:19). He works to blind men's eyes (2 Corinthians 4:4) and deceives them to the point of rejecting the truth (2 Thessalonians 2:9-10). The war is one of truth versus deception, good versus evil, right versus wrong, the Lamb versus the dragon.

"Then I heard a loud voice saying in heaven, 'Now salvation, and strength, and the kingdom of our God, and the power of His Christ have come, for the accuser of our brethren, who accused them before our God day and night, has been cast down. And they overcame him by the blood of the Lamb and by the word of their testimony, and they did not love their lives to the death. Therefore rejoice, O heavens, and you who dwell in them! Woe to the inhabitants of the earth and the sea! For the devil has come down to you, having great wrath, because he knows that he has a short time'" (vv.10-12).

Satan was cast down and his power over death was defeated by the resurrection of Christ (1 Corinthians 15:54 ff; Hebrews 2:14 ff). The kingdom of God – the church of Christ – was established on His resurrection, the death He endured could not prevail against Him (cf. Matthew 16:18-19). Saints can now overcome the accuser "by the blood of the Lamb and by the word of their testimony, and they did not love their lives to the death."

He accuses: "Your sins are too great to be forgiven." "You are not worthy to become a child of God." "You can never measure up to living the Christian life." Christ intercedes (1 John 2:1-2). We are redeemed by the precious blood of the Lamb (1 Peter 1:18-19), and by the precious love of the Lamb (Revelation 1:5-6; Romans 5:8).

The devil deceives (John 8:44; Revelation 12:9): "You are just fine just like you are." "God does not exist." "Jesus was just a man." "All religions are the same." Christ gives truth (John 8:31-32). "For the law was given by Moses, but grace and truth came by Jesus Christ" (John 1:17). Jesus came into the world to "bear witness to the truth" (John 18:37). We purify our souls by obeying the truth (1 Peter 1:22, 25). The gospel is the Christian's word of testimony.

Satan offers the world and its kingdoms (Matthew 4:8) – but it is a world which will vanish away (1 John 2:15-17). Satan can offer temporary riches and fame (Hebrews 11:25; Romans 6:21). Satan can offer fleeting wealth and power. Christ offers life everlasting (Matthew 10:28-30; John 14:1-3; Revelation 22:14, 17).

To "love not their life" is to be "faithful unto (even to the point of) death" (Revelation 2:10). These saints were not living merely for the here and now. Christians of every age should have the same mindset, for we are fighting to overcome the same adversary. *"Shall we be carried to the skies on flowery beds of ease, when others fought to win the prize and sail the stormy seas?"*

The Woman Persecuted (vv. 13-17)

"Now when the dragon saw that he had been cast to the earth, he persecuted the woman who gave birth to the male Child. But the woman was given two wings of a great eagle, that she might fly into the wilderness to her place, where she is nourished for a time and times and half a time, from the presence of the serpent" (vv.13-14).

Satan is a deceiver (v.9), an accuser (v.10), and a persecutor (v.13) of God's people. But through Christ he can be defeated. He persecuted the woman who gave birth to the male Child, yet the woman was divinely protected with "two wings of a great eagle."[2] She was enabled to fly into the wilderness and escape his persecution. Such has been the unfolding drama of Revelation chapters 6-11. The church has been viciously persecuted by Satan and yet divinely protected by God. The mention of the wilderness should invoke the readers to consider Israel's exodus from Egypt into the wilderness for protection.

The woman is nourished in the wilderness for "a time and times and half a time" or three and one-half years. The church is being protected during the time of the destruction of Jerusalem and the Jewish state. Chapter twelve is summarizing the previous chapters and segueing into the following chapters.

---

[2] The OT often speaks of wings as a God-given source of strength and shelter (e.g., Isaiah 40:3; Psalm 17:8; 36:7; 57:1).

"So the serpent spewed water out of his mouth like a flood after the woman, that he might cause her to be carried away by the flood. But the earth helped the woman, and the earth opened its mouth and swallowed up the flood which the dragon had spewed out of his mouth. And the dragon was enraged with the woman, and he went to make war with the rest of her offspring, who keep the commandments of God and have the testimony of Jesus Christ" (vv.15-17).

The devil could not prevail against the woman (God's plan of redemption), the Child (God's only begotten Son), or her offspring (the church). His attempts (e.g., the flood spewed from his mouth, cf. Daniel 9:26) were thwarted. Christianity was to spread beyond the borders of Judea and throughout the world, just as Jesus said it would (Acts 1:8). This enraged the devil "and he went to make war with the rest of her offspring." Satan's continued war against the church in the Roman world and beyond will be the subject of chapters 13-20:10 leading to his ultimate and final defeat.

Application for Today

Chapter twelve reminds us of the nefarious lengths to which Satan will go to stop the Lord's will from being done. He will attack God's people collectively and individually through deception, accusation, and persecution. Christians must be aware and stand on guard against the "wiles of the devil" (Ephesians 6:11).

Just as our blessed Lord overcame the devil's temptations so too can we. But victory will not be achieved with half-hearted faith and lack of self-discipline. Faith remains the victory for overcoming the world. Faith must be trained and exercised through studying God's word, endurance of trials, prayer, and practice. Times of temptation and trials brought on by the adversary should not provoke us to abandon God but to draw ever nearer to Him.

He knows the enemy we face and the depths to which he will sink to ensnare us. At all times, He cares for us (1 Peter 5:7). We will find our heavenly Father's grace to be sufficient to resist the devil (2 Corinthians 12:9). Moreover, He will not allow us to be tested above our ability to endure, as He knows it (1 Corinthians 10:13; Psalm 11:5). "Preserve me, O God, for in thee do I put my trust" (Psalm 16:1).

As we survey the world in its present condition, this "present evil age," we find both the subtle and overt tactics of the devil on full display. His deception runs rampant over the earth. Yet, in view of his assured defeat, all he can do is "believe and tremble." To be sure, he is powerful, but he is not all-powerful. He has great knowledge to conquer souls, but he is not all-knowing. Neither is he omnipresent. Neither he nor his angels can be everywhere at all times. He cannot come into your heart and mind without an invitation. He cannot wreck your life unless you allow him. But he is persistent. Even though he was stopped from devouring the Child and prevented from destroying the woman of chapter twelve, his wrath only burned hotter. His zeal and thirst for blood is insatiable. He could not destroy the church through the Jews in Jerusalem (chaps. 6-11); from this point, he will focus his efforts on destroying the church through the mightiest empire ever to exist at that time, Rome (chaps. 13-19). However, God knows and reveals the ending of the story to John. He will triumph over the devil and all who are His children will share the victory.

Therefore, "Be strong in the Lord and the power of His might." Resist him steadfastly in the faith. Overcome his evil just as our brethren did "by the blood of the Lamb and by the word of their testimony, and they did not love their lives to the death." Find protection and nourishment from the Lord, for He is good. "Be sober, be vigilant; because your adversary the devil walks about like a roaring lion, seeking whom he may devour" (1 Peter 5:8).

Chapter Thirteen

The Revelation received by John did not end with the destruction of Jerusalem. In fact, from the perspective of historical chronology, the destruction of Jerusalem occurred before the writing of Revelation. Revelation was written during the reign of Domitian (81-96 AD), and we believe around the time of 95 AD. Jerusalem was destroyed in 70 AD. Thus, chapters 6-11 depict something that already occurred for the original readers. But why?

The church faced three great persecutions in the first century. The first, at the hands of the Jews in Judea ended with the destruction of the Jerusalem. The second and third persecutions came by the hands of Rome through the diabolical schemes of two emperors especially – Nero (54-68 AD) and Domitian. God used Rome to destroy Jerusalem much like He used Babylon in the OT (586-7 BC); and just as God overthrew Babylon in the OT (cf. Isaiah 13; Jeremiah 51), He promised to overthrow Rome in Revelation.

In chapter twelve the devil's attempts to destroy the woman, the Child, and her offspring (God's plan of redemption, Christ, and the church) were defeated and the church was protected during the time of Jerusalem's destruction. The chapter closes as Satan is enraged by his defeat and "went to make war with the rest of her offspring" – the church in the Roman world.

Beginning in chapter thirteen Satan plans to use Rome (the beast of the sea) and the imperial cult (the beast of the earth) to accomplish his victory over the church. At the time of writing, the church was in the throngs of a pagan, polytheistic Roman society indoctrinated with the propaganda of false religion, superstition, and feigned patriotism. Through prayer, the faithful saints were sending a distress signal to heaven. God had answered their S.O.S before when He ended the Jewish persecution. In the forthcoming chapters, we will read about God's answer to their cry of distress and the end of Roman persecution as well.

The Beast from the Sea (vv. 1-10)

"Then I stood on the sand of the sea. And I saw a beast rising up out of the sea, having seven heads and ten horns, and on his horns ten crowns, and on his heads a blasphemous name" (v.1).

The representation of the empire as a beast reminds us of Daniel 7:1-8 wherein Daniel dreamed of four beasts, each representing a different world empire (Daniel 7:17). The fourth beast of Daniel's dream depicted Rome, which is the beast of the sea in Revelation (cf. Daniel 7:3, 7-8; 19-28).[1] This interpretation also agrees with the descriptions of the beast later in Revelation 17:3 ff.

The beast comes from the sea.[2] The waters of the sea remain most mysterious, dark, fretful, powerful, and mostly uncharted. Perhaps this is the reason for the beast rising from the sea as it adds to the mystery and fierceness of the creature. The "cosmic sea" is believed to symbolize a "continued threat the forces of chaos pose against God and creation…The calmness of the sea symbolizes the absence of evil and chaos…After the consummation there is no longer a sea (Revelation 21:1), which symbolizes no more actual or possible threat to the creation and sovereignty of God."[3]

He is seen **"having seven heads and ten horns, and on his horns ten crowns."** These emblems should be connected to **"his**

---

[1] Ladd, 179.

[2] The sea was the origin for the world powers of Daniel 7:3 as well. Other OT passages picture a monster from/in the sea causing chaos yet being subdued by God (Job 26:12; Psalm 74:12-14; 89:9-10; Isaiah 51:9).

[3] *DBI,* 675.

power, his throne, and great authority" (v.2). In OT apocalyptic writings, heads denoted kingdoms, horns denoted power, and crowns denoted authority. The beast in Revelation 13 has more horns (power) and crowns (authority) than heads (kingdoms). This seems to suggest that some of the rulers or periods of rule characterized by this beast were more powerful and had greater authority than others. Yet, all of them shared in common the blasphemous name they wore.

The heads on the beast could symbolize different Caesars and emperors of Rome. They might also symbolize the various vasal kingdoms subjugated to the empire's dominion.

"Now the beast which I saw was like a leopard, his feet were like the feet of a bear, and his mouth like the mouth of a lion. The dragon gave him his power, his throne, and great authority" (v.2).

Once more we see an allusion to Daniel's dream of four beasts in this description. The beast has the swiftness of a leopard, the power of a bear, and the ferocity of a lion – a dreadful foe indeed!

It is most important, however, to recognize that the dragon gave the beast his power. The evil manifested by Rome should be directly attributed to the source of its authority. Recall how Satan offered Christ the kingdoms of the earth as part of his temptation (Matthew 4:1-11). Many leaders and nations today are receiving their power from the dragon as well. Satan's sway over the nations has ever been the case. His influence remains today. The beast of the sea is Satan's representative on earth. He is doing his master's bidding.

We find this imagery pertaining to the beast in Daniel as well. "A king shall arise, Having fierce features, Who understands sinister schemes. His power shall be mighty, but not by his own power; He shall destroy fearfully, And shall prosper and thrive;

He shall destroy the mighty, and also the holy people. Through his cunning He shall cause deceit to prosper under his rule; And he shall exalt himself in his heart. He shall destroy many in their prosperity. He shall even rise against the Prince of princes; But he shall be broken without human means." (Daniel 8:23-25).

"And I saw one of his heads as if it had been mortally wounded, and his deadly wound was healed. And all the world marveled and followed the beast" (v.3).

This aspect of the vision likely alludes to the historical record of Rome in warfare. Rome was not undefeated in battle, but it remained unconquered in warfare. At various times in Rome's history, it may have seemed that the defeat and death of Rome was imminent only for Rome to recover and triumph. One might point to Hannibal and the Punic Wars, or the Germanic "Barbarian" wars. A better case may be made for the Roman civil war which followed Nero's suicide.[4] Based on the writings of Tacitus, others have speculated that the wounding and subsequent healing of the beast refers to a prevalent superstition during that time in which it was thought that Domitian was Nero reincarnated.[5]

Another possible explanation for the wounding and healing of the beast pertains to the persecution of the church. The death of Nero created a lull in Roman persecution – the wounding – but the rise of Domitian brought back persecution with a vengeance – the healing.[6]

"So they worshiped the dragon who gave authority to the beast; and they worshiped the beast, saying, 'Who is like the beast? Who is able to make war with him?'" (v.4)

---

[4] Paul, 231.
[5] Hailey, 286.
[6] Thompson, 109.

Remaining victorious and even increasing in might, caused the citizens of Rome to worship the dragon (the source) and the beast (the empire/emperor). However, the devil is ultimately the object of every false religion, and such paganism is rooted in his evil agenda.

"And he was given a mouth speaking great things and blasphemies, and he was given authority to continue for forty-two months" (v.5).

Once more we have an allusion to the fourth beast of Daniel (Daniel 7:21, 25). In Daniel, the beast was to persecute the saints for "a time, times, and half a time" or three and one-half years. In Revelation the span is forty-two months or three and one-half years. When we combine this time span to the previous three and one-half years of Revelation 11:2, 3 and 12:6 we arrive at a total of seven years. In apocalyptic literature, the number "seven" denotes completes. The sum of the two periods in Revelation likely denotes the full extent of persecution against the first century church.

"Then he opened his mouth in blasphemy against God, to blaspheme His name, His tabernacle, and those who dwell in heaven. It was granted to him to make war with the saints and to overcome them. And authority was given him over every tribe, tongue, and nation" (vv.6-7).

The beast speaks against God, His tabernacle (the church), and those who dwell in heaven (martyred saints). He is tasked with making war with the saints to overcome them.

Daniel's dream foresaw John's vision. The two speak of the same beast (Rome) and its persecution of the kingdom. Daniel's fourth beast would "be different from all other kingdoms, And shall devour the whole earth, Trample it and break it in pieces...He shall speak pompous words against the Most High,

Shall persecute the saints of the Most High, And shall intend to change times and law. Then the saints shall be given into his hand, For a time and times and half a time" (Daniel 7:23 ff.).

In this passage we read that the beast "opened his mouth in blasphemy against God, to blaspheme His name, His tabernacle, and those who dwell in heaven. It was granted to him to make war with the saints and to overcome them. And authority was given him over every tribe, tongue, and nation." The two passages are speaking of the same kingdom and its authority to wage a blasphemous war against God and His people.

"All who dwell on the earth will worship him, whose names have not been written in the Book of Life of the Lamb slain from the foundation of the world" (v.8).

Within the historical context of Revelation and first century Rome, the practice of emperor worship is the clear meaning behind this statement. Emperor deification and worship began in Rome when the senate declared Caesar to be *Devus Julius* or "god Julius." Augustus Octavian then began calling himself *Devi Filius* or "son of a god."

Augustus would go on to create the early guidelines for the imperial cult, while being sure to include Roma, the female goddess who personified the Roman state. The Roman citizens were instructed to worship Roma and Julius. The cult of Roma would later be blended with the cult of the emperor in their temples, sacrifices, prayers, and rituals. Emperor worship continued throughout first century Rome during the reigns of Tiberius, Caligula, Claudius, Nero, Vespasian, Titus, Domitian, Nerva, and Trajan with varying obligations, strictness, and intensity of enforcement.

The "book of life" is also found in Daniel 12:1 and is connected to the period of Roman rule. Only those who are written in the book of life have the promise of protection from the beast.

"If anyone has an ear, let him hear. He who leads into captivity shall go into captivity; he who kills with the sword must be killed with the sword. Here is the patience and the faith of the saints" (vv.9-10).

Just as Daniel foretold, the fourth beast in Daniel's dream, and the beast of the sea in John's vision, will be defeated by the Lord (Daniel 12:1 ff.). He who lived by the sword would die by it also. "Here is the patience and faith of the saints." The people of God are called to endure until these things shall be finished (Daniel 12:7).

The Beast from the Earth (vv. 11-15)

"Then I saw another beast coming up out of the earth, and he had two horns like a lamb and spoke like a dragon" (v.11)

By the descriptions which follow pertaining to the work of the beast of the earth, it appears clearly that this beast symbolizes the priests and ringleaders of the Roman imperial cult. By the time of Revelation, the imperial cult had spread quickly throughout the empire and became a tool to unite its people. Imperial cult centers became rallying points for the citizenry to express devotion to the emperor and to Rome. In time, emperors increased the influence of the imperial cult so that the cult effectively became a state religion and a test of loyalty.

This beast resembles a lamb but speaks like a dragon. The characteristics of false religions are summed up by this description. The beast appears harmless but is truly of the devil. Speaking like a dragon would include false doctrines, lies, manipulations, and blasphemies.

"And he exercises all the authority of the first beast in his presence, and causes the earth and those who dwell in it to worship the first beast, whose deadly wound was healed" (v.12).

His objective is to lead men to worship the first beast – i.e., the Roman state as it was embodied in its rulers. "This passage deals with the power of the second beast, the organization set up to enforce Caesar worship throughout the empire."[7]

Concerning the signs and wonders performed by the beast, "Everywhere there were statues of the emperor in the presence of which the official act of worship was carried out. In all ancient religions the priests knew how to produce signs and wonders; they knew well how to produce the effect of a speaking, image. Pharaoh had had his magicians in the time of Moses, and the imperial priesthood had its experts in conjuring tricks and ventriloquism and the like."[8]

Moreover, "This beast brings it about that those who will not worship will be killed. That was, in fact, the law. If a Christian refused to make the act of worship to Caesar, he was liable to death. The death penalty was not always carried out; but, if a Christian had not the mark of the beast, he could not buy or sell. That is to say, if a man refused to worship the emperor, even if his life was spared, he would be economically ruined."[9]

"He performs great signs, so that he even makes fire come down from heaven on the earth in the sight of men" (v.13).

Just as Pharoah's magicians were able to perform their mischief up to a point, so too is the beast of the earth allowed to deceive through seemingly "great signs." Paul spoke of the man of sin, the son of perdition coming "according to the working of Satan, with all power, signs, and lying wonders" (2 Thessalonians 2:9).

---

[7] William Barclay, *The Revelation of John* (Philadelphia: Westminster Press, 1976), 89.

[8] Ibid.

[9] Ibid.

The connection here with the man of sin in 2 Thessalonians may be deeper than a mere resemblance. While the man of sin likely personifies all false religions generally, Paul could have been speaking in 2 Thessalonians of the tactics and agenda of the imperial cult leaders of that day.

"And he deceives those who dwell on the earth by those signs which he was granted to do in the sight of the beast, telling those who dwell on the earth to make an image to the beast who was wounded by the sword and lived. He was granted power to give breath to the image of the beast, that the image of the beast should both speak and cause as many as would not worship the image of the beast to be killed" (vv.14-15).

As we read the description of the beast of the sea, consider Paul's words from 2 Thessalonians 2:7-12 (ESV): "For the mystery of lawlessness is already at work. Only he who now restrains it will do so until he is out of the way. And then the lawless one will be revealed, whom the Lord Jesus will kill with the breath of his mouth and bring to nothing by the appearance of his coming. The coming of the lawless one is by the activity of Satan with all power and false signs and wonders, and with all wicked deception for those who are perishing, because they refused to love the truth and so be saved. Therefore, God sends them a strong delusion, so that they may believe what is false, in order that all may be condemned who did not believe the truth but had pleasure in unrighteousness."

Here is a summary of the works of the beast of the earth from Revelation:

- He has two horns like a lamb (appearing innocent) and speaks like a dragon (lies, blasphemies, etc.).

- He exercises all the authority of the first beast in his presence (his authority is derived from the first beast, the empire of Rome).
- He causes (makes) the earth and those who dwell in it to worship the first beast.
- He performs great signs.
- He deceives those who dwell on the earth by those signs which he was granted to do in the sight of the beast.
- He tells those who dwell on the earth to make an image to the beast.
- He was granted power to give breath (life) to the image of the beast. Without the imperial cult the practice of emperor worship would have died. The cult gave voice to the notion of the emperor being a god.
- He would cause as many as would not worship the image of the beast to be killed.

Now consider the remarks made about the man of sin in 2 Thessalonians 2:

- He will lead a rebellion against God.
- He will oppose and exalt himself against every so-called god or object of worship, so that he takes his seat in the temple of God, proclaiming himself to be God.
- He was already at work.
- The Lord Jesus would kill him with the breath of his mouth by the appearance of his coming.
- The coming of the lawless one is by the activity of Satan with all power and false signs and wonders, and with all wicked deception for those who are perishing, because they refused to love the truth and so be saved.
- Those who follow him believe what is false and are condemned having pleasure in unrighteousness.

The similarities between the characters in these two passages are striking. Perhaps this is why many commentators view the beast of the earth as the Anti-Christ,[10] seeing that the Anti-Christ is also their understanding of the man of sin. However, when we take into account the figure of speech known as personification, we can see these two characters represent all false religions generally, and perhaps specifically, both refer to the imperial cult of Rome.

The Mark of the Beast (vv. 16-18)

"He causes all, both small and great, rich and poor, free and slave, to receive a mark on their right hand or on their foreheads, and that no one may buy or sell except one who has the mark or the name of the beast, or the number of his name" (vv.16-17).

Speculations run wild for the mark of the beast. The meaning can be simplified with a cross-reference to a previous passage in Revelation. In chapter 7:2-4 we read of the sealing of the servants of God. Their sealing distinguished them as belonging to God. Here the beast of the earth seals or marks those who are obedient to him. Unless they obey, they will be prohibited from buying and selling.

Throughout history unjust governments have used their society's economic freedom as a means of manipulating their citizens. Such was the case in Rome. The economic freedom of any person unwilling to worship the emperor was being manipulated. Christians were viewed as enemies of the state for not participating in this idolatry and worshipping the image of the emperor. They were threatened with economic boycott, confiscation of property, imprisonment, and death.

---

[10] Kealy, 174 ff.

"Here is wisdom. Let him who has understanding calculate the number of the beast, for it is the number of a man: His number is 666" (v.18).

Greek and Roman letters have numerical equivalents. We still use Roman numerals today. Seeing that Revelation was written in Greek, we should stay with the Greek numbering system.

Alexander Campbell did so in his debate with Purcell. He deciphered the letters to mean "the Latin Kingdom" or Rome. He was debating a Catholic bishop who took offense to his work, nevertheless it does add up. "The fifteen Greek letters making 'the Latin Kingdom' (*he Latine Basileia*) have numeral value in order as follows: 8, 30, 1, 300, 10, 50, 8, 2, 1, 200, 10, 30, 5, 10, and 1, totaling 666."[11]

Whether or not this is the true meaning remains a mystery. The connection to Rome is sure and for Christians of that time, an application to emperor worship was obvious.

Application for Today

It is interesting to note that John did not call Nero or Domitian by name in this chapter, or Rome, or for that matter, anywhere in Revelation. Neither did he mention Jerusalem or the identity of Thyatira's Jezebel by name. John was inspired to speak in coded language for the protection of the church. The brethren undoubtedly knew of whom he spoke.

Nevertheless, he did identify Satan by name. In dealing with people in government who were evil, John dealt with the source of the evil – Satan. If Satan's agenda can be stopped, then the wicked people promoting it will also be stopped. We should keep this point in mind as we oppose Satan's seat in civil government

---

[11] Cited by Hugo McCord, "The Number 666, the Mark of the Beast, and the 144,000" in *Difficult Texts of the New Testament Explained* (ed. Wendell Winkler) (Tuscaloosa, AL: Winkler, 1981), 402-5.

today. If the gospel is preached and obeyed, Satan will be defeated one soul at a time. The most effective thing any Christian can do for a government, or its citizenry, is to bring them to Christ.

We should also remember the ferocity, power, and authority of the beast. Christians were facing the most powerful empire in human history and the head of which hated them. While it may not seem like a fair fight and these brethren were at a severe disadvantage, the heavenly allies helping the church were more powerful than the adversaries opposing it. God will always prevail and all those who are His will rejoice together in His victory.

Lastly, consider the beast of the earth and his work as a propagandist for the beast of the sea. Domitian had his cult, Hitler had Goebbels, and rulers today have their talking heads. The propaganda of the beast serves to remind us that not everything we hear is true, right, or good. Yet, God's word will forever remain good, right, and true (cf. Ephesians 5:9). If one is trying to decide if a thing is of God or not, he must ask, "Is it good, right, and true?" God's way will always be all three. By so doing, the false propagandas of the world can be shunned, and the truth of God can be followed.

Chapter Fourteen

In chapter thirteen we found the unholy trinity of the dragon (Satan), the beast of the sea (the Roman Empire), and the beast of the earth (the imperial cult) arrayed for battle and united in cause with the intention of waging war for the destruction of the Lord's church. Their legions are identified with the beast whose mark they bore. The foe has been introduced and depicted from its diabolical leader to its vast power on earth as a formidable opponent to God's kingdom and His plans for the world. Who could stand against such an enemy? And how might a triumphant stand be made? As the tension builds and the prosecution of the war looms, our answer is provided in this chapter.

The answer is given as we behold with John the Lamb of God who stands on Zion's glorious summit with a sea of saints before Him – the first fruits of the gospel, the 144,000 (cf. 7:4 ff.) – who have overcome the previous persecution in Judea and are ready to spread the everlasting gospel to "every nation, tribe, tongue, and people." God has defeated one enemy in settling the persecution the Judean Jews brought against the first century church. He will now see to the cessation of the onslaught perpetrated by Satan through the hands of Rome's seemingly limitless might. God will do so through the grace of His providence and change the world forever by the preaching of His word.

The Lamb and the 144,000 (vv. 1-5)

"Then I looked, and behold, a Lamb standing on Mount Zion, and with Him one hundred and forty-four thousand, having His Father's name written on their foreheads" (v.1).

The Lamb has been previously identified in 5:6 ff. as Christ. That Jesus is standing on the location where the temple in Jerusalem was destroyed signifies to us that He has prevailed over one enemy and now has His eyes set on another.

With Him stand the 144,000 of 7:4 ff. Recall that these are they who were sealed by God "of all the tribes of the children of Israel" (7:4). They are the first fruits of the gospel as it was preached first to the Jew. Depicted in this image is the faithful church of God who have endured one persecution and now stand with the Lamb ready to execute His cause against the unholy trinity. Just as the legions under the sway of the devil bear the mark of the beast, the 144,000 have their Father's name written upon their foreheads. They are His family, His children, begotten by Him.

"And I heard a voice from heaven, like the voice of many waters, and like the voice of loud thunder. And I heard the sound of harpists playing their harps" (v.2).

A majestic voice, loud like the sound of many waters and of thunder (cf. 1:15; 6:1), echoes from heaven. The sound of harps once more accompanies the Lamb (cf. 5:8). In celebration of assured victory over the dragon and his beasts of sea and earth the harps will again sound (15:2). Yet, in Babylon (Rome) there will be no such celebration (18:22).

Those who use mechanical instruments of music in worship to God find authority for the practice with the harps that are used in heaven. In answering this argument, several different approaches may be taken. It can be argued that it is unclear whether these instruments are literal or figurative. It can be argued that by opening the door to instruments based on Revelation, we open the door to altars, tabernacles, incense, and such like. However, the point remains that no angel, apostle, or prophet, has testified that instrumental music should be used in New Testament worship.[12]

"They sang as it were a new song before the throne, before the four living creatures, and the elders; and no one could learn that song except the hundred and forty-four thousand who were redeemed from the earth" (v.3).

A new song is heard by John. The song signifies the special covenant relationship between the 144,000 and the Lord as "no one could learn it" except them. The song is "before the throne" and before the elders and living creatures introduced in chapter 4.

Many precious promises of "new" things are found in the NT. Let us recall the new birth, the new covenant, the new and living way, the new heavens and earth. Truly, the mercies of God are new every morning (Lamentations 3:23). Saints will have a new song to praise Him forevermore in heaven.

"These are the ones who were not defiled with women, for they are virgins. These are the ones who follow the Lamb wherever He goes. These were redeemed from among men, being first fruits to God and to the Lamb. And in their mouth was found no deceit, for they are without fault before the throne of God" (vv.4-5).

The character of the 144,000 is above reproach. They have not been defiled by women but are pure virgins. When we compare this statement with Paul's in 2 Corinthians 11:2, we can understand this chastity is spoken of in a spiritual sense. Note: "For I am jealous for you with godly jealousy. For I have betrothed you to one husband, that I may present you *as* a chaste virgin to

---

[12] The passages which instruct the church pertaining to the music they must render are found in Romans 15:9, 11; 1 Corinthians 14:15, 26; Ephesians 5:19; Colossians 3:16; Hebrews 2:12; James 5:13.

Christ." They did not become spiritual adulterers, as others, through friendship with the world (James 4:4). As good sheep, they followed the Shepherd wherever He went, through thick and thin, in times of peace and persecution. They took up their crosses and followed Him (Matthew 16:24) and were thus redeemed from among men (cf. Ephesians 1:7). To be redeemed is to be purchased[13] or "bought back." Man is sold under sin and bought back by the purchased price of Christ's blood. To be redeemed from among men is not to say that they had once been purchased by men as slaves, but that from among sinful humanity they have been bought by the blood of Christ.

The 144,000 are the first fruits to God and the Lamb. Seeing that the gospel was preached first to the Jews of Judea (cf. Acts 1:8; 2:1 ff.), these would have been Jewish Christians who remained faithful to Christ. In their mouth was found no deceit. These souls were honest and humble people of God, serving Him faithfully with moral purity, steadfastness, and integrity. Truly, this is the kind of army the Lord uses to defeat His foes.

The Proclamations of Three Angels (vv. 6-13)

"Then I saw another angel flying in the midst of heaven, having the everlasting gospel to preach to those who dwell on the earth—to every nation, tribe, tongue, and people— saying with a loud voice, 'Fear God and give glory to Him, for the hour of His judgment has come; and worship Him who made heaven and earth, the sea and springs of water'" (vv.6-7).

Several key facts pertaining to the message of Revelation are contained in this section of the text. First, we have the proclamation of the everlasting gospel. The preaching of the gospel precedes God's judgment of sinful men. We have seen this repeatedly

---

[13] Comfort, 847.

throughout Revelation. God grants opportunity for repentance and ample warnings before He destroys.

We should also note that this gospel is an "everlasting gospel." The word of God lives and abides forever (1 Peter 1:23). While earthly dominions, governments, and laws rise and fall, God's word is forever established in heaven (Psalm 119:89). This gospel is for the eternal benefit of "every nation, tribe, tongue, and people." God is without respect of persons (Acts 10:34; Romans 2:11) and He desires that all men should be saved and come to the knowledge of the truth – this gospel (1 Timothy 2:4). Jesus tasted death for every man (Hebrews 2:9).

Even the citizens of Rome who were given over to emperor worship could repent and obey the gospel. In fact, many Romas and even palace guards were obedient to the gospel (cf. Acts 28:30-31; Philippians 1:12-13).

"And another angel followed, saying, 'Babylon is fallen, is fallen, that great city, because she has made all nations drink of the wine of the wrath of her fornication'" (v.8).

God can speak of things that have not happened as though they have already transpired (Romans 4:17). "Babylon is fallen," is the proclamation of the second angel. The gospel of Christ has been preached and now the people have been warned. God's longsuffering kindness toward man is evident in this passage (2 Peter 3:9). After offering salvation and providing the warning of impending doom, the only act of divine justice remaining is that of judgment. Rome will be made to drink the wine which she has been serving. God will mix it in full strength and pour it upon them. The images to follow of the seven bowls/vials of wrath will present the outpouring of the wrath of God.

"Then a third angel followed them, saying with a loud voice, 'If anyone worships the beast and his image, and receives his mark on his forehead or on his hand, he himself shall also drink of the wine of the wrath of God, which is poured out full strength into the cup of His indignation'" (vv.9-10).

Anyone who chose not to heed the warnings of God, repent, and obey the gospel "shall also drink of the wine of the wrath of God" which is to be poured out in "full strength into the cup of His indignation." The "full strength" of God's wrath is not limited to this world only, but also extends throughout eternity, as is seen in the next verse.

"He shall be tormented with fire and brimstone in the presence of the holy angels and in the presence of the Lamb. And the smoke of their torment ascends forever and ever; and they have no rest day or night, who worship the beast and his image, and whoever receives the mark of his name" (v.11).

Consider the facts of hell stated in this verse. These rebellious souls who "worship the beast and his image, and whoever receives the mark of his name" will be tormented "with fire and brimstone in the presence of the holy angels and in the presence of the Lamb." Fire and brimstone were elements often used to convey God's judgment upon sinful men in scripture (Psalm 11:6; Isaiah 30:33; 34:9; Ezekiel 38:22; Luke 17:29).

(1) "The smoke of their torment ascends forever and ever." Not only is the smoke eternal, but also the torment. The scriptures speak of the eternality of hell frequently and clearly (cf. Matthew 25:46; 2 Thessalonians 1:7-9).

(2) "They shall have no rest day or night." In hell there will be no rest, comfort, or reprieve from the torment to be endured.

"Here is the patience of the saints; here are those who keep the commandments of God and the faith of Jesus" (v.12).

The saints can endure the sufferings inflicted upon them by those who worship the beast and faithfully keep the commandments of God because they know God will avenge them. They do not have to take matters into their own hands. God will repay. "Beloved, do not avenge yourselves, but rather give place to wrath; for it is written, 'Vengeance is Mine, I will repay,' says the Lord" (Romans 12:19). "Here is the patience of the saints."

"Then I heard a voice from heaven saying to me, Write: 'Blessed are the dead who die in the Lord from now on.' 'Yes,' says the Spirit, 'that they may rest from their labors, and their works follow them'" (v.13).

In juxtaposition to the torment of the worshippers of the beast, we have the blessedness of the saints. Not all dead are blessed, only the dead "who die in the Lord." Consider their characteristics:

(1) They died in the Lord. For one to die in the Lord, he must first live in the Lord. He must be in Christ (Galatians 3:26-27). He must remain in Christ (Revelation 2:10).

(2) They rest from their labors. For one to rest from labor, he must first labor. The Christian faith is an active, even pro-active, religion. Christ's disciples are devoted to keeping His mission and ministry alive through preaching the gospel (Mark 16:15) and a commitment to good works (cf. Matthew 5:16; Ephesians 2:10; Titus 2:14).

(3) Their works do follow them. The life of the faithful Christian becomes his legacy to be handed down from generation to generation. Not only will his works follow him on earth, but they will also follow him to judgment (cf. Matthew 25:31-40).

While the wicked are cursed with sleepless torment, the righteous are blessed in a state of perpetual rest and peace. All men could know this blessedness, but only those who do the will of the Father will experience it (cf. Matthew 7:21-23).

Reaping the Earth's Harvest (vv. 14-16)

"Then I looked, and behold, a white cloud, and on the cloud sat One like the Son of Man, having on His head a golden crown, and in His hand a sharp sickle" (v.14).

After God has revealed what He is going to do, He does it. We see Christ – "One like the Son of Man" – adorned with a golden crown (the victor's crown) wielding in His hand a sharp sickle.

He appears on a white cloud as is often the scene in scripture of divine judgment (cf. Matthew 24:30; Revelation 1:7). "A number of passages associate God's appearance as a warrior with the cloud...Clouds serve as God's war chariot in the imagination of the OT poets and prophets (Psalm 18:9; 68:4; 104:4; Daniel 7:13; Nahum 1:3)."[14]

"And another angel came out of the temple, crying with a loud voice to Him who sat on the cloud, 'Thrust in Your sickle and reap, for the time has come for You to reap, for the harvest of the earth is ripe'" (v.15).

The time for reaping has come. An angel comes from the heavenly temple and with a loud voice relates the message to "Thrust in Your sickle and reap, for the time has come for You to reap, for the harvest of the earth is ripe." There will be no more delay. God's time to judge Domitian and his empire is at hand.

"So He who sat on the cloud thrust in His sickle on the earth, and the earth was reaped" (v.16).

---

[14] *DBI*, 157. See also Isaiah 19:1-2.

The parable of the wheat and the tares presents a similar picture for the end of time (cf. Matthew 13:24-30). The reaping to be done in view of the present context in Revelation is that of divine judgment on Rome.

Reaping the Grapes of Wrath (vv. 17-20)

"Then another angel came out of the temple which is in heaven, he also having a sharp sickle. And another angel came out from the altar, who had power over fire, and he cried with a loud cry to him who had the sharp sickle, saying, 'Thrust in your sharp sickle and gather the clusters of the vine of the earth, for her grapes are fully ripe'" (vv.17-18).

In keeping with the reaping metaphor and imagery, "another angel came out of the temple which is in heaven, he also having a sharp sickle." And yet another angel appears from the altar in heaven with power over fire. He communicates to the first angel, "Thrust in your sharp sickle and gather the clusters of the vine of the earth, for her grapes are fully ripe." The time is now. The hour of judgment has come upon the enemies of God.

We should keep in mind that this is not the final judgment of mankind, but God's judgment against the beasts and their followers – "against the city." Final judgment will come in Revelation 20:11-15).

"So the angel thrust his sickle into the earth and gathered the vine of the earth, and threw it into the great winepress of the wrath of God. And the winepress was trampled outside the city, and blood came out of the winepress, up to the horses' bridles, for one thousand six hundred furlongs" (vv.19-20).

The forthcoming judgment is depicted as the "great winepress of the wrath of God." Here is how the wine of God's wrath which is to be outpoured is made. John foresaw the winepress as being trampled – i.e., the grapes in the winepress – outside the city (beyond the city limits of Rome). Blood overflowed from the winepress "up to the horses' bridles, for one thousand six hundred furlongs" – roughly 4-5 feet deep for 200 miles. As with other images in Revelation, we would do well not to consider this literally exact. It signifies the vast number of souls pressed in the winepress of God's judgment. Such was the extent of the forces arrayed for battle against the Lord's church. It would have seemed insurmountable. Yet, with God all things are possible (Matthew 19:26) and only by Him will victory be attained.

Application for Today

The first century church faced tremendous odds in dire circumstances. Their perseverance puts to shame the one who claims, "Oh, if conditions were only better, what a Christian I could be!" When facing persecution from foes powerful and ruthless, these brethren could have doubted the presence of God. Such was the case for many first century Christians. Yet, we find the Lamb standing triumphant, ready to engage the enemy, surrounded by a host of saints who likewise are ready to do His will.

Revelation 14 presents to us in vivid visions the unstoppable and decisive judgment of God against the wickedness of humanity and the strategies of the devil. However, His judgment would not come without first granting the opportunity for lost souls to repent. The gospel would be preached, the rebellious would be warned, and the impenitent would be judged.

We know this to be true of God's judgments throughout the scriptures. We also know this to be true of God's ultimate judgment of the world. The two-edged sword that is the word of God provides both the promises and salvation of the gospel and the warnings of retribution and punishment for the wicked. Mankind may have many excuses to offer on the day of final judgment, but as was the case with Rome, he cannot say he was not offered a better ending and that he was not forewarned of the greatest of the wrath of God.

Chapter Fifteen

In chapter fourteen John witnessed the climax of the conflict with Rome before it occurred. Chapter fifteen will continue John's visions from the previous chapter and serve to introduce the actual judgments of God as they are poured out through seven bowls of wrath. The victory has been foretold and the devastation of Rome's defeat has been foreseen. Now, the commencement of the war will be described. The wine has been mixed and now it is time to pour.

Special attention should once again be given to the realm from whence the war commences – heaven. The battle on earth began in the heavenly places (Ephesians 6:12; Revelation 12:7 ff.). It is a spiritual war conducted on earth. The forces of God and the forces of the devil are contesting over the future of the church, the kingdom of God on earth. The events which transpire on earth extend far beyond the natural realm. What can be witnessed by humanity is the manifestation and confirmation of the spiritual war being waged for the souls of men.

Prelude to the Bowl Judgments (vv. 1-8)

"Then I saw another sign in heaven, great and marvelous: seven angels having the seven last plagues, for in them the wrath of God is complete" (v.1).

Seven angels will carry the seven last plagues to complete the wrath of God on Rome. The scene pictured in this verse will continue into chapter sixteen. These seven plagues will complete

God's wrath on Domitian's reign and once for all end his persecution of the church. Consider the confidence with which these words are spoken. No doubt or speculation is heard or hinted at in this proclamation. God's mind is settled. His wrath will be such as to end Domitian's reign. And, there is nothing Satan, Domitian, or the imperial cult can do to stop it.

"And I saw something like a sea of glass mingled with fire, and those who have the victory over the beast, over his image and over his mark and over the number of his name, standing on the sea of glass, having harps of God" (v.2).

In contrast to the turbulent and chaotic sea from which the beast arose, the saints stand on a sea of glass. It is calm, still, and sound. Moreover, it is mingled with fire. Fire is essential to the process of making glass. Through a painstaking process the unstable element of sand becomes the stable element of glass when mingled with fire.

Perhaps a greater significance is being alluded to in this vision. The saints passed through the fire of persecution to stand before God on this marvelous sea of glass. It is beautiful, heavenly. Yet, the platform has been forged by fire. Truly, "We must through many tribulations enter the kingdom of God" (Acts 14:22).

"They sing the song of Moses, the servant of God, and the song of the Lamb, saying 'Great and marvelous are Your works, Lord God Almighty! Just and true are Your ways, O King of the saints!' Who shall not fear You, O Lord, and glorify Your name? For You alone are holy. For all nations shall come and worship before You, For Your judgments have been manifested'" (vv.3-4)

The songs being sang point to their Jewish heritage (the song of Moses), and their Christian faith (the song of the Lamb). As we have noted in our comments on the 144,000, we are again reminded of the Jewish origins of the church of Christ. Moreover, included in this number would have been the faithful of Israel who were ultimately redeemed by the blood of Christ (cf. Romans 3:21ff; Hebrews 9:15).

They praise God for His works that are great and marvelous and for His ways which are just and true. He is almighty, King of the saints. He alone is holy and deserving of worship from all nations. His judgments have been made known.

"After these things I looked, and behold, the temple of the tabernacle of the testimony in heaven was opened. And out of the temple came the seven angels having the seven plagues, clothed in pure bright linen, and having their chests girded with golden bands" (vv.5-6).

Angels adorned with girded chests of golden bands proceed from the heavenly temple. Many times, throughout scripture God's dwelling is referred to as His temple, or His heavenly temple. We have seen this in Revelation as well.

These angels are proceeding from the presence of God having seven plagues which will be poured out from seven bowls of wrath in the next chapter.

"Then one of the four living creatures gave to the seven angels seven golden bowls full of the wrath of God who lives forever and ever" (v.7).

In addition to introducing the seven bowls in this verse, the eternality of God is restated. Throughout Revelation we are reminded of the eternal nature of the Godhead. Very few people can speak of the reign of Domitian, and the empire of Rome vanished centuries ago. Yet, God lives forever, Jesus remains the name above every name, the Holy Spirit's inspired word is the most read book in the history of the world, and the church presses on.

"The temple was filled with smoke from the glory of God and from His power, and no one was able to enter the temple till the seven plagues of the seven angels were completed" (v.8).

We find similar scenes in the OT temple (cf. Exodus 40:34-35; 1 Kings 8:10-11; 2 Chronicles 5:13). "The description may be a collective echo of similar OT descriptions of God's presence in the earthly temple."[15]

However, Ezekiel 10:2-4 may provide more understanding for the nature of this scene than all other references. In that passage, the angels of Ezekiel's first vision have reappeared. The man clothed in linen who had marked the remnant in Jerusalem is instructed to scatter coals of fire upon the city to signify its destruction by fire. Just as in Revelation, God's angels were there to assist Him in executing His judgment. "The Ezekiel 10 scene is an introduction to an announcement of judgment, which brings it even closer to the function of the similar vision in Revelation 15 so that the former becomes analogous to the latter."[16]

Angels will also be present in the Lord's return and destruction of earth. The archangel will signal the Lord's return with a shout (1 Thessalonians 4:16). Angels will sweep the earth gathering the elect (Matthew 13:39; Jude 14) and separating the wicked from the righteous (Matthew 13:40–41).

Application for Today

Chapter fifteen speaks of many of the most glorious attributes of God. We must remember these things. This chapter reminds us of the beauty of heaven and perhaps of the difficulty with which the righteous will be saved (1 Peter 4:18). Perhaps most of all, this chapter speaks to us of the deliberate wrath of God. He makes no

---

[15] Beale, 1134.
[16] Ibid.

hasty or rash decisions to judge even the most sinful men. All these things are to be kept in mind and heart as we contemplate our relationship with the eternal Almighty.

Chapter Sixteen

Chapter sixteen concludes the series of seals, trumpets, and bowls (vials) signifying God's judgments on those who persecuted His church. Just as the trumpets echoed the plagues of judgment in Exodus, so too will the bowls of wrath (cf. Psalm 78:44 ff.).

The bowls of wrath are poured out on Rome, "upon the men who had the mark of the beast and those who worshiped his image" (v.2). We will also find Armageddon mentioned for the first time in this chapter. Keep in mind that studying Revelation within its first century context will remain a key to interpreting and correctly understanding the meaning of the seven bowls of wrath.

The punishments poured out upon Rome represent their "moral, intellectual, religious, and spiritual environment."[1] It would be extremely difficult, even impossible, to attempt to attach these plagues with literal events in Rome's history. Just as with the plagues of chapter eight, we must keep in mind that these judgments are intended to mirror the Exodus plagues and symbolize God's punishments on Rome for their many perversions.

In many ways, "the divine judicial hardening of mankind due to sin and rebellion against God is in view."[2] God is delivering them over to reap what they have sown. They preferred to serve Satan, the beast, and the false prophet, now we will see how that service became a curse rather than a blessing. They will receive

---

[1] Coffman, 349.
[2] Ibid., 350.

their "just due" which is the total pollution of their moral, intellectual, spiritual, and religious environment signified in these plagues.[3]

First Bowl: Loathsome Sores (vv. 1-2)

"Then I heard a loud voice from the temple saying to the seven angels, 'Go and pour out the bowls of the wrath of God on the earth.' So the first went and poured out his bowl upon the earth, and a foul and loathsome sore came upon the men who had the mark of the beast and those who worshiped his image" (vv.1-2).

Seven angels are directed from the temple in heaven (cf. Isaiah 66:6) to pour out the bowls of God's wrath and judgment "upon the men who had the mark of the beast and those who worshiped his image." The passage refers to the Romans who had been practicing emperor worship as part of the Roman imperial cult. They are plagued with foul and loathsome sores modeled after the Egyptian plague of boils (Exodus 9:8-11).

"These are the things which specially characterize them and mark them off from other men. There are then some evils which afflict those who give themselves over to wickedness but do not affect other men."[4] Especially is this true with sins of a sexual nature and the physical plagues to be endured through their transmitted diseases. Also, sins rooted in addiction to drugs and alcohol can cause numerous physical calamities to the body. Indeed, "the way of the unfaithful is hard" (Proverbs 13:15).

We should continue to observe how this first plague was not intended to destroy these perverse and rebellious souls but to bring them to their senses and repentance. The judgements poured out

---

[3] Ibid., 351.
[4] Morris, 193. E

from the bowls of wrath will intensify just as the judgments revealed through the opening of the seven seals and the sounding of the seven trumpets. However, after ample time and opportunity for correction is granted, ultimate destruction will come.

Second Bowl: The Sea Turns to Blood (v. 3)

"Then the second angel poured out his bowl on the sea, and it became blood as of a dead man; and every living creature in the sea died" (v.3).

When the second trumpet sounded (8:8-9), the sea turned to blood. The waters and life of the sea can provide food and nourishment and wealth to humankind, or they can be turned to blood and death. One of the ways the sea was turned to blood, figuratively speaking, was through naval warfare, piracy, and slave trade.

Rome's allies, the Cilician pirates, supplied much of their slave labor. Not only were vessels attacked at sea, but these pirates were apt at "masquerading as legitimate merchants to lure unsuspecting citizens toward their ships. The pirates would announce some quantity of goods they had for sale, wait until a good number of people had either boarded the ship or gathered near to it, and then haul as many as possible aboard and sail away...Rome did nothing to stop this practice or curtail piracy in any way because now they were benefiting from it. The Cilician pirates were, in effect, working for the Roman Empire."[5]

The judgments of God against Jerusalem from the second trumpet are being repeated here (cf. 8:8). This repetition will follow in the third bowl as well.

Third Bowl: The Waters Turn to Blood (vv. 4-7)

---

[5] Joshua J. Mark, "Pirates in the Ancient Mediterranean" (World History Encyclopedia, Online, Published August 19, 2019).

"Then the third angel poured out his bowl on the rivers and springs of water, and they became blood. And I heard the angel of the waters saying: 'You are righteous, O Lord, The One who is and who was and who is to be, Because You have judged these things. For they have shed the blood of saints and prophets, And You have given them blood to drink. For it is their just due.' And I heard another from the altar saying, 'Even so, Lord God Almighty, true and righteous are Your judgments'" (vv.4-7).

Just as with the sounding of the third trumpet (8:10-11), the fresh waters are plagued. The meaning of this plague is also intended to mirror God's judgment upon Egypt (Exodus 7:14 ff.). No longer will the rivers and streams provide fresh water. Just as they have shed blood, those bearing the mark of the beast will be made to drink blood. The response from the angel helps to explain the meaning of the third bowl.

Note: "You are righteous, O Lord, The One who is and who was and who is to be, Because You have judged these things. For they have shed the blood of saints and prophets, And You have given them blood to drink. For it is their just due."

God was rendering to them according to their deeds. They shed the blood of the saints, now they will be made to drink blood. God's judgment is righteous in repaying their "just due." Those who shed innocent blood in their devotion to the beast will be forced to reap what they have sown. They have lived by the sword, they will die by the sword (Matthew 26:52).

Fourth Bowl: Men Are Scorched (vv. 8-9)

"Then the fourth angel poured out his bowl on the sun, and power was given to him to scorch men with fire. And men were scorched with great heat, and they blasphemed the name of

God who has power over these plagues; and they did not repent and give Him glory" (vv.8-9).

There is no darkness or shade, just immense, scorching fire, and heat – a prelude to their eternity! Pictured here is a waterless world filled with immense fire and heat. Such was Christ's depiction of hell in His story of the rich man and Lazarus (Luke 16:23-24).

The result of their preview of eternal torment: they blasphemed the name of God, and they did not repent and give Him glory. Each of these judgments is leading toward their ultimate end. With each bowl of wrath an opportunity to repent remains, but they would not. As with Pharoah and Egypt, each plague only served to further harden the hearts of the rebellious.

Fifth Bowl: Darkness and Pain (vv. 10-11)

"Then the fifth angel poured out his bowl on the throne of the beast, and his kingdom became full of darkness; and they gnawed their tongues because of the pain. They blasphemed the God of heaven because of their pains and their sores, and did not repent of their deeds" (vv.10-11).

The fifth bowl brought darkness and continued pain. Once more the Exodus plagues are herein mirrored (Exodus 10:21 ff.). This plague serves to predict their eternity. Hell will be a place of outer darkness with weeping and gnashing of teeth (Matthew 22:13). God is allowing them to reap as they have sown, suffer the consequences of sin in this life, and offer the opportunity to realize the tremendous effects of sin so that He might bring them to repentance and avoid these effects for eternity. Yet, "They blasphemed the God of heaven because of their pains and their sores, and did not repent of their deeds."

Sixth Bowl: Euphrates Dried Up (vv. 12-16)

"Then the sixth angel poured out his bowl on the great river Euphrates, and its water was dried up, so that the way of the kings from the east might be prepared. And I saw three unclean spirits like frogs coming out of the mouth of the dragon, out of the mouth of the beast, and out of the mouth of the false prophet. For they are spirits of demons, performing signs, which go out to the kings of the earth and of the whole world, to gather them to the battle of that great day of God Almighty. 'Behold, I am coming as a thief. Blessed is he who watches, and keeps his garments, lest he walk naked and they see his shame.' And they gathered them together to the place called in Hebrew, Armageddon" (vv.12-16).

Here we have a plague unique to the bowls of wrath with the drying of the Euphrates River. It was dried for a purpose, "so that the way of the kings from the east might be prepared." The reason for the preparation of the way is so that the kings of the earth could be gathered for battle at the place called "Armageddon." God is providing the way for the Dragon's allies to be assembled and collectively destroyed. As in Joel 2:11 and Zephaniah 1:14, when Israel's enemies are gathered and destroyed, this also is called "the great day of God Almighty."[6]

Similarly, in 1Kings 22, a false spirit in the mouth of Ahab's prophets led him into war to be slain.[7] The kings of the earth are here deceived into battle by "three unclean spirits like frogs coming out of the mouth of the dragon, out of the mouth of the beast, and out of the mouth of the false prophet. For they are spirits of demons, performing signs."

---

[6] For further reference, another OT parallel can be found in Zechariah 12-14.
[7] Beale, 1136.

We are again reminded of one of the Exodus plagues in the plague of the frogs (Exodus 8:1-15; Psalm 104:30). Just as Pharoah had his magicians, the imperial cult had its lying priests. The spirit of demons performing signs is frequently mentioned in the NT. The frogs symbolize something unclean and defiled. Their work is one of unrighteous deception as they are used by the devil to harden men's hearts into warring against the saints (2 Thessalonians 2:9).

The place of Armageddon and the battle which ensued there must be considered with the same approach taken when interpreting the previous signs of this chapter. Supporting this view is the fact that no literal place known as Armageddon ever existed. Armageddon in Hebrew translates as Mt. Megiddo. There is no mountain of Megiddo. It must be considered as a metaphorical rather than a literal location.

Megiddo is an ancient city located in northern Israel in the Jezreel Valley. It was an important city and was the site of many battles. Its history serves to add meaning to the interpretation of this text. Israel was attacked by enemies at Megiddo, also in connection to the Euphrates River (cf. 2 Kings 23; 2 Chronicles 35; see also Zechariah 12).

Just as Deborah's forces were greatly outnumbered at Megiddo – and if not for the mighty hand of God would have been destroyed (Judges 4, 5) – so too must the Lord be trusted to deliver His saints from Domitian persecution. God is willing to keep His covenant with His people. He is faithful. Even though we may find ourselves in times of great persecution from an enemy that has greatly outnumbered us, we will be victorious. Christians are indeed "kept by the power of God" (1 Peter 1:5). He will conquer and banish the adversary – saving His people at last.

Christians should view the Battle of Armageddon in context of the spiritual war being waged – good vs. evil, the church vs. Rome, the apostles vs. the imperial cult, God vs. Satan. It is a spiritual conflict and earth is the battlefield. The war is being waged in the hearts and minds of men and therefore, is executed in the deeds of mankind.

Seventh Bowl: The Earth Utterly Shaken (vv. 17-21)

"Then the seventh angel poured out his bowl into the air, and a loud voice came out of the temple of heaven, from the throne, saying, 'It is done!' And there were noises and thunderings and lightnings; and there was a great earthquake, such a mighty and great earthquake as had not occurred since men were on the earth. Now the great city was divided into three parts, and the cities of the nations fell. And great Babylon was remembered before God, to give her the cup of the wine of the fierceness of His wrath. Then every island fled away, and the mountains were not found. And great hail from heaven fell upon men, each hailstone about the weight of a talent. Men blasphemed God because of the plague of the hail, since that plague was exceedingly great" (vv.17-21).

Once more we read the language of divine judgment. These verses provide vivid apocalyptic terms of judgment and destruction leading to the ultimate victory of God's people over their enemies. "Noises, thunderings, and lightnings" denote acts of divine judgment throughout scripture and the book of Revelation, as do earthquakes (cf. Ezekiel 38:19-22).

The city called "Babylon" is divided and allied cities fall. Here we have the overthrow of Rome pictured and more will be said of its fall in the forthcoming chapters. That the "islands fled away" and the "mountains were not found" is language signifying societal upheaval as part of the divine judgment. The hail from heaven reminds us of the Exodus plague of hail (Exodus 9), but its size emphasizes the severity of the judgment.

What is the result of God's judgment? "Men blasphemed God because of the plague of the hail, since that plague was exceedingly great." Here we see that this is not the final judgment of the world, but the judgment of Rome. At the final judgment, none will blaspheme, but all will confess (Romans 14:11). Throughout the seven bowls of wrath, sinful man was given opportunity and motivation to repent through punishment. However, rather than repent and obey God, these men who wore the beast's mark increasingly hardened the hearts and entrenched themselves in their foolish pride while anticipating a deliverance that would never come.

Application for Today

Let us offer a personal application from this chapter. What must we do when our sins find us out and we are made to reap what we have sown? Did our Lord not teach us to repent or perish (Luke 13:3, 5)? Did John not also teach us of a sin unto death (1 John 5:16)?

Repentance is a change of will that produces a change of life and is brought about by godly motivations. Three godly motivations which induce repentance are (1) godly sorrow (2 Corinthians 7:10); (2) the fear of the Lord (Jude 22); (3) the goodness of the Lord (Romans 2:4). We should not consider sorrow for sin, fear of the Lord, nor the goodness of the Lord to be repentance, but such emotions serve as motivating factors which will induce the sinner to repent. As stated, repentance is a change of life, not the causes which bring about the change.

The message of repentance is one of the great sources of hope for the human soul. God is gracious in granting us the opportunity for "repentance unto life" (Acts 11:18). He is longsuffering, not willing that any should perish, but that all should come to repent-ance (2 Peter 3:9).

Sin is disgraceful and disappointing. Hardness of heart toward sin is damnable. Let us strive to have godly sorrow leading to re-pentance (2 Corinthians 7:10), humble ourselves, and find grace in the eyes of God (James 4:6-10).

Chapter Seventeen

Chapter seventeen is a continuation of chapter sixteen and back to chapter fourteen, as it foretells the destruction of Rome, Babylon, the Mother of Harlots. This chapter will depict Rome as the great harlot sitting upon a scarlet and purple beast. Much symbolism is contained in this relatively short chapter. However, for the reader's benefit much of it can be explained from within the text of Revelation itself.

Before proceeding to our comments upon the text, let us consider a fascinating cross-reference from Daniel 7. Daniel saw "the four winds of heaven were stirring up the Great Sea. And four great beasts came up from the sea, each different from the other" (vv.2-3). The beasts are described in all their fury and terror and represent coming kingdoms of mankind. The most dreaded beast was the last of the four and depicted Rome.

Daniel's dream also portrayed a vision of "the Ancient of Days." Seated upon His throne, "His garment was white as snow, And the hair of His head was like pure wool. His throne was a fiery flame, Its wheels a burning fire; A fiery stream issued And came forth from before Him. A thousand thousands ministered to Him; Ten thousand times ten thousand stood before Him" (v.9 ff.).

As one beast (kingdom) was destroyed, and "the rest of the beasts, they had their dominion taken away," the Ancient of Days, "was given dominion and glory and a kingdom, That all peoples, nations, and languages should serve Him. His dominion is an everlasting dominion, Which shall not pass away, And His kingdom the one Which shall not be destroyed" (v.14).

While suffering grief, Daniel was assured that the "saints of the Most High shall receive the kingdom, and possess the kingdom forever, even forever and ever" (v.18). He saw that the fourth beast (kingdom) "was making war against the saints, and prevailing against them, until the Ancient of Days came, and a judgment was made in favor of the saints of the Most High, and the time came for the saints to possess the kingdom" (v.19 ff.).

As we consider Revelation seventeen, we are reading the fulfillment of Daniel 7. Four kingdoms rose and fell according to the prophecies of Daniel from the time of Nebuchadnezzar's Babylon. History's accounting of these kingdoms follows: Babylon, Medo-Persia, Greece, and Rome. During the days of the fourth kingdom (Rome), God's kingdom would be established (cf. Daniel 2:44). However, it was not without difficulty. Rome spoke "pompous words against the Most High" and persecuted the saints. Daniel foretells the events which occurred during the life of John, the early church, and the book of Revelation. This section in Daniel foreshadowed the events now being described in the book of Revelation.

The Scarlet Woman and the Scarlet Beast (vv.1-6)

"Then one of the seven angels who had the seven bowls came and talked with me, saying to me, 'Come, I will show you the judgment of the great harlot who sits on many waters, with whom the kings of the earth committed fornication, and the inhabitants of the earth were made drunk with the wine of her fornication'" (vv.1-2).

Our comments on these verses will begin with an interpretation of the symbols. Once more, John was "in the Spirit" (cf. 1:10) and an angel is used to "show" John the vision of the judgment to come. The judgment in view is not the final judgment of the world, as it is to come in Revelation 20:11-15. The "great harlot" is later revealed as being "that great city which reigns over the kings of the earth" (v.18). In the context of the first century, this could only refer to Rome. The "many waters" upon which she sits is later revealed as being the "peoples, multitudes, nations, and tongues" over which Rome rules (v.15). If we put this into literal terms, it might read something like this: "Come, I will show you the judgment of Rome who rules over many peoples, multitudes, nations, and tongues."

The reason stated for Rome's judgment is that she has "committed fornication with the kings of the earth, and the inhabitants of the earth were made drunk with the wine of her fornication." Similar language is used to describe the spiritual wickedness and judgment of Tyre (Isaiah 23:15-18) and Nineveh (Nahum 3:3-4). Using these OT cross-references helps us to understand that the harlotry and fornication mentioned is of a spiritual nature and represents the seduction of false religion. Rome was certainly guilty of this sin by seducing the nations under their control to worship their emperors past and present.

"So he carried me away in the Spirit into the wilderness. And I saw a woman sitting on a scarlet beast which was full of names of blasphemy, having seven heads and ten horns. The woman was arrayed in purple and scarlet, and adorned with gold and precious stones and pearls, having in her hand a golden cup full of abominations and the filthiness of her fornication. And on her forehead a name was written:

MYSTERY, BABYLON THE GREAT,
THE MOTHER OF HARLOTS
AND OF THE ABOMINATIONS
OF THE EARTH."

The wilderness or "desert place" to which John traveled describes a place uninhabited by man.[1] The wilderness is also the place where the woman of Revelation 12 found safety from the

---

[1] A similar scene is found in Isaiah 21:1 ff.

dragon (cf. 12:14). As previously noted, the scenes of chapter 12 denote God's protection over His eternal plan to save man. The "offspring" of the women are those who keep His commandments, i.e., Christians. They are protected from the devil in the wilderness having fled from Jerusalem (chap. 11-12).

Where might the church flee for rest from persecution in the Roman world of the first century? In this place of quite seclusion and rest from the dragon, John sees "a woman sitting on a scarlet beast which was full of names of blasphemy, having seven heads and ten horns." The devil has found his way into the wilderness (the Gentile world) and the woman is **"drunk with the blood of the saints and with the blood of the martyrs of Jesus. And when I saw her, I marveled with great amazement" (vv. 3-6).**

Chapter seventeen will provide the student of Revelation with several interesting contrasts between good and evil. God's salvation – pure religion – is described as a virgin in chapter 12. Here, we find the devil's plan of destruction described as **"a woman was arrayed in purple and scarlet, and adorned with gold and precious stones and pearls, having in her hand a golden cup full of abominations and the filthiness of her fornication."** She is the mother of harlots and of the abominations of the earth. Whereas the woman of chapter 12 is the mother of those who keep the commandments of the Lord.

Being evil can be a lucrative business and bring much earthly power. The harlot is **"arrayed in purple and scarlet, and adorned with gold and precious stones and pearls, having in her hand a golden cup..."** Roma, the female goddess of Rome also seems to provide an interesting parallel to this vision. The devil is using the power, wealth, and influence of Rome to martyr the saints of God.

The beast on which the woman sits is described as scarlet in color and **"full of names of blasphemy, having seven heads and ten horns."** The beast will **"ascend out of the bottomless pit and go into perdition" (v. 8).** In Revelation 20:1-3, 7-10, the beast is revealed as Satan. The statement of this passage is looking ahead to Satan's scheme and what will come near the end of time. In contrast to Him "who is, was, and is to come" the beast "was, is not, and will ascend." Christ will descend from heaven while the beast will ascend from the bottomless pit.

The scarlet beast is full of blasphemy. He has seven heads and ten horns. The seven heads are seven mountains on which the woman sits. Mountains are symbolic of kingdoms in the OT (cf. Jeremiah 51:25; Ezekiel 35:3; Zechariah 4:7).[2] That there are *seven* mountains or "kingdoms" denotes the completeness of the rule the beast has had over the kingdoms of the earth. The horns are later revealed to be kings who are allied with the beast (v.12).

If we put this scene into literal language, it might read something like this: "I saw Rome in all its wealth and splendor sitting upon Satan, being carried by him as a woman upon a beast. All the earthly kingdoms with her, and they were powerful. And they were all guilty of murdering the saints of God. They were speaking blasphemous words, benefiting, and boasting about what they were doing. But I was assured that their end would come."

The Meaning of the Woman and the Beast (vv.7-18)

"But the angel said to me, 'Why did you marvel? I will tell you the mystery of the woman and of the beast that carries her, which has the seven heads and the ten horns. The beast that you saw was, and is not, and will ascend out of the bottomless pit and go to perdition. And those who dwell on the earth will marvel, whose names are not written in the Book of

---

[2] Beal, 1138.

Life from the foundation of the world, when they see the beast that was, and is not, and yet is" (vv.7-8).

In verse 7, the angel begins explaining the vision to John. Relying on chapter 20 for our explanation, we realize that the beast is Satan. The angel continues, **"Here is the mind which has wisdom: The seven heads are seven mountains on which the woman sits. There are also seven kings. Five have fallen, one is, and the other has not yet come. And when he comes, he must continue a short time. The beast that was, and is not, is himself also the eighth, and is of the seven, and is going to perdition" (vv.9-11).**

Concerning the seven kings, "five have fallen, one is, and the other has not yet come." The number of kings totals seven. And while the number seven signifies completeness in apocalyptic prophecy, something deeper and more literal may be denoted. Five kings/kingdoms who were guilty of persecuting the people of God have fallen. Commentators have attempted to connect these kings with Roman emperors but fall short as there had been more than five emperors by the time of Revelation. However, if we look back into the OT, we will find exactly five world powers who persecuted the people of God – Egypt, Assyria, Babylon, Persia, and Greece. Each of these had fallen by the first century. One kingdom "is" and that would be Rome. One is to come, and it is mentioned in Revelation 20:7 as Gog and Magog.

Consider also, "The beast that was, and is not, is himself also the eighth, and is of the seven, and is going to perdition." Here Satan is among the seven kings/kingdoms. Truly, wherever and whenever an earthly kingdom exists that is intent on destroying the people of God, Satan is among them.

"The ten horns which you saw are ten kings who have received no kingdom as yet, but they receive authority for one

hour as kings with the beast. These are of one mind, and they will give their power and authority to the beast. These will make war with the Lamb, and the Lamb will overcome them, for He is Lord of lords and King of kings; and those who are with Him are called, chosen, and faithful" (vv.12-14).

The symbol of the ten horns likely refers to the vassal kingdoms of Rome. They had no real dominion apart from Rome, but were allies, nonetheless, having one mind. They received power and authority from the beast (the devil) and made war with the Lamb. To war against the church is to war against the Christ (cf. Acts 9:4-5). John is assured that the Lamb will overcome them.

Another possible interpretation is that these horns refer to some of the previous emperors of Rome. Some had a longer reign and more power than others.

"Then he said to me, 'The waters which you saw, where the harlot sits, are peoples, multitudes, nations, and tongues. And the ten horns which you saw on the beast, these will hate the harlot, make her desolate and naked, eat her flesh and burn her with fire. For God has put it into their hearts to fulfill His purpose, to be of one mind, and to give their kingdom to the beast, until the words of God are fulfilled. And the woman whom you saw is that great city which reigns over the kings of the earth'" (vv.15-18).

Internal conflict among the vassal kingdoms is foretold in this passage. The angel explains, "the ten horns which you saw on the beast, these will hate the harlot, make her desolate and naked, eat her flesh and burn her with fire." Rebellion within Rome is foretold. Rebellion, revolution, civil war, and usurpation blanketed the history of Rome from the time of its beginning until its demise. Moreover, a brief survey of Rome's history over the next four centuries will uncover scores of internal conflicts in the empire. "For

God has put it into their hearts to fulfill His purpose, to be of one mind, and to give their kingdom to the beast, until the words of God are fulfilled." Amen.

Application for Today

From the Garden of Eden down through the stream of time even until the present hour, it may be observed without exception that when good is found in the world so also is evil. Light and darkness co-exist. God's light shines in darkness and will ultimately prevail over the darkness.

In the chapter just concluded we have observed the interesting and contrasting symbol of two women. One represents God's plan and is virtuous and pure (chap. 12). The one in this chapter represents Satan's plan and is unfaithful and treacherous. Much like Solomon's contrasts of wise and foolish women in Proverbs, the use of personification in Revelation helps us to identify the contrast between good and evil. Mankind rests between the two. Sound doctrine which cannot be denied tugs at the light residing in man's conscience, while the devil's blasphemies pull him toward darkness. Souls of every age must decide which voice will prevail personally. Ultimately, God will prevail eternally as He has throughout history. However, each person must decide if He is to prevail personally.

For those who allow the devil's blasphemies to prevail, this chapter provides their sad existence and demise. Just as with the ten horns representing kingdoms, their existence is one of internal conflict. Just as the five kingdoms which fell, their demise is sure. The Lamb will prevail. The fate of Rome and every empire on the ash heap of history which defied the living God illustrates this. God's message in Revelation must be heard and kept in the heart of every individual person, nation, and government. Truly, "blessed is he."

Chapter Eighteen

Chapter eighteen continues the apocalyptic description of the fall of Domitian's Rome from chapters sixteen and seventeen. The conclusion to this portion of Revelation will be provided in chapter nineteen. An angel will announce the fall of Babylon "the great city" – i.e., Rome. Rome's fall is precipitated by its wickedness. The cause for its destruction was given in the previous chapter. This chapter will focus primarily on the results. Rome's demise is settled in heaven, and it will be told as though it has already occurred, reminding us of the surety and absoluteness of God's word.

Concerning Rome's fall, Revelation is depicting how "Rome fell from its position as the world's leading city of commerce and wealth and as the capital of a world empire whose religious life centered upon pagan god-Caesar worship."[1]

In prophetic manner, the chapter describes "the ultimate collapse of a monstrous antichristian world order determined to defeat the purpose of God in history. It is not personal vindictiveness but loyalty to God and His great redemptive purpose that moves the seer to deliver a prophetic oracle in the accepted literary genre of his predecessors."[2]

The Fall of Babylon the Great (vv.1-8)

"After these things I saw another angel coming down from heaven, having great authority, and the earth was illuminated with his glory" (v.1).

---

[1] Harkrider, 208.
[2] Mounce, 321.

The great authority of the angel has no doubt been vested in him by God. He is granted the authority necessary to proclaim the destruction of Rome. The earth is illuminated with his glory, signifying that he has come from God. He is reflecting the radiance and glory of God.[3] The expression indicates that this angel is particularly important.[4]

"And he cried mightily with a loud voice, saying, 'Babylon the great is fallen, is fallen, and has become a dwelling place of demons, a prison for every foul spirit, and a cage for every unclean and hated bird!'" (v.2)

The angel's proclamation echoes that of Isaiah 21:9, "Babylon is fallen, is fallen! And all the carved images of her gods He has broken to the ground." Rome's fall is said to have already occurred. John is not writing historically, but prophetically. Paul noted that God "calls those things which do not exist as though they did" (Romans 4:17). John is doing that here. "The city's doom is still future but it is so certain that it can be spoken of as already accomplished."[5] The culmination of Rome's destruction occurs when the beast and false prophet are finally defeated (see 19:19-21).

The great city will become desolate and (1) a dwelling place of demons; (2) a prison for every foul spirit and (3) a cage for every unclean and hated bird. It is not a habitable place for Christians to be sure! It is a dwelling place of devils. When in an environment such as this, Christians must be on guard against the pervasiveness of worldly lusts and temptations to do evil. It is a prison for every foul spirit. One can easily get the picture that Satan has not only a foothold in the city but is at home there. His demons are caged

---

[3] Ibid., 322.

[4] Morris, *Revelation*, 214.

[5] Ibid., 215.

there, even "haunting" the place.[6] It is a society devoid of God and all that is good and true and right. One can picture vultures and the like lurking and perched over the city. The stench of death in the air. "Such birds commonly haunt deserted places, and this will be the significance of the term."[7] Rome would become a deserted place when compared to her former glory.

"For all the nations have drunk of the wine of the wrath of her fornication, the kings of the earth have committed fornication with her, and the merchants of the earth have become rich through the abundance of her luxury" (v.3).

The angel now summarizes the reason for the city's condition. (1) All the nations have drunk of the wine of the wrath of her fornication (cf. Hosea 4:10; Jeremiah 3:2). (2) The kings of the earth have committed fornication with her. And (3) the merchants of the earth have become rich through the abundance of her luxury.

The nations under her sway have been corrupted by her and have been intoxicated by her wicked influence. The kings over these nations are "in bed" with her. They are active participants and share in her sin. The merchants (businessmen) have no problem with her wickedness as they are profiting financially from it. The riches they have accumulated have blinded their eyes to the evil which made them rich. For them, the ends justify the means.

"And I heard another voice from heaven saying, 'Come out of her, my people, lest you share in her sins, and lest you receive of her plagues" (v.4).

As with Lot in Sodom, the people of God are instructed to leave the wicked city and all her evil influence. It was no time to come to terms with the wickedness surrounding them or to compromise with the evil doers. We find the instruction to flee from

---

[6] Ibid.
[7] Ibid.

evil throughout the NT as well (cf. 2 Corinthians 6:14; Ephesians 5:11; 1 Timothy 5:22). The idea conveyed is clearly one of separation. Be separate from the evil in this city and thus avoid the destruction to come upon it. Join with them, however, and their fate will be yours.

"The persecuted church has always faced the temptation to compromise with worldliness and thus ease the tension of living in a hostile environment. Separation is the order of the day: sometimes physical, always ideological."[8]

"For her sins have reached to heaven, and God has remembered her iniquities" (v.5).

A similar statement is found in Jeremiah 51:9 concerning Babylon in the OT. An OT statement from Moses comes to mind when reading this verse, "Be sure your sin will find you out" (Numbers 32:23). And "God will not acquit the wicked" (Exodus 23:7; Nahum 1:3).

"Render to her just as she rendered to you, and repay her double according to her works; in the cup which she has mixed, mix double for her" (v.6).

The charge here is likely to the avenging angels soon to act. The pronoun "you" is an addition found in later manuscripts. Rome is soon to experience a double portion of the grief and pain she has inflicted on the saints (cf. Jeremiah 50:29). God is rendering to Rome their "just due" (16:6).

"In the measure that she glorified herself and lived luxuriously, in the same measure give her torment and sorrow; for she says in her heart, 'I sit as queen, and am no widow, and will not see sorrow.' Therefore her plagues will come in one day—death and mourning and famine. And she will be utterly

---

[8] Mounce, 324.

burned with fire, for strong is the Lord God who judges her"' **(vv.4-8).**

Punishment will be enacted quickly – "in one day" bringing death and mourning by famine and fire. It is the Lord who is judging her. "From the viewpoint of man, the length of their reign and ultimate downfall may seem long; but from heaven's viewpoint, the time is brief in God's overall plan. The central message is that the destruction is certain and will be complete."[9]

The judgment Rome had rendered to the saints will be returned in double measure. She caused death and mourning, now she will experience it. She brought famine to God's people through economic persecution, now she will starve. She burned Christians alive, now she will burn (cf. Jeremiah 51:25 ff.).[10] "In ancient times the smoke of a burning city signaled its collapse...In the case of Rome it is the Lord God in His strength who will bring about judgment by fire."[11]

The World Mourns Babylon's Fall (vv. 9-20)

"The kings of the earth who committed fornication and lived luxuriously with her will weep and lament for her, when they see the smoke of her burning, standing at a distance for fear of her torment, saying, 'Alas, alas, that great city Babylon, that mighty city! For in one hour your judgment has come"' **(vv.9-10).**

This section of Revelation appears to be modeled after Ezekiel's lamentation over Tyre (Ezekiel 27).[12] Here we find the

---

[9] Harkrider, 208.

[10] A comparison to this passage is also found in Isaiah 47:7-8.

[11] Mounce, 327.

[12] See also the imagery of fire used in divine judgment in Isaiah 34:10; Ezekiel 28:18; 2 Thessalonians 1:8-9; 2 Peter 3:12.

world leaders lamenting over the sudden and unexpected fall of Rome, the trade center of the ancient world. The hour of persecution appears to be balanced by an hour of retribution.[13]

As the Austrians and Ottomans would have mourned the fall of Germany in World War I, the kings of the earth mourned the demise of Rome. She was their military ally. With Rome's fall came uncertainty. What would become of these kings? Who would protect them? Who would fill the void left behind?

"And the merchants of the earth will weep and mourn over her, for no one buys their merchandise anymore: merchandise of gold and silver, precious stones and pearls, fine linen and purple, silk and scarlet, every kind of citron wood, every kind of object of ivory, every kind of object of most precious wood, bronze, iron, and marble; and cinnamon and incense, fragrant oil and frankincense, wine and oil, fine flour and wheat, cattle and sheep, horses and chariots, and bodies and souls of men" (vv.11-13).

"No less than twenty-nine commodities are listed, ranging from gold, fine linen, scented wood, to cattle, slaves, and the souls of men."[14] "Scholars estimate about 10% (but possibly up to 20%) of the Roman empire's population were enslaved. This would mean, for an estimated Roman empire population of 50 million (in the first century AD) between five and ten million were enslaved. This number would have been unequally distributed across the empire, with a higher concentration of enslaved people in urban areas and in Italy."[15] The inventory is also very similar to the one found in Ezekiel 27.

---

[13] Mounce, 329.
[14] Harkrider, 209.
[15] https://www.britishmuseum.org/exhibitions/nero-man-behind-myth/slavery-ancient-rome

The merchants of the earth became rich from Roman prosperity. Their mourning could be likened to the mourning of a casino owner over the death of an addicted gambler or a drug dealer mourning the loss of the junkie. The mourning is not due to a sense of sincere grief but due to the loss of personal and financial gain.

"The fruit that your soul longed for has gone from you, and all the things which are rich and splendid have gone from you, and you shall find them no more at all" (v.14).

The mourning merchants longed for the things they stood to lose. They would be pierced through with many sorrows due to the loss of their material wealth (1 Timothy 6:9-10). Rome's power was connected to their vast wealth. To destroy the one must also include the destruction of the other.

"The merchants of these things, who became rich by her, will stand at a distance for fear of her torment, weeping and wailing, and saying, 'Alas, alas, that great city that was clothed in fine linen, purple, and scarlet, and adorned with gold and precious stones and pearls! For in one hour such great riches came to nothing.' Every shipmaster, all who travel by ship, sailors, and as many as trade on the sea, stood at a distance and cried out when they saw the smoke of her burning, saying, 'What is like this great city?'" (vv.14-18).

Each group sees Rome's fall in terms of its own interests.[16] None of Rome's riches could save her in the day of God's avenging justice. Her splendor has perished. The great city is brought to nothing. Nations which base their prestige and prominence on the world stage would do well to consider the fall of Rome.

"They threw dust on their heads and cried out, weeping and wailing, and saying, 'Alas, alas, that great city, in which

---

[16] Ibid., 331.

all who had ships on the sea became rich by her wealth! For in one hour she is made desolate"' (v.19).

The loss of wealth was devasting to those who had been made rich by Rome. Again, the lamentation draws a comparison to the lament over Tyre (Ezekiel 27). Tyre was a prominent and wealthy nation (cf. Isaiah 23:8). They had created a fortress for themselves through their wealth (2 Samuel 24:7). Yet, Tyre also delighted in the downfall of Judah. Therefore, the Lord promised their destruction. The fall of Tyre would have a ripple effect down the coastline upon all the kings and inhabitants of that region. The destruction of Tyre would be complete and without a remnant for the possibility of return. Ezekiel 27 contains a lamentation for Tyre from its merchants. It was a great kingdom filled with beauty, riches, and power. Yet, Tyre would be overthrown during the height of their wealth, prominence, and power. Such a defeat is very uncommon, but not beyond the power of the Lord. Even though they were a nation of wealth and influence, God would take this opportunity to punish them also for their sins by the hand of Nebuchadnezzar.

"Rejoice over her, O heaven, and you holy apostles and prophets, for God has avenged you on her!" (v.20).

While the kings and merchants of the earth mourn, heaven and saints rejoice. Much can be gleaned about the character of a person, institution, or civilization by observing the type of people who mourn in death.

If a funeral is filled with elderly people, it is likely the deceased was elderly as well, and so on. If the funeral is full of saints mourning the soul of a beloved person, it is likely that person was a faithful Christian. If the funeral is full of non-believers, with very few Christians in mourning, it is likely the deceased was not a Christian. And, if Christians are made to rejoice over the death of another, it is certain that person or institution was no friend of the church.

Here, "The church victorious is to rejoice that God the righteous judge has turned back the evidence laid against believers and in turn has served to bring judgment upon the accuser himself."[17] Moreover, "This is not the expression of glee over the fall of a great city or people, but a rejoicing over the defeat of evil and the victory of righteousness."[18]

The question of "How long?" (6:10-11) has been answered. "The time has now come that they should rejoice, not because the souls of men are lost, but that the cause of righteousness has at last been vindicated."[19]

Finality of Babylon's Fall (vv. 21-24)

"Then a mighty angel took up a stone like a great millstone and threw it into the sea, saying, 'Thus with violence the great city Babylon shall be thrown down, and shall not be found anymore. The sound of harpists, musicians, flutists, and trumpeters shall not be heard in you anymore. No craftsman of any craft shall be found in you anymore, and the sound of a millstone shall not be heard in you anymore. The light of a lamp shall not shine in you anymore, and the voice of bridegroom and bride shall not be heard in you anymore. For your merchants were the great men of the earth, for by your sorcery all the nations were deceived. And in her was found the blood of prophets and saints, and of all who were slain on the earth'" (vv. 21-24).

---

[17] Ibid., 332.
[18] Hailey, 369.
[19] Harkrider, 210.

An object lesson is provided to John by the angel with the casting of a millstone into the sea. Rome will be cast down in a similar manner. It will sink to rise no more. The action signifies the disappearance of Rome as a world power. The entire economy and the joys of everyday life have ceased. The description in this passage echoes several OT judgment passages as well (cf. Isaiah 24:8; Jeremiah 25:10; Ezekiel 26:13). Rome is now viewed as a deserted and lonely metropolis.[20]

"The god-Caesar system that opposed the one true God of heaven shall be found no more at all. As a spiritual Babylon which influenced the world through its wickedness, Rome satisfies this prophecy. No longer will the Lord Caesars reign and a religion that worshipped them be enforced! No longer is the persecution against God's people being controlled by this capital city of wickedness. She lost the glory of a city that ruled the world and would never again be restored to the power she once had. The arrogant, rebellious Rome of John's day will be no more at all."[21]

The reason is also stated once more: "for by your sorcery all the nations were deceived. And in her was found the blood of prophets and saints, and of all who were slain on the earth." The deception of Rome, much like with Egypt before the fall of Judah, had lulled the nations into a false sense of security, leading them to believe she was truly the "eternal city."

"By the time Revelation was written, Rome was the seat from which emanated the law of the empire. In her was authority to stop any persecution or to advance it. Therefore Rome was to blame for allowing Christians to be slain throughout the empire, thus figuratively in her was found the blood of all that were slain upon the earth."[22] Jesus made a similar statement regarding "the blood of

---

[20] Mounce, 334.
[21] Harkrider, 211.
[22] Ibid., 212.

Abel to the blood of Zechariah who perished between the altar and the temple. Yes, I say to you, it shall be required of this generation" (Luke 11:51).

Looking ahead, when the next chapter closes with the defeat of the beast, false prophets, and wicked allies, the portion of the Revelation pertaining to the destruction of Rome is completed. Chapter 20 will focus on events prior to the Lord's return and the final judgment of humanity. Chapters 21-22 will cover various facts and descriptions concerning life after earth with the new heavens and new earth.

Application for Today

It has been said that God answers prayer in three ways: yes, no, and wait. The saints were made to wait, to endure the hardship pressed upon them by Domitian. Yet, just as God delivered the church from the hands of Jewish persecutors (ch.11), He promised to deliver them from Roman oppression. His response was not immediate and explanations for this are found throughout the NT (cf. James 1:2-4; 1 Peter 5:9-10). However, when it came, His justice was meted out quickly and fully and finally.

When Rome ultimately fell, it fell forever. It went the way of Egypt, Assyria, Babylon, Persia, and Greece. The great Empire of Rome is now part of history, cast into the sea, never to rise again.

The church, however, is spreading over the face of the earth. Congregations of the Lord's church continue to be established worldwide. The gospel will continue to cover the earth as the waters cover the sea until our Lord returns. He will be worshipped and honored and praised throughout eternity. Yet, centuries have passed since anyone bowed a knee in worship to a Roman emperor. Let that settle our hearts as we serve the Lord.

Chapter Nineteen

Chapter nineteen will provide us with visions of the final defeat of Babylon (Rome), the beast (the emperor), and the false prophet (the imperial cult). Rome's allies will also be defeated. Again, we must remember the fall of Rome is described in apocalyptic form. The chapter is full of symbolism, and it will be vital to the reader's understanding of the text to interpret correctly the various symbols contained therein.

Only by remembering the content of Revelation thus far, and not straying from the context of the previous chapters, will we reach a correct interpretation of the symbolism of chapter nineteen. Our conclusions must be consistent with the immediate context, the content of the book, and the sum of scripture ultimately.

Chapter nineteen also presents the betrothal of the bride (the church) to the groom (Christ). John will continue to use the OT as the basis for what is said as many allusions to the prophetic writings and the history of the OT will be revisited.

Heaven Exults over Babylon (vv. 1-10)

"After these things I heard a loud voice of a great multitude in heaven, saying, 'Alleluia! Salvation and glory and honor and power belong to the Lord our God! For true and righteous are His judgments, because He has judged the great harlot who corrupted the earth with her fornication; and He has avenged on her the blood of His servants shed by her'" (vv.1-2).

In response to the command to "Rejoice" over the fall of Rome, the first chorus of "alleluia" is raised. It is a fitting climax to the section of Revelation which began in 13:1. The word "alleluia" is derived from the Hebrew words (*halal* and *Jah*), meaning "praise Jehovah or Yahweh" and is translated "praise the LORD" throughout the Psalms (cf. Psalm 106:48).

The Lord is praised for His salvation, glory, honor, power, and true and righteous judgments. He has avenged the blood of His servants by defeating her, proving He is worthy to be praised. The vision that began with the promise of judgment for the harlot city (17:1 ff.), now ends with the celebration of the fact.[1]

"This victory has been anticipated in the destiny of the saints who were sealed (7:11 ff.), in the story of Satan's being cast out of heaven (12:10 ff.), in the song of victory parallel to this at the seventh trumpet (11:15-18), and in the new song of the martyrs in 15:3,4. In all of these, the reign, kingdom, or authority of the Lord is promised. What has been so anticipated is now a fact."[2]

"Again they said, 'Alleluia! Her smoke rises up forever and ever!' And the twenty-four elders and the four living creatures fell down and worshiped God who sat on the throne, saying, 'Amen! Alleluia!' Then a voice came from the throne, saying, 'Praise our God, all you His servants and those who fear Him, both small and great!'" (vv.3-5)

The fate of the city is sealed with fire and smoke, as was the case with Jerusalem (11:13-19). "John's readers would perhaps recall the oracle of Isaiah against Edom in which the enemy's land is to burn night and day and 'its smoke shall go up forever' (Isaiah 34:8-10; cf. Revelation 14:11)."[3]

Again, praise is in order. This time the twenty-four elders and four living creatures join the chorus. The voice calling for the praise is likely on of the heavenly beings surrounding the throne.

---

[1] Roberts, 157.
[2] Ibid.
[3] Mounce, 338.

All of God's servants are to praise Him, both small and great (cf. Psalm 115:13). "Their future in the spiritual realm is eternal life, whereas the future of the beast and those who worshipped him and his image is as smoke rising up forever and ever, eternal punishment (14:9-11; 20:10; Matthew 25:46)."[4]

"And I heard, as it were, the voice of a great multitude, as the sound of many waters and as the sound of mighty thunderings, saying, 'Alleluia! For the Lord God Omnipotent reigns! Let us be glad and rejoice and give Him glory, for the marriage of the Lamb has come, and His wife has made herself ready.' And to her it was granted to be arrayed in fine linen, clean and bright, for the fine linen is the righteous acts of the saints" (vv.6-8).

The third chorus of "alleluia" is one of unanimous praise from a great multitude. God is praised for His established reign on the earth, "For the Lord God Omnipotent reigns!" His reign brings gladness and joy to the heart of the believer. He is to be given glory for His salvation and enduring mercy and righteousness. The kingdoms of men will not stand, but His kingdom shall endure forever. Domitian had taken for himself the title of "Lord and God." He is now defeated and the true "Lord God Almighty" remains.

Following the third alleluia chorus, is the marriage of the Lamb. In ancient times a marriage consisted of two things: a betrothal and the ceremony. The betrothal was public. One who was betrothed (espoused) was considered to be the bride even before the marriage ceremony and supper (cf. Deuteronomy 22:23-24; Matthew 1:18, 20). The passage under consideration depicts the betrothal of the church to Christ (5:6). The marriage metaphor expresses the relationship of Christ to His church as in Ephesians

---

[4] Harkrider, 214.

5:32 (cf. Matthew 22:2 ff.; Romans 7:4; 2 Corinthians 11:2). We find the metaphor used for God's relationship with Israel in the OT as well (cf. Isaiah 1:21; 50:1; 54:5-7; Jeremiah 2:2, 32; Ezekiel 16; Hosea 2:5, 19). Later in Revelation (21:2, 9), the metaphor will be fully realized in heaven. At this point, the wedding is spoken of proleptically for the period of blessedness to follow the final judgment (Revelation 21-22).

The bride had to be properly adorned for her groom when he came in his best attire, accompanied by his friends and family to receive his bride. He would come to her home and then take her to his home with festivities lasting several days. In the marriage metaphor of this chapter, the bride (the church) is adorned in "fine linen, clean and bright, for the fine linen is the righteous acts of the saints." This statement also helps to explain the attire worn by the heavenly saints throughout the book (3:4; 6:11; 7:14; 16:15). The symbol is also found in the OT (cf. Genesis 35:2; Isaiah 52:1; Zechariah 3:4). During this betrothal period, the bride must make herself ready by arraying herself in righteous apparel (cf. Ephesians 5:27; Matthew 22:1-13).

Moreover, a dowry was paid for the bride. Christ has paid the dowry by His blood (Ephesians 1:7; 5:25; Acts 20:28). The church is now sealed with the earnest payment of the Holy Spirit until the redemption of the purchase (Ephesians 1:14).

"Then he said to me, 'Write: 'Blessed are those who are called to the marriage supper of the Lamb!' And he said to me, 'These are the true sayings of God.' And I fell at his feet to worship him. But he said to me, 'See that you do not do that! I am your fellow servant, and of your brethren who have the testimony of Jesus. Worship God! For the testimony of Jesus is the spirit of prophecy'" (vv.9-10).

Here we find the fourth of the seven beatitudes in Revelation (cf. 1:3; 14:13; 16:15; 19:9; 20:6; 22:7, 14). The blessings which are bestowed in these beatitudes are true for they are the sayings of God, who cannot lie (Titus 1:2; Hebrews 6:18).

John responds to this scene by falling at the feet of the heavenly messenger to worship him. Perhaps he mistook the speaker for the Lord. The messenger's statement that he is John's "fellow servant, and of your brethren who have the testimony of Jesus" could allude to a fellow saint in heaven or to an angel. Man must be careful not to regard too highly the messenger. The worship of angels is prohibited (Colossians 2:18) as is the worship of men (Acts 10:25).

The testimony of Jesus is referred to as "the spirit of prophecy" by the messenger. Christ in the flesh is the embodiment of prophecy and the message attested by Him is the essence of prophetic proclamation. Man must worship God, the giver of prophetic revelation, and not the angel, who is merely the interpreter of visions (cf. Hebrews 1:7, 14).[5] This scene does much harm to the cultish doctrines which assert that Christ was only a chief angel and not Deity.

Christ on a White Horse (vv. 11-16)

"Now I saw heaven opened, and behold, a white horse. And He who sat on him was called Faithful and True, and in righteousness He judges and makes war. His eyes were like a flame of fire, and on His head were many crowns. He had a name written that no one knew except Himself. He was clothed with a robe dipped in blood, and His name is called The Word of God. And the armies in heaven, clothed in fine linen, white and clean, followed Him on white horses. Now out of His mouth goes a sharp sword, that with it He should strike the nations.

---

[5] Mounce, 342.

And He Himself will rule them with a rod of iron. He Himself treads the winepress of the fierceness and wrath of Almighty God. And He has on His robe and on His thigh a name written:

'KING OF KINGS AND
LORD OF LORDS.'"

For the third time, heaven opens. On this occasion, it is not for John to enter, but for Christ to exit. He appears as the great defender of God's cause in this conflict with Babylon and her allies. "The imagery and its terminology are drawn primarily from two OT sources. The first is the war hymn of Psalm 2; the second is the numerous prophetic passages describing the holy war of God in the last days (e.g., Isaiah 8:9 ff; 17:12, 24; 29:7 ff; 59:15-20; 63:1-6; Joel 3:9-21; Ezekiel 38-39)."[6]

The twelve-fold description of Christ is vivid and significant in its apocalyptic style and application.

- **He is riding white horse.** The first of the four horsemen was also seen riding a white horse (6:2). It is likely that the horseman was a depiction of Rome. The rider now is Christ. Rome was allowed to conquer as a means of defeating Jewish persecution of the church. Christ has now come forth to conquer the beast and her allies. It is the symbol of victorious conquest.[7]

- **He is called Faithful and True.** Christ did not abandon His people to Rome. He is faithful and true (1:5; 3:7, 14; cf. Psalm 96:13).

- **In righteousness He judges and makes war.** The conquering work of Christ is manifested in His judgment and in His prosecution of this holy war. These two functions are also united

---

[6] Roberts, 163.
[7] Mounce, 343.

in various OT apocalyptic passages (cf. Joel 3:12; Daniel 7:13, 21, 26; Ezekiel 38-39).[8]

- **His eyes were like a flame of fire.** We find this depiction of Christ earlier in Revelation as well (1:14; 2:18). Nothing has been hidden from Him (Hebrews 4:13) and His gaze is fixed on the battle at hand.

- **On His head were many crowns.** In 6:2 and 14:14, Christ is seen wearing the victor's crown (*stephanos*). Here He is wearing many crowns of royalty (*diadema*). His crown of thorns has been exchanged for unlimited, universal, and ultimate sovereignty.[9]

- **He had a name written that no one knew except Himself.** This reminds us of the promise of a new name to be given to the faithful (2:17). This could be a parallel to the sacred name of God, YHWH, the tetragrammaton. It was a name too holy to pronounce, for fear of profaning it, hence the vowel markings were omitted by the Hebrew scribes.

- **He was clothed with a robe dipped in blood.** Commentators suggest two valid possibilities here. The blood could be His own and serves to remind us of His atonement. Or it could be the blood of battle and His garment is stained with the blood of His enemies.

- **His name is called "The Word of God."** See John 1:1, 14, 18; 14:9. He is the living embodiment of God's revelation.

- **Out of His mouth goes a sharp sword, that with it He should strike the nations.** We are reminded of the characteristic sharpness of God's word (Hebrews 4:12) and its place in the armament of the Christian (Ephesians 6:17). In this passage, His word strikes the nations. His word is conquering the world and defeating His enemies (1:16; 2:12). "With the

---

[8] Roberts, 163.
[9] Harkrider, 219.

breath of His lips He slays the wicked" (Isaiah 11:4). We are also reminded of the nature of this war. We do not fight with swords and spears (Isaiah 2:4), but with the spiritual armor of God.

- **He will rule them with a rod of iron.** An OT parallel is found in Isaiah 11:4. He will reign over the nations with strength, and iron rod and scepter (cf. 2:27; 12:5; Psalm 2:9; 110:1-7; Isaiah 11:1-5).[10] His judgment, word, and rule cannot be bent.
- **He treads the winepress of the fierceness and wrath of Almighty God.** He executes God's vengeance on the nations for their rebellions and wickedness (cf. 14:19-20; Isaiah 63:1-7).
- He has on His robe and on His thigh a name written: **"KING OF KINGS AND LORD OF LORDS."** This title occurs in 17:14; 1 Timothy 6:15; Deuteronomy 10:17; and Daniel 2:47. Here it signifies the universal sovereignty of Christ and His triumph over evil. "He will smite the nations, break them with a rod of iron, and tread the winepress of His fierce wrath because all power is His and all the nations are subject to the might of His righteous retribution."[11]

His armies also appear with Him in this scene. They are in heaven and clothed in fine linen, white and clean, following Him also on white horses. These are not armies of earth but proceed from heaven. "This was a conflict in the heavenly realm. This spiritual conflict is won by Jesus, but all who 'follow the Lamb wherever He goes' (14:4) share in Christ's victory over the forces of evil."[12] Their adornment of fine linen, white and clean, denotes their righteous lives by virtue of their justification in Christ (cf. 6:11; 7:14; 19:8).[13]

---

[10] Ibid., 220.
[11] Mounce, 347.
[12] Harkrider, 220.
[13] Roberts, 165.

The Beast, False Prophet, and Armies Defeated (vv. 17-21)

"Then I saw an angel standing in the sun; and he cried with a loud voice, saying to all the birds that fly in the midst of heaven, 'Come and gather together for the supper of the great God, that you may eat the flesh of kings, the flesh of captains, the flesh of mighty men, the flesh of horses and of those who sit on them, and the flesh of all people, free and slave, both small and great'" (vv.17-18).

Having battled against Christ, the dead would lie unburied and left as food for the wild birds (cf. Genesis 40:19; 1 Samuel 17:44; Jeremiah 7:33; 16:3-9; Matthew 24:28). "God will be victorious over His enemies, both small and great (cf. Ezekiel 39:17-22).[14]

Moreover, "the contrasting suppers depicted in this chapter are worthy of note. The marriage supper of the Lamb is for the victorious righteous saints. The supper of the great God prepared for vultures is composed of all the ungodly who conspired to harm the Lord's cause."[15]

"And I saw the beast, the kings of the earth, and their armies, gathered together to make war against Him who sat on the horse and against His army. Then the beast was captured, and with him the false prophet who worked signs in his presence, by which he deceived those who received the mark of the beast and those who worshiped his image. These two were cast alive into the lake of fire burning with brimstone. And the rest were killed with the sword which proceeded from the mouth of Him who sat on the horse. And all the birds were filled with their flesh" (vv.19-21).

The Battle of Armageddon has arrived. The kings of the earth and their armies have gathered to make war against Christ.

---

[14] Harkrider, 222.
[15] Ibid.

"Though they join forces, the wicked will not go unpunished" (Proverbs 11:21). The battle began to be foretold in 16:13-16 and again in 17:12-14. "For the third time these are revealed with their armies (plural) to make war against the warrior-king and His army (singular)...It seems clear that we have now come to the actual battle of Har-Megedon which is fought to decide who is the King of Kings – Christ, or the world-caesars and potentates."[16]

Caution must be exercised when interpreting this battle scene, but seldom seems to be among enthusiasts of Revelation. "While the events portrayed in apocalyptic language are to be taken with all seriousness, they are not to be taken literalistically."[17] Armageddon portrays the defeat of Rome, the imperial cult, and her allies, "but does not require that we accept in a literal fashion the specific imagery with which the event is described."[18]

"Great world wars have required years to fight and many volumes to describe, but interestingly, this conflict has no details of the actual war. There is no prolonged battle. It is no contest. Victory in Christ is certain and swift."[19]

The "beast was captured" (cf. 13:1 ff). The false prophet, the one responsible for persuading men to worship the beast and bear his mark, was also captured. "These two were cast alive into the lake of fire burning with brimstone." The beast and the false prophet will later be joined in the lake of fire (hell) by the devil (20:10), death and hades (20:14), and all evil men (21:8). It is described as a place of ceaseless and dreadful torment throughout

---

[16] Hailey, 387.
[17] Mounce, 349.
[18] Ibid.
[19] Harkrider, 222.

scripture (cf. Matthew 5:22; 24:51; 25:30, 41, 46; Mark 9:43; Revelation 14:11).[20]

"And the rest were killed with the sword which proceeded from the mouth of Him who sat on the horse. And all the birds were filled with their flesh."

All who arrayed themselves for battle against God are destroyed in an act of divine retribution and righteous vindication of the true kingdom of the true God. "The kingdom of God which Rome attempted to stamp out, still stands"[21] but the empire of Rome is nothing more than an insert in the annuls of world history.

The visions and message of Daniel 7-12 is fulfilled. "In this defeat and destruction is revealed the destiny of all such powers that should ever arise to fight against God and His kingdom. This is God's guarantee of victory to the saints who lived then and to all who would come after them, even until the end of time."[22]

Application for Today

Revelation has depicted retrospectively the fall of Jerusalem and those who persecuted the church for its first forty-years. Now the Apocalypse has portrayed prospectively the fall of Rome, the second entity to persecute the church in the first century. God has affirmed His love and protection for His people. Much like the book of Job, no explanation is given for why He allowed His people to suffer. Perhaps no explanation is necessary. Christians live in a world hostile to the purposes of God. We will be made to suffer from time to time as a result of being in "this present evil world." Consider Paul's words of reality and comfort when contemplating these things (2 Timothy 3:12; Romans 8:18).

---

[20] See also Isaiah 24:21-22 for an OT reference.
[21] Harkrider, 223.
[22] Hailey, 388.

Chapter Twenty

The Bible is not a book to be decoded but rightly divided (2 Timothy 2:15). The exegesis of this text merits our seeking to understand the meaning of a prophecy, figure, or picture overall, rather than becoming too concerned with applying a literal meaning to every detail. One will fail to see the whole picture when overly consumed by every brush stroke or miss the forest for the trees so to speak.

Revelation 20:1-10 is the primary text used to support millennial theories as it is the only place where the millennium is found in scripture. Premillennialists believe chapter nineteen depicted the second coming of Christ. For them, His coming is chapter 20 would be a second return of Christ. However, scripture only speaks of Christ coming "once more" (Hebrews 12:27) and a "second time" (Hebrews 9:28), never "twice more" or a "third time."

For us to come to a correct understanding of this passage, let us look at the overall content, theme, and message of Revelation. Here is a brief outline of the book: [1]

- Chapter 1: Introduction to Revelation

- Chapters 2-3: Christ addressed the seven churches of Asia Minor.

- Chapter 4: God appeared on His throne.

- Chapter 5: Christ appeared as a Lamb and received the scroll.

---

[1] Much of this chapter is taken from: Andrew D. Erwin, *According to His Promise: Studies in the Last Things* (Charleston, AR: Cobb Publishing, 2022).

- Chapters 6-7: The seals were broken, and the contents of the scroll were revealed.

- Chapters 8-11: The seven trumpets sounded, and the first enemy (Jerusalem/Jewish persecution of the church) was defeated.

- Chapter 12: The woman with Child was protected from the serpent. God's plan of redemption was protected.

- Chapter 13: A new enemy appeared as a beast rising from the sea accompanied by a beast of the earth (Roman persecution).

- Chapters 14-19: Seven bowls of wrath were poured out upon Rome and the second persecution of the early church came to an end.

In chapter twenty, the final overthrow of Satan is presented in apocalyptic form. We will launch into the study while also maintaining its harmony with other plainly stated passages. From the text, Satan's power is limited by the power of God. God is and will always be more powerful than the adversary. Satan cannot prevent the final judgment. God will render to everyone according to their deeds (Romans 2:6). But before final judgment is rendered, Satan will attempt one final effort to defeat God and His eternal purposes.

Satan Bound 1,000 Years (vv. 1-3)

"Then I saw an angel coming down from heaven, having the key to the bottomless pit and a great chain in his hand. He laid hold of the dragon, that serpent of old, who is the Devil and Satan, and bound him for a thousand years; and he cast him into the bottomless pit, and shut him up, and set a seal on him, so that he should deceive the nations no more till the thousand years were finished. But after these things he must be released for a little while" (vv.1-3).

The chapter begins with an angel binding Satan with a great chain. He is called the "serpent of old," a clear reference to Genesis and the Genesis 3:15 prophecy.[2]

The angel that bound Satan is not identified other than that he came down from heaven. He was an agent of the purpose of God. God's purpose was to bind Satan. It is certain that God's power is greater than Satan's. While we are not certain of the exact identity of the angel, we can be certain that his mission was to bind or *prohibit* the devil from accomplishing his evil deception over the nations.

The writer of Hebrews stated Christ's mission for coming into the world when he wrote, "Inasmuch then as the children have partaken of flesh and blood, He Himself likewise shared in the same, that through death He might destroy him who had the power of death, that is, the devil, and release those who through fear of death were all their lifetime subject to bondage. (Hebrews 2:14-15). Christ also said He would "bind the strong man" (Matthew 12:29).

In Christ, all nations of the earth can be blessed not only with salvation, but also with knowledge, so that Satan "*should not*" be able to continue deceiving the nations (v.3). When man obeys the gospel he not only is called out of the darkness of sin, but also the darkness of ignorance (1 Peter 2:9), thus rendering the devil powerless in his ability to deceive. Satan should not be able to deceive the children of God. That is not to say that he *cannot*, but he *should not be able* to deceive us and turn us from God if we continue growing in His grace and knowledge (compare with 2 Peter 3:15-18). It is the truth that sets us free (John 8:31-32). Therefore, this

---

[2] We find other NT reference to angels who sinned being bound in prison in 2 Peter 2:4 and Jude 6.

binding of Satan would symbolize the power of Christ's redemptive work and gospel among the nations so as to prohibit the deceiving/persecuting work of Satan.

"What does the binding of Satan mean? His being loosed must be the opposite of his being bound. When loosed, he immediately sought to gather the nations and bring them against the camp of the saints (20:7-9). His being bound must mean that for a thousand years he could not bring the nations against the saints in persecution, as he had done before being bound...The thousand years may be symbolic of a long period of time."[3]

Throughout Revelation, Satan has been free to inflict severe persecution upon the church. God allowed Satan to be released in chapter nine. Revelation 20 begins with Satan being bound by God for a symbolic period of 1,000 years, denoting a period of peace for the church. The number 1,000 is often used symbolically in scripture (cf. Job 9:3; Psalm 50:10; 105:8). Satan is bound "so that he should deceive the nations no more till the thousand years were finished. But after these things he must be released for a little while." When released, he will go about deceiving the nations, gathering allies, and seeking to destroy the saints (20:7-9).

The Saints Reign with Christ 1,000 Years (vv. 4-6)

"And I saw thrones, and they sat on them, and judgment was committed to them. Then I saw the souls of those who had been beheaded for their witness to Jesus and for the word of God, who had not worshiped the beast or his image, and had not received his mark on their foreheads or on their hands. And they lived and reigned with Christ for a thousand years. But the rest of the dead did not live again until the thousand years were finished. This is the first resurrection. Blessed and

---

[3] Owen Olbricht, *Beyond Death's Door* (Delight, AR: Gospel Light, 1997), 79.

holy is he who has part in the first resurrection. Over such the second death has no power, but they shall be priests of God and of Christ, and shall reign with Him a thousand years" (vv.4-6).

During this period of peace, the roles have been reversed. The martyred saints are now reigning and judging with Christ, rather than being judged by antagonistic powers. Judgment was committed to them (cf. 1 Corinthians 6:2; Matthew 19:28; Matthew 12:41). Christ's rule has been established on the earth (cf. Isaiah 2:1-4) and His people share in the privilege of His providence. The one who overcomes and keeps His works unto the end is given "power over the nations" (Revelation 2:26).

Satan's power to deceive to the extreme potential he used with Rome is prohibited. His power is limited when the gospel is heard and obeyed and as one grows in the grace and knowledge of the Lord; but we know that Satan's deceptive power continues working in those who refuse to hear the gospel. Paul taught that this would grow worse and worse until the return of Christ (2 Timothy 3:13).

Two parties are presented in v. 4: (1) the faithful martyrs; and (2) those that worshipped the beast and received his mark. The faithful martyrs lived and reigned with Christ for 1,000 years. "This is the first resurrection." Christ has been reigning on His throne since He ascended into heaven; and Satan's deceptive power has been bound or *prohibited* through the spread of the gospel. The binding of Satan should also be considered as a figurative description of his being restricted from using a world power like Rome to stamp out the preaching of the word.

Just as the number 1,000 conveys completeness and perfection in other passages (e.g., Job 9:3; Psalm 50:10; 105:8), it would seem to convey completeness as pertaining to the reign of the martyred saints – i.e., the Christian age – in this passage. Martyred souls are pictured living and reigning with Christ. They are priests and kings of God and Christ (1:6). The second death of 20:14 has no power over them.[4]

The reign of the saints who endure has been promised throughout the book of Revelation (see 2:10-11; 2:26; 3:21). Now we are assured that the promise is kept. While they were humiliated by Rome in this life, they are now exalted by Christ in eternal life.

In v. 5 we read the statement, "This is the first resurrection." John refers to those martyred souls who lived or *came to life* and reigned with Christ as the first resurrection. The text says nothing of this being a bodily or literal resurrection. If it is not a bodily resurrection it must be a figurative resurrection.

Their reign began after the destruction of Rome (Babylon). The importance of the first resurrection is thus magnified in v. 6: "Blessed and holy is he that hath part in the first resurrection: on such the second death has no power, but they shall be priests of God and of Christ and shall reign with him a thousand years." These souls who endured Rome's persecution are now seen reigning with the Lord. The "second death" – hell – has no power over them.

One possible explanation for the "first resurrection" is that the spirit of the martyred saints has been revived in the church post-Roman persecution. "The spirit of the martyrs is revived and lives in the church. The souls of the martyrs live because the church is composed of those who love Christ better than goods or liberty or

---

[4] The second death made clear in the text itself. Note: "Death and hell were cast into the lake of fire. This is the second death" (20:14). The lake of fire – eternal damnation – is the second death. All men are appointed to physical death, but only the lost are appointed to the second death.

life."[5] The church is thus "filled with the spirit of the ancient martyrs."[6] Just as Elijah came in spirit and power before Christ and in the presence of John the Baptist, and just as God opened the graves of Israel and returned them to their homeland after Babylonian captivity (Ezekiel 27:12-14), the spirit of the martyred saints is revived in those dedicated to the reign of Christ over the earth.[7]

Another possible explanation, and perhaps not mutually exclusive, is that the first resurrection comes at baptism.[8] A resurrection to newness of life does occur at baptism (see John 3:3-5; Romans 6:3-7; Ephesians 2:1, 4-6; and Colossians 2:12-13). After baptism, the second death no longer has power over the individual.

Revelation 20:5 should be understood almost as a parenthetical statement (cf. NIV). The "rest of the dead" refers to those who *did* receive the mark of the beast and worship his image. Their diabolic influence will be revived and "live again" in spirit with those who will ally themselves with Satan and surround the camp of the saints upon his release from the bottomless pit.

Satan's Final Act of Rebellion Is Crushed (vv.7-10)

"Now when the thousand years have expired, Satan will be released from his prison and will go out to deceive the nations which are in the four corners of the earth, Gog and Magog, to gather them together to battle, whose number is as the sand of the sea. They went up on the breadth of the earth and surrounded the camp of the saints and the beloved city. And fire came down from God out of heaven and devoured them. The devil, who deceived them, was cast into the lake of fire and

---

[5] B.W. Johnson, *Vision of the Ages* (Delight, AR: Gospel Light, n.d.), 339.
[6] Ibid.
[7] Ibid., 340-1.
[8] Erwin, 94.

brimstone where the beast and the false prophet are. And they will be tormented day and night forever and ever" (vv.7-10).

Satan was bound "so that he should deceive the nations no more till the thousand years were finished. But after these things he must be released for a little while."[9] Satan's binding brought about a period of peace and growth for the church and greater potential for the spreading of the gospel. When he is freed from his binding, he returns to his purpose of trying to stamp out Christianity.

Satan enlists and empowers Gog and Magog. Gog and Magog were enemies of Israel in Ezekiel 38–39. Gog was the "rosh prince" the "head prince" or "chief prince" (see ESV) in the land of Magog, over the cities of Meshech and Tubal. No record exists outside of scripture for these places or this prince. It could be that Gog and Magog in Ezekiel are descendants of Japheth (European people). Remember that Magog, Meshech, and Tubal were sons of Japheth (Genesis 10). The Israelites were the sons of Shem.

From the Ezekiel prophecy we are reminded that the people of God will face tremendous enemies. When considering the figurative nature of these passages, we can realize the leader will not necessarily have the name "Gog" or fight with literal bows and arrows. Rather, Ezekiel 38-39 represents a prophecy of a climactic struggle between the forces of good and evil. Gog personifies the head of the forces of evil which are intent on destroying the people of God.

Here are a few more details from Ezekiel concerning Gog and Magog:

---

[9] Compare this to 2 Thessalonians 2:1-12 and 2 Timothy 3:13 as the idea of evil and false doctrine being prevalent on the earth at the return of Christ.

- God's people have returned to their homeland and are living in peace (38:8, 11).

- A greedy assailant has devised an evil plan (38:10) to make war with the people of God who are living in peace and nearly defenseless (38:11-13).

- The enemy will find allies from the various nations to form a mighty army (38:5-6, 9, 15). The people of God are thus surrounded by enemies and doomed for destruction (38:9, 16). Israel would be surrounded by Gomer (North), Persia (East), Ethiopia (South), and Libya (West).

- God is against this prince and his nation. He will be the one to lead this enemy and his allies into battle for the purpose of destroying them (38:1-4; 39:1-4).

- God will intervene and protect His people (38:18-39:8)! He will wage war against Gog like He did against Sodom and Gomorrah (38:21-23).

- Every man's sword would be against his brother (v.21).

- All the nations of the earth will see how God protects His people and glorify His name (38:16, 23, 39:7, 21, 27). The victory would magnify the Lord and He would be sanctified and known in the eyes of many nations. They would know that He is the Lord.

- The deeds and fate of this enemy had also been foretold by previous prophets (38:17).

- Gog and his armies would fall in Israel. Israel would learn not to profane the holy name of God anymore. The nations would know that God is the Holy One. Gog's defeat would be great and final. Description is given for the amounts of weapons recovered and used for firewood. The plunderer was plundered (39:1-10).

- Gog and his armies would be buried in Israel, the land they came to conquer. The place they would be buried would be called Hamon Gog – "the multitude of Gog." The land would be unclean while these corpses and bones were on the ground. People would have to be selected to touch and bury the remains (39:11-16) in keeping with the law of Moses (cf. Num. 19:11).

- The once mighty army would become food for the fowls, the fish, and the beasts (39:17-20).

- Upon the victory, God would be glorified among all the nations. The house of Israel would reaffirm their conviction in God. The Gentiles would know that Israel was God's special nation, and that the reason for their captivity was because of their unfaithfulness. They would also know that He was still protecting them in their homeland (39:21-29).

The message from Ezekiel and also Revelation would not necessarily have to refer to one single event, king, or dominion. Rather, the text could simply refer to God's protection of His people from the forces of evil no matter how great. "…if the passage is apocalyptic, the identity of Gog becomes meaningless. He represents every force of evil that is marshalled against God. It is immaterial whether or not Ezekiel had in mind a historical prototype."[10]

---

[10] Andrew W. Blackwood, Jr., *Ezekiel: Prophecy of Hope* (Grand Rapids, MI: Baker Book House, 1965), 227.

Ezekiel's Gog and Magog were part of the last enemies to be defeated before Israel could settle peacefully in their land. In Revelation, likewise the camp of the saints and the beloved city is surrounded. God's people are outnumbered, and defeat seems imminent for them until the Lord intervenes for one final time in earth's history. The symbolism is clear: the enemies of the Israel of God (see Galatians 6:16) are destroyed in Revelation just as they were in Ezekiel.

Satan's final act of rebellion will be defeated with fire from heaven, alluding to the second coming of Christ. Christ will come in flaming fire. The earth will be destroyed by fire (see 2 Thess. 1:7-9; 2 Peter 3:10-13).

The binding of Satan is going to end according to the text. The terms fulfilled, finished, and expired are all used to denote the end of this period. Satan will be loosed for "a little season" to go out and deceive the nations. It appears he will do so to an extent similar to the level of deception he exercised with Rome. Perhaps this is how the "seducers" Paul mentioned will become worse and worse before the return of Christ. The only way Satan's deception will come to an ultimate end is with fire from heaven and the final judgment.

The Great White Throne Judgment (vv. 11-15)

"Then I saw a great white throne and Him who sat on it, from whose face the earth and the heaven fled away. And there was found no place for them. And I saw the dead, small and great, standing before God, and books were opened. And another book was opened, which is the Book of Life. And the dead were judged according to their works, by the things which were written in the books. The sea gave up the dead who were in it, and Death and Hades delivered up the dead who were in them. And they were judged, each one according to his

works. Then Death and Hades were cast into the lake of fire. This is the second death. And anyone not found written in the Book of Life was cast into the lake of fire" (vv.11-15).

Revelation 20 closes as earth and heaven have fled away. The heavens and the earth will be destroyed at the return of Christ (cf. 2 Peter 3:10-13). The dead are judged according to their works (cf. Ecclesiastes 12:14; Romans 2:6; 2 Corinthians 5:10) and according to the books that were opened (cf. John 12:48). Anyone not found written in the Book of Life (3:5) was cast into the lake of fire which is the second death. The lake of fire is the eternal prison for the beast and false prophet.

Some distinction is made throughout Revelation between the bottomless pit and the lake of fire. Perhaps the bottomless pit where Satan was bound and from which he was released is the realm of "Death and Hades" mentioned here.

The final judgment will occur after the heaven and earth have fled away (see Hebrews 1:11-12). Judgment will be rendered according to the word of God and according to our works. The righteous were addressed first and the wicked last just as in Matthew 25:31-46. Every one of us will have to give an account for what we have done, whether it is good or evil (2 Corinthians 5:10). Every knee shall bow and every tongue shall confess (Romans14:11). It will be a day in which all who have ever lived will receive justice. The Lord says, "And behold, I am coming quickly, and My reward is with Me, to give to everyone according to his work" (Revelation 22:12). All evidence will be brought to light. "For God will bring every work into judgment, including every secret thing, whether it is good or whether it is evil" (Ecclesiastes 12:14).

Men cannot hide themselves from God. "And there is no creature hidden from His sight, but all things are naked and open to the eyes of Him to whom we must give account" (Hebrews 4:13). We cannot succeed in hiding our sins from God. "For if our heart condemns us, God is greater than our heart, and knows all things" (1 John 3:20). As with Achan in Joshua 7, "Woe to those who seek deep to hide their counsel far from the Lord, and their works are in the dark; they say, 'Who sees us?' and, 'Who knows us?'" (Isaiah 29:15). God is there! God sees and God knows; and God will bring every secret thing to judgment.

Eternity will follow the final judgment. In chapters 21–22 heaven, the home of the saved, will be revealed as a "new heavens and new earth."

Application for Today

Chapter twenty reveals to us that Satan's work is not finished with the downfall of Rome. However, the same can be said for God's work. The chapter affords Christians a measure of optimism considering the binding of Satan and reigning with Christ. The chapter also brings to mind the certainty of Satan's last-ditch effort to deceive the nations and turn them against Christ which is to occur at a future time. No more information is clearly given.

In the case of Revelation 20, it is just as important to realize what the passage does not say as it is to realize what it does say. The passage does not say anything about Jesus returning to earth. The passage does not say that Jesus will reign on earth. It does not say that Jesus will reign for 1,000 years. Only the reign of the martyred saints is mentioned.

Revelation 20 does not say that Jesus will reign in Jerusalem. Moreover, the passage does not say that Jesus will wait until then to reign on David's throne. Christ is now reigning on David's throne. God's throne (see 1 Kings 1:32-40; 1 Chronicles 29:23) would be established forever (2 Samuel 7:12-17; Psalm 89:3-4; 28-37; Isaiah 9:6-7; Jeremiah 23:5-6; Daniel 2:44). This promise is fulfilled in Christ (Isaiah 22:22; Luke 1:31-33; Acts 2:24 ff.; Acts 13:16 ff.; 2 Timothy 2:8).

God's temple is now restored in Christ as promised (Amos 9:11-12; Zechariah 6:12-13; Acts 15:13-19; see also 1 Corinthians 3:16-17; 1 Peter 2:5; Hebrews 8:1-2). God's family is now enlarged to include the Gentiles (Isaiah 11:1-5, 10; 42:1-9; 49:1-6, 8, 19-22; 54:2-3, 62:2). The family was enlarged beginning with the house of Cornelius (Acts 10). The new name was then given (Isaiah 56:5; 62:2; 65:15; Acts 11:26).

Christ now reigns over His kingdom (1 Corinthians 15:22). Jesus has said His kingdom is not of this world (John 18:36). Christ does not rule from Jerusalem (Jeremiah 22:30), but from heaven seated at the right hand of God (Hebrews 1:3; 8:1; 12:2, 25). Jesus has been crowned "Lord and Christ" and "King of Kings and Lord of Lords" – "Thy throne, O God, is forever and ever: a scepter of righteousness is the scepter of thy kingdom" (Hebrews 1:8, KJV).

Chapter Twenty-One

Chapters 21 and 22 present in apocalyptic prose the radiance and splendor of heaven. The natural order has given way to the heavenly realm. The final judgment has occurred. Satan, sin, and the workers of iniquity have been vanquished and one eternal day commences.

As we study chapter twenty-one, we must maintain the connection with the previous chapter and the book of Revelation overall. Moreover, we need to realize the similarities between the close of Revelation and the close of Ezekiel. Ezekiel 40-48 presents a vivid symbolic prophecy, describing the glorious return of the exiles from Babylon to the Promised Land. They would again enjoy the presence of God, the beauty of a rebuilt city and temple, and land ownership.

The name of the city in Ezekiel is profoundly stated: "THE LORD IS THERE" (48:35). God was waiting on His children to come home. God was waiting to renew His covenant with them. God was waiting to bless them. God was there, ready to restore His plan through Israel to bless all nations of the earth through the advent of His only begotten Son.

As Revelation closes, we find the new Jerusalem situated on a new earth with a new heaven above it. The Lord is there too!

All Things Made New (vv. 1-8)

"Now I saw a new heaven and a new earth, for the first heaven and the first earth had passed away. Also there was no more sea. Then I, John, saw the holy city, New Jerusalem, coming down out of heaven from God, prepared as a bride adorned for her husband. And I heard a loud voice from heaven saying, 'Behold, the tabernacle of God is with men, and He will dwell with them, and they shall be His people. God Himself will be with them and be their God. And God will wipe away every tear from their eyes; there shall be no more death, nor sorrow, nor crying. There shall be no more pain, for the former things have passed away'" (vv.1-4).

In Revelation 21:1-2, we find the first heaven and the first earth passing away, just as Peter described in greater detail (2 Peter 3:10-13). We find that the new earth differs from the old earth as there is no longer any sea. The new heavens are also different from the old heavens as they are without the sun and the moon (cf. 21:23). The sun and the moon, along with all the host of the heavens, passed away with a great noise ("roar," NASB), and the elements were destroyed with intense heat. As Jesus said, Peter and John affirm, "...heaven and earth will pass away" (Matthew 24:35).

The Jerusalem of chapter 11 is replaced with a "New Jerusalem, coming down out of heaven from God, prepared as a bride adorned for her husband." The purpose of the vision appears to be to cement the fact that "the tabernacle of God is with men, and He will dwell with them, and they shall be His people."

Saints are once more reassured that "God Himself will be with them and be their God. And God will wipe away every tear from their eyes; there shall be no more death, nor sorrow, nor crying. There shall be no more pain, for the former things have passed away" (cf. 7:14-17).

"Then He who sat on the throne said, 'Behold, I make all things new.' And He said to me, 'Write, for these words are true and faithful'" (v.5).

It is difficult for humans to begin to conceive the possibilities of this statement. Isaiah and Paul said as much we they wrote, "Eye has not seen, nor ear heard, Nor have entered into the heart of man The things which God has prepared for those who love Him" (Isaiah 64:4; 1 Corinthians 2:9). In the context we have already found a new heavens, new earth, new Jerusalem, and essentially a new experience of life, free from pain, sorrow, fear, sin, and death.

"And He said to me, 'It is done! I am the Alpha and the Omega, the Beginning and the End. I will give of the fountain of the water of life freely to him who thirsts. He who overcomes shall inherit all things, and I will be his God and he shall be My son. But the cowardly, unbelieving, abominable, murderers, sexually immoral, sorcerers, idolaters, and all liars shall have their part in the lake which burns with fire and brimstone, which is the second death'" (vv. 6-8).

Several tremendous statements of fact are expressed in these verses. In the first place, "It" life, world affairs, etc., it is not done or finished until the Lord says, "It is done!" He will prove to every creature that He is "the Alpha and the Omega, the Beginning and the End." He will have the final say.

Secondly, a precious promise is restated as He offers to "give of the fountain of the water of life freely to him who thirsts." Only the Lord has the power to make this offer and He alone can keep it.

A third statement of fact is stated again in the form of a promise: "He who overcomes shall inherit all things, and I will be his God and he shall be My son." In this promise we have the theme of Revelation being essentially expressed. In fact, the passage under consideration (21:6-8) provides the theological basis or theme for the book of Revelation.

A fourth fact is found in the warning of verse 8: "But the cowardly, unbelieving, abominable, murderers, sexually immoral, sorcerers, idolaters, and all liars shall have their part in the lake which burns with fire and brimstone, which is the second death." Heaven will be free from any temptation to sin. Anyone who would tempt others to sin will be cast out at the final judgment. Anyone who refused to repent and drink from the fountain of the water of life will be cast out and have no part in the eternal reward the Lord will extend to His people.

The New Jerusalem (vv. 9-21)

"Then one of the seven angels who had the seven bowls filled with the seven last plagues came to me and talked with me, saying, 'Come, I will show you the bride, the Lamb's wife.' And he carried me away in the Spirit to a great and high mountain, and showed me the great city, the holy Jerusalem, descending out of heaven from God, having the glory of God. Her light was like a most precious stone, like a jasper stone, clear as crystal. Also she had a great and high wall with twelve gates, and twelve angels at the gates, and names written on them, which are the names of the twelve tribes of the children of Israel: three gates on the east, three gates on the north, three gates on the south, and three gates on the west. Now the wall of the city had twelve foundations, and on them were the names of the twelve apostles of the Lamb. And he who talked with me had a gold reed to measure the city, its gates, and its wall. The city is laid out as a square; its length is as great as its breadth. And he measured the city with the reed: twelve thousand furlongs. Its length, breadth, and height are equal. Then he measured its wall: one hundred and forty-four cubits, according to the measure of a man, that is, of an angel. The construction of its wall was of jasper; and the city was pure gold, like clear glass. The foundations of the wall of the city were adorned with all kinds of precious stones: the first foundation was jasper, the second sapphire, the third chalcedony, the fourth emerald, the fifth sardonyx, the sixth sardius, the seventh chrysolite, the eighth beryl, the ninth topaz, the tenth chrysoprase, the eleventh jacinth, and the twelfth amethyst. The twelve gates were twelve pearls: each individual gate was of one pearl. And the street of the city was pure gold, like transparent glass."

Just as Ezekiel provides in apocalyptic terms the description and dimensions of the new temple in a restored homeland, so too does John describe the new Jerusalem for his readers. Ezekiel's vision begins with him being transported to a high mountain. He meets an angelic figure with measuring instruments in hand. John is also carried away "in the Spirit to a great and high mountain," to see "the great city, the holy Jerusalem, descending out of heaven from God, having the glory of God." John will also be given measuring instruments and instructed to measure what he sees.

John is amazed first by the light emanating from it as "a most precious stone, like a jasper stone, clear as crystal." He observes "she had a great and high wall with twelve gates, and twelve angels at the gates, and names written on them, which are the names of the twelve tribes of the children of Israel: three gates on the east, three gates on the north, three gates on the south, and three gates on the west."

In the new Jerusalem honor is given to the redemption story, particularly the role of Israel from which the OT and Christ came. Honor is also given to the apostles as "the wall of the city had twelve foundations, and on them were the names of the twelve apostles of the Lamb." The size of the city and the gates is significantly larger than the dimensions in Ezekiel. There is room for all to enter and remain. The rooms for the priests could have the same meaning. Jesus said, "In my Father's house are many rooms" (John 14:2, ESV).

The beauty of the new Jerusalem is beyond any city ever known on earth. It is heavenly and its Builder and Maker is God.

The Glory of the New Jerusalem (vv. 22-27)

"But I saw no temple in it, for the Lord God Almighty and the Lamb are its temple" (v.22).

On this point we find a major distinction given between the visions of Ezekiel and Revelation. The Revelation vision had no temple, "for the Lord God Almighty and the Lamb are its temple." Such a distinction denotes to us that while the visions may be similar and provide similar hope to its readers, they are not referring to the same scene.

"The city had no need of the sun or of the moon to shine in it, for the glory of God illuminated it. The Lamb is its light" (v.23).

Clearly, the new Jerusalem "is not a picture of renovation of this earth, but of the disappearance of this earth and sky."[1] The sun and moon have been placed in the natural realm to mark time, and time will cease to function in eternity – a point which is repeated by John again in 22:5.[2] The wording of the verse is based on the Isaiah 60:19 prophecy: "The sun shall no longer be your light by day, Nor for brightness shall the moon give light to you; But the Lord will be to you an everlasting light, And your God your glory."

"And the nations of those who are saved shall walk in its light, and the kings of the earth bring their glory and honor into it" (v.24).

---

[1] A.T. Robertson, *The General Epistles and the Apocalypse* in Word Pictures in the New Testament: vol. 6, (Nashville, TN: Sunday School Board of the Southern Baptist Convention, 1933), 466.

[2] Simon J. Kistemaker, *Revelation* (Grand Rapids, MI: Baker, 2001), 573.

We have read much about the corrupt kings of the earth in Revelation. But this statement reminds us that not all kings are corrupt. May God bless every nation with leadership that someday will walk in heaven's light and "bring their glory and honor into it."

"Its gates shall not be shut at all by day (there shall be no night there)" (v.25).

In heaven eternal there will be no need to shut the gates. There will be no threat from enemies outside to capture and destroy. Rather, all who enter, **"shall bring the glory and the honor of the nations into it. But there shall by no means enter it anything that defiles, or causes an abomination or a lie, but only those who are written in the Lamb's Book of Life" (vv.26-27).**

Application

The application portion for this chapter will be kept brief as such descriptions of heaven should remind the readers of Revelation of the importance of living a faithful Christian life. Who would not want to go to heaven? Who could possibly want to go to hell? Men must be convinced of the certainty of eternity and the only two possible destinations. Truly, if heaven is lost, everything is lost. Nothing should matter more.

Chapter Twenty-Two

In chapter twenty-two, the angel continues to provide a guided tour for John of the heavenly vision he is experiencing. In the previous chapter, the prophecies of Ezekiel (and many from Isaiah) played a significant role in the description of the scenes. In chapter twenty-two, the reader will be reminded of Eden, as John's vision presents Eden restored in the new earth.

The final chapter of Revelation will offer motivation for faithful Christians to endure and overcome through Christ. It will also contain words of warning, encouragement, and blessings. It is not only the last chapter of Revelation; it is the final chapter of God's message to man – the Bible. The ending of scripture is therefore linked to the beginning. God creates a new Eden for man to dwell. However, the serpent will not have access to this Eden. Moreover, no tree of the knowledge of good and evil appears, only the tree of life in full bloom.

The River of Life (vv. 1-5)

"And he showed me a pure river of water of life, clear as crystal, proceeding from the throne of God and of the Lamb. In the middle of its street, and on either side of the river, was the tree of life, which bore twelve fruits, each tree yielding its fruit every month. The leaves of the tree were for the healing of the nations. And there shall be no more curse, but the throne of God and of the Lamb shall be in it, and His servants shall serve Him. They shall see His face, and His name shall be on their foreheads. There shall be no night there: They need no lamp nor light of the sun, for the Lord God gives them light. And they shall reign forever and ever" (vv.1-5).

The vision of heaven continues with a scene of **"a pure river of water of life, clear as crystal, proceeding from the throne of God and of the Lamb" (v.1).** Jesus embodied the water of life while on earth (cf. John 4:14; John 7:38-39). The heavenly reality of His words now appears to John.

John will then see **"the tree of life, which bore twelve fruits, each tree yielding its fruit every month. The leaves of the tree were for the healing of the nations" (v.2).** Life is restored in the water and in the tree which bears its fruit year-round with an abundant supply.[1] Heaven is also depicted not only for its beauty and life, but for its healing, the "healing of the nations." The Great Physician provides healing to His people in this life and the life to come. Heaven will be a place where the broken-hearted are forever healed (cf. Luke 4:18).

"And there shall be no more curse, but the throne of God and of the Lamb shall be in it, and His servants shall serve Him (v.3)." Corresponding to the healing provided is the promise of "no more curse." The curse mentioned refers to man's curse which resulted from the fall in Eden (Genesis 3:14-19). The role of the triumphant church is one of serving Him forever. "Undoubtedly John means to imply that the heavenly worship of the Father and the Son comes naturally out of the transformation of the redeemed, who have now been changed into the likeness of His glorious body (Philippians 3:21)."[2]

"They shall see His face, and His name shall be on their foreheads" (v.4). In this life, no man can see His face and live (Exodus 33:20), but in heaven every person will be able to commune directly with God in the holiest of holies. Truly, "Blessed are the pure in heart, For they shall see God" (Matthew 5:8). They

---

[1] Morris, 256.
[2] Roberts, 194.

will be sealed by the name of God on their foreheads, denoting their allegiance to Him as in the sealing of the 144,000 (7:3 ff.).

"There shall be no night there: They need no lamp nor light of the sun, for the Lord God gives them light. And they shall reign forever and ever" (v.5). Two facts are restated in this verse for emphasis. (1) There shall be no night there. God will provide the light and He will always be there. He will never leave. (2) The residents of the celestial city will reign forever and ever. The saints will be made priests and kings, reigning as victors over the devil forever.

These affirmations bring to a close John's vision of heaven. Beginning in verse 6, an epilogue of the book of Revelation will commence.[3]

The Time Is Near (vv. 6-11)

"Then he said to me, 'These words are faithful and true.' And the Lord God of the holy prophets sent His angel to show His servants the things which must shortly take place" (v.6).

As John closes his prophecy to the seven churches, he offers final assurances, warnings, and blessings. The contents of his work are "true and faithful" for they come from Him who is "Faithful and True" (19:11). These things (the deliverance from persecution) "must shortly take place" (1:1; 1:3). Domitian's reign of terror would soon end.[4]

"Behold, I am coming quickly! Blessed is he who keeps the words of the prophecy of this book" (v.7).

Once more we have one of the seven beatitudes found in Revelation. A blessing is to be bestowed upon all who will keep (hold

---

[3] Paul, 363.

[4] We believe Revelation to have been written in 95 AD. Domitian's death came in 96.

fast to) the words of the prophecy of this book (the book of Revelation). The message of Revelation would be of little value to those who rejected the faith to appease the emperor. The blessing of deliverance both now and forever is offered to those who will remain faithful.

"Now I, John, saw and heard these things. And when I heard and saw, I fell down to worship before the feet of the angel who showed me these things. Then he said to me, 'See that you do not do that. For I am your fellow servant, and of your brethren the prophets, and of those who keep the words of this book. Worship God'" (vv.8-9).

"To the reader's surprise, John falls down a second time to worship the angel, and again receives a reprimand (19:10). The greatest of God's servants are not to be worshiped, for worship is reserved for God alone."[5] While we do not know John's reason for doing this, other than possibly being swept up with emotion, we do find a point of emphasis in the reprimand occurring a second time. It should be clear that the worship of men or angels or anything other than God is strictly forbidden.

"And he said to me, 'Do not seal the words of the prophecy of this book, for the time is at hand. He who is unjust, let him be unjust still; he who is filthy, let him be filthy still; he who is righteous, let him be righteous still; he who is holy, let him be holy still'" (vv.10-11).

The time was at hand. The prophecy given to John was not to be sealed but read, preached, heard, and heeded. What might a person do with the message of Revelation? A man's response to God's message has no bearing on the veracity of it. By writing the words, "He who is unjust, let him be unjust still; he who is filthy, let him be filthy still; he who is righteous, let him be righteous

---

[5] Harkrider, 256.

still; he who is holy, let him be holy still," John is essentially saying, "Do as you will." If the reader was determined to remain on a course of unrighteousness despite the message given by God, so be it. He would not be forced to obey. However, if the reader was pursuing righteousness, "let him be righteous still." Stay the course. Keep the faith. Receive the crown (cf. 2 Timothy 4:7-8).

Jesus Testifies to the Churches (vv. 12-17)

"And behold, I am coming quickly, and My reward is with Me, to give to every one according to his work. I am the Alpha and the Omega, the Beginning and the End, the First and the Last" (vv.12-13).

Notice the facts stated in this statement by Christ:

(1) I am coming quickly. His judgment on Domitian, his imperial cult, and Rome would come quickly.

(2) He will judge righteously both now and forever, rendering to every man according to his work. Whenever divine judgment is mentioned in scripture, especially eternal judgment, it is based on the life of the individual being judged. The doctrine of inherited sin is greatly defeated when we realize that we are not going to be held accountable for the guilt we inherited, but for the guilt we accrued through our personal rebellion to God's will.

(3) Christ is "Alpha and Omega, the Beginning and the End, the First and the Last." Christ is at the beginning and ending of the world. He is at the beginning and ending of divine revelation. He is at the beginning and ending of the redemption story.

"Blessed are those who do His commandments, that they may have the right to the tree of life, and may enter through the gates into the city. But outside are dogs and sorcerers and sexually immoral and murderers and idolaters, and whoever loves and practices a lie" (vv.14-15).

Here we have another beatitude from Revelation which again marks the distinction between the two groups of people who have comprised humanity's existence on earth. In one group we find those who obey God and are blessed. In the other group we find those who have rebelled against God and are cursed. These two groups reach back to Cain and Abel and run as a continuous thread throughout scripture.

"I, Jesus, have sent My angel to testify to you these things in the churches. I am the Root and the Offspring of David, the Bright and Morning Star" (v.16).

"These things" – the words of Revelation – were to be testified in the churches of Asia first, and then to all churches of Christ until the end of time. Jesus identifies Himself once more as the "Root and the Offspring of David, the Bright and Morning Star" (cf. 5:5; 2:28). He has the credentials of history and heaven to speak the words of the prophecy of this book.

"And the Spirit and the bride say, 'Come!' And let him who hears say, 'Come!' And let him who thirsts come. Whoever desires, let him take the water of life freely" (v.17).

It is stunning to see God's word to man close with an invitation to come and take of the water of life freely. The invitation demands something of man and his freewill. He must "come." He must decide to take of the water of life. He may do so "freely."

God is not forcing man to accept Him. He is inviting Him. Man must accept the invitation.

A Warning (vv. 18-19)

"For I testify to everyone who hears the words of the prophecy of this book: If anyone adds to these things, God will add to him the plagues that are written in this book; and if

anyone takes away from the words of the book of this prophecy, God shall take away his part from the Book of Life, from the holy city, and from the things which are written in this book" (vv.18-19).

"Now is added a warning from the Lord Himself that the prophecy of the book is not to be tampered with, either by deleting from, adding to, or changing it. A similar command and warning had been given concerning the law (Deuteronomy 4:2; 12:32; Proverbs 30:5 ff.) and the gospel (Galatians 1:6-9). God's spiritual and moral truth must be neither altered nor perverted; it must be faithfully handed on from one generation to another. The principle applies to all the Word of God, but here Jesus is speaking particularly of this book, the Revelation."[6]

The Lord gave Israel the first covenant and then made it "old" by giving to mankind a second covenant, the New Testament (Hebrews 8:13; 9:15). To go beyond that would be transgression (2 John 9-11). Revelation is the final book of God's final word to mankind (Hebrews 1:1-2). It is certainly fitting and necessary that it should close with a warning concerning additions or subtractions to it.

Moreover, we must not think of man beyond what is written (1 Corinthians 4:6). No man, council, church, or creed has the authority to go beyond divine revelation in issuing doctrines, rites, sacraments, tenets, or decrees. We must be sure to speak only the things which have been learned from an accurate handling of the word of God (2 Timothy 2:15; 2 Peter 3:15-18).

A Promise and Blessing (vv. 20-21)

"He who testifies to these things says, 'Surely I am coming quickly,' Amen. Even so, come, Lord Jesus!" (v.20).

---

[6] Hailey, 432-3.

Revelation and the Bible closes with a word of promise and a blessing. "Surely I am coming quickly." Throughout Revelation the message of God's decisive action and certain vindication of His people has been made clear. The suffering endured by the saints would last a little longer (2:10), but it was soon to end. With a seeming sigh of relief, John adds, "Even so, come, Lord Jesus!" John speaks for all Christians under duress and who are enduring the pain, grief, and tragedy associated with this world as it abides "under the sway of the wicked one" (1 John 5:19). He speaks for all Christians who are longing for the home of the soul and to rest in the arms of the Lord.

"The grace of our Lord Jesus Christ be with you all. Amen" (v.21).

The final verse of Revelation, and the Bible, is a word of blessing. May we consider this carefully. The last written words given by the inspiration of the Holy Spirit are words of blessing, great and meaningful words of blessing.

No greater blessing could be bestowed upon a Christian than to simply say, "The grace of our Lord Jesus Christ be with you." There is no word more vivid or rich in our language than "grace." No word is its equivalent. It brings to our heart thoughts of kindness, goodness, and mercy to those who most need it and least deserve it.

Grace is at the core of God's being. God is grace. God's grace has appeared through His delight, of His accord, through His own yearning heart, and due to His sleepless ministry of mercy to man. The gospel reveals the character of God and of His grace, embodied and illustrated in the life and death of His incarnate Son.

God's grace brings salvation to all men (Titus 2:11-12). The grace of God forbids us from living in sin (Romans 6:1-2). By grace He instructs us to deny sin. The grace of God teaches us how to live. The grace of God teaches us about the present age and the age to come. By the grace of God, we are alive today and we can be just as right with God as we desire to be. Amen.

Application for Today

When looking for practical significance and daily application of the twenty-second chapter of Revelation, we need not look too far. The chapter is bubbling over with tremendous encouragement and applications to be made. Two of the seven beatitudes from Revelation are also found in the chapter (vv.7,14), encouraging the readers to keep the words of the prophecy and obey the commandments of the Lord.

We are allowed to visualize heaven in all its beauty. We are given promises of a restored Edenic homeland that will last forever with God. We are told who will be there and who will not. Readers are assured of Christ's impending deliverance from persecution and His sovereignty over the world. Instruction is provided for handling the book of Revelation and the Bible. An invitation to eternal life is extended. And lastly, a blessing of grace is bestowed.

As we bring our study to an end, a more fitting final word cannot be found than the one John offered to his readers. We now offer it for you. **"The grace of our Lord Jesus Christ be with you all. Amen"**

Bibliography

Archer, Gleason L. *Encyclopedia of Bible Difficulties*. Grand Rapids, MI: Zondervan, 1982.

Barclay, William. *The Revelation of John*. Philadelphia, PA: Westminster Press, 1976.

Baukham, Richard. *The Theology of the Book of Revelation*. Cambridge, UK: Cambridge University Press, 1993.

Beale, G.K., and D.A. Carson. *Commentary on the New Testament Use of the Old Testament*. Grand Rapids, MI: Baker Academic, 2007.

Beasley-Murray, G.R. "Revelation," *The IVP Dictionary of the New Testament*. Downers Grove, IL: IVP, 2004.

Berry, George Ricker. *Interlinear Greek-English New Testament*. Grand Rapids, MI: Baker, 1984.

Blackwood, Andrew W., Jr. *Ezekiel: Prophecy of Hope*. Grand Rapids, MI: Baker Book House, 1965.

Borchert, G.L. "Laodicea," *ISBE*, vol. 3, Revised Edition. Grand Rapids, MI: Eerdmans, 1986.

Boring, M. Eugene. *Revelation*, ICS. Louisville, KY: John Knox Press, 1989.

Bruce, F.F. "Laodicea," *ABD*, vol. 4. New York, NY: Doubleday, 1992.

Bullinger, E.W. *Figures of Speech Used in the Bible*. Grand Rapids, MI: Baker Book House, 2003.

Chesser, Frank. *The Man of Chebar: A Study of Ezekiel*. Huntsville, AL: Publishing Designs, 2018.

Cobb, Bradley S. *War in Heaven War on Earth*. Charleston, AR: Cobb, 2022.

Comfort, Philip W. *The New Testament Text and Translation Commentary*. Carol Stream, IL: Tyndale House, 2008.

Erwin, Andrew D. *According to His Promise: Studies in the Last Things*. Charleston, AR: Cobb Publishing, 2022.

Ford, J. Massyngberde. *Revelation*, ABC. Garden City, NY: Doubleday, 1975.

Gasque, W. Ward "Philadelphia," *ABD*, vol. 5. New York, NY: Doubleday, 1992.

Hailey, Homer. *Revelation: An Introduction and Commentary*. Grand Rapids, MI: Baker Book House, 1979.

Hendrickson, William. *More Than Conquerors*. Grand Rapids, MI: Baker, 1979.

Jenkins, Ferrell. *The Old Testament in the Book of Revelation*. Marion, IN: Cogdill Foundation, 1972.

Johnson, B.W. *Vision of the Ages*. Delight, AR: Gospel Light, n.d.

Jones, Brian W. "Domitian," *ABD*, vol. 2. New York, NY: Doubleday, 1992.

Jones, Donald L. "Roman Imperial Cult," *ABD*, vol. 5. New York, NY: Doubleday, 1992.

Kaiser, Walter C., Jr., Peter H. Davids, F.F. Bruce, and Manfred T. Brauch, *Hard Sayings of the Bible*. Downers Grove, IL: IVP, 1996.

Kealy, Sean P. *The Apocalypse of John*. Collegeville, MN: Liturgical Press, 1990.

Kent, Charles Foster. *The Work and Teachings of the Apostles*. New York, NY: Charles Scribner's Sons, 1916.

Kistemaker, Simon J. *Revelation*. Grand Rapids, MI: Baker, 2001.

Ladd, George Eldon. *A Commentary on the Revelation of John*, Grand Rapids, MI: Eerdmans, 1972.

Mark, Joshua J. "Pirates in the Ancient Mediterranean" World History Encyclopedia, Online, Published August 19, 2019.

McClintock, John and James Strong, *Cyclopedia of Biblical, Theological, and Ecclesiastical Literature*, vol. 7. Grand Rapids, MI: Baker, 1981.

McCord, Hugo. "The Number 666, the Mark of the Beast, and the 144,000" in *Difficult Texts of the New Testament Explained* (ed. Wendell Winkler). Tuscaloosa, AL: Winkler, 1981.

McDowell, Edward A. *The Meaning and Message of the Book of Revelation*. Nashville, TN: Broadman, 1951.

Metzger, Bruce M. *A Textual Commentary on the Greek New Testament*. New York, NY: United Bible Societies, 1971.

_____. *Breaking the Code: Understanding the Book of Revelation*. Nashville, TN: Abingdon, 1993.

Morgan, G. Campbell. *The Letters of Our Lord*. London, UK: Pickering & Inglis, n.d.

Morris, Leon. *Apocalyptic*. Grand Rapids, MI: Eerdmans, 1972.

_____. "John the Apostle," *ISBE*, vol.2, Revised Edition. Grand Rapids, MI: Eerdmans, 1982.

_____. *The Revelation of St. John*, TNTC. Grand Rapids, MI: Eerdmans, 1980.

Mounce, Robert H. *The Book of Revelation*, NICNT. Grand Rapids, MI: Eerdmans, 1977.

North, Robert. "Pergumum," *ISBE*, vol. 3, Revised Edition. Grand Rapids, MI: Eerdmans, 1986.

_____. "Philadelphia," *ISBE*, vol. 3, Revised Edition. Grand Rapids, MI: Eerdmans, 1986.

_____. "Thyatira," *ISBE*, vol. 4, Revised Edition. Grand Rapids, MI: Eerdmans, 1986.

Olbricht, Owen. *Beyond Death's Door.* Delight, AR: Gospel Light, 1997.

Osborne, Grant R. *Revelation: Verse by Verse.* Bellingham, WA: Lexham Press, 2016.

Paul, Ian. *Revelation,* TNTC. Downer's Grove IL: IVP Academic, 2018.

Petrillo, Denny *Ezekiel*, TFTC. Searcy, AR: Resource Publications, 2004.

Rienecker, Fritz and Cleon Rogers. *Linguistic Key to the Greek New* Testament. Grand Rapids, MI: Zondervan, 1980.

Roberts, J.W. *Revelation*, LWC. Austin, TX: Sweet, 1974.

Robertson, A.T. *The General Epistles and the Apocalypse* in

Word Pictures in the New Testament: vol. 6. Nashville, TN: Sunday School Board of the Southern Baptist Convention, 1933.

Roper, David L. *Revelation 1-11*, TFT. Searcy, AR: Resource Publications, 2002.

Ryken, Leland. *How to Read the Bible as Literature.* Grand Rapids, MI, Zondervan, 1984.

_____, James C. Wilhoit, Tremper Longman, "Stars" *DBI.* Downer's Grove, IL: 1998.

Schaff, Philip. *History of the Christian Church: Apostolic Christianity AD 1-100*, vol.1. New York: Scribner's, 1889.

Stalker, James. *The Two St. Johns of the New Testament.* New York, NY: American Tract Society, 1895.

Stambaugh, John E. "Thyatira," *ABD*, vol. 6. New York, NY: Doubleday, 1992.

Summers, Ray. *Worthy Is the Lamb.* Nashville, TN: Broadman & Holman, 1951.

Thiessen, H.C. *Introduction to the New Testament.* Grand Rapids, MI: Eerdmans, 1966.

Thompson, W.S. *Comments on the Revelation.* Memphis, TN: Southern Church Publications, 1957.

Vine, W.E. *Vines' Expository Dictionary of New Testament Words.* McLean, VA: MacDonald, n.d.

Wallace, Foy E., Jr. *The Book of Revelation.* Nashville, TN: Foy E. Wallace, Jr., Publications, 1966.

West, W.B., Jr. *Revelation through First Century Glasses*. Nashville, TN: Gospel Advocate, 1997.

Wilcock, Michael. *The Message of Revelation: I Saw Heaven Opened*, BST. Downers Grove, IL: IVP, 1975.

Youngblood, Ronald F. (Editor) "John the Apostle," *Nelson's New Illustrated Bible Dictionary*. Nashville, TN: Thomas Nelson, 1995).

www.ingramcontent.com/pod-product-compliance
Lightning Source LLC
LaVergne TN
LVHW051225080426
835513LV00016B/1413